Conversations with E. L. Doctorow

Literary Conversations Series

Peggy Whitman Prenshaw
General Editor

Photo credit: © Nancy Crampton

14. XII. 1999

Conversations with E. L. Doctorow

Edited by
Christopher D. Morris

Dear Maria —

Wishing you a Merry Christmas and a joyous Holiday Season.
Good start in the New Millenium!

Fondly,
Michael

University Press of Mississippi
Jackson

Books by E. L. Doctorow

Welcome to Hard Times, New York, Simon & Schuster, 1960
Big as Life, New York, Simon & Schuster, 1966
The Book of Daniel, New York, Random House, 1971
Ragtime, New York, Random House, 1975
Drinks before Dinner, New York, Random House, 1979
Loon Lake, New York, Random House, 1980
Lives of the Poets, New York, Random House, 1984
World's Fair, New York, Random House, 1985
Billy Bathgate, New York, Random House, 1989
Poets and Presidents, New York, Random House, 1993
The Waterworks, New York, Random House, 1994

http://www.upress.state.ms.us

Copyright © 1999 by University Press of Mississippi
All rights reserved
Manufactured in the United States of America

02 01 00 99   4 3 2 1

Library of Congress Cataloging-in-Publication Data

Doctorow, E. L., 1931–
    Conversations with E. L. Doctorow / edited by Christopher D.
Morris.
        p. cm. — (Literary conversations series)
    Includes bibliographical references and index.
    ISBN 1-57806-143-1 (alk. paper). — ISBN 1-57806-144-X (pbk. :
alk. paper)
    1. Doctorow, E. L., 1931–   —Interviews. 2. Novelists,
American—20th century—Interviews.   3. Fiction—Authorship.
I. Morris, Christopher D. II. Title. III. Series.
PS3554.03Z465   1999
813'.54—dc21   99-12235
                                                       CIP

British Library Cataloging-in-Publication Data available

Contents

Introduction

In assessing the career of E. L. Doctorow, many readers share the impression that not since the late work of Twain has an American writer presented such compelling images of the country suffering from an incurable corruption of its ideals. In *Welcome to Hard Times* (1960), the Emersonian doctrine of self-reliance embodied in the narrator, Blue, is shown to be ludicrously naive, self-deluded, impotent in the face of evil, perhaps even complicit with it. In *The Book of Daniel* (1971) the stripping-away of all patriotic pretensions reveals America to be just one more example of history's relentless demonstration that state power exists for its own sake. In *Ragtime* (1975) America's power elite literally gets away with murder, and the national ethos bears an uncanny resemblance to those spiritual frauds exploiting the credulous that Houdini discovers everywhere. In *The Waterworks* (1994) the ruling class's instinct for self-preservation mobilizes both science and the political system in support of a quest for immortality that would not hesitate to commandeer the body parts of orphans, if necessary, in prolonging its senescence another day. At the same time, these terrifying characterizations of America—the list could be extended with even darker examples—are presented in narratives of such acknowledged technical sophistication that readers are often left not only appalled at the scene of corruption but also dazzled with doubt as to its meaning. Does any character within a work retain the integrity America has lost? Can art, after all, provide an alternative to the society it so passionately condemns? Does the novels' collective indictment come from some privileged source or voice readers can accept as authentic? For the answers to such questions readers and literary critics—whether of Doctorow, Twain, Dreiser, or others—have sought clues first from the novels and, where these have proven inadequate or contradictory, from statements made by the author. Hence the enduring appeal of the literary interview, a form which seems to hold forth the grail of the reader's quest—an unequivocal answer to reading dilemmas.

When I asked Doctorow about interviews, he had this to say about the prospect of a collection such as this one:

Perhaps looking at several interviews together would be a good idea, because one could see different aspects of the same writing mind and find things that the subject-writer, of the interviews as it were, never intended. So in that sense, one could consider a collection of interviews as kind of a solipsistic novel and treat it on that basis . . . But all in all I think the reader would do better to read books than interviews.

Doctorow's nuanced answer here, worth studying in some detail on its own account, derives in part from his conviction, expressed on numerous occasions, that "fiction is a system of knowledge"; thus interviews, even if they are new forms of fiction, may also be occasions for learning. On the other hand, the author's comments may disclose "things that the subject-writer, of the interviews as it were, never intended"; and this concession immediately raises the issue of intentionality and interpretation. Are the author's interview-responses, after all, privileged and final interpretations of his works? And what of Doctorow's implication that a collection of interviews like this one may be merely a "solipsistic novel"? Just how *can* such a new fiction teach? As if in response to these imponderables, Doctorow's response to my question clearly reflects a preference for the book instead of the interview.

Nowhere is this preference more evident than in Doctorow's responses to questions about his life. Many interviews take note of the basic facts—his Depression-era childhood in the Bronx, his education at Kenyon College with the New Critic John Crowe Ransom, his work as an editor. These and other details, summarized in the "Chronology," are by now familiar to readers and critics, though for Doctorow himself they are irrelevant to the understanding of his work. "The minute you ask a question about a writer's life," he told Bruce Weber, "you're not dealing with the book. In one sense, we deny authors by wanting to know about them. In another, we learn to ignore them the same way. I'll tell you right now that more people in this country who think of themselves as cultured know that Faulkner was a heavy drinker than have read *Light in August*." Doctorow's rigorous separation between his life and his work, perhaps influenced by contact with Ransom, has been repeated in many interviews, especially those concerned with *World's Fair*. Although other interviewers have confirmed my own impression of Doctorow as being patient and responsive to questions about his personal life, he is equally firm in insisting on their irrelevance.[1]

Of course, Doctorow shares his belief in the autonomy of the art-object with numerous twentieth-century, non-confessional writers; however, he takes the idea of the artist's separation from his works more seriously than many do and adopts an extremely open, flexible, and receptive stance toward interpretation. After listening to Doctorow's exploratory comments on *Loon Lake,* Victor S. Navasky concluded, "Mr. Doctorow makes it quite clear that, as far as he is concerned, his theories about his books are no more qualified than anyone else's. He is, in the words of a mutual friend, a walking refutation of the intentional fallacy." Readers of this volume will find Navasky's conclusion confirmed in the number of times Doctorow replies to a suggested interpretation with responses like "maybe so" or "probably" or "you could make that case." Of course, it is crucial to recognize that such responses in no way constitute *endorsements* of an interviewer's ideas. Instead, Doctorow's unusual openness in the discussion of his works may be a measure of the unbridgeable distance he often observes between the act of writing and everything else, including interviews or literary criticism. In his concluding remarks to Bruce Weber, he claimed the "most important lesson I've learned is that planning to write is not writing. Outlining a book is not writing. Researching is not writing. Talking to people about what you're doing, none of that is writing. Writing is writing." If there is a constant in Doctorow's interviews, it is this deep gulf between the act of writing and everything else. "When you're finished with a book," he told Michelle Tokarczyk, "nothing will ever match the experience you've had writing it." Doctorow is resolute in his conviction that his work never grows out of a plan, a theory, an ideology or an agenda, but instead "takes it own course." Other buried personifications for writing appear on many occasions: "it generated itself, made its own rules" or "that was a gift the book gave me." It is clear from the frequency of such tropes that for Doctorow the act of writing transcends the act of talking about it; he even associates writing with life itself, an implication being that the prospect of not writing is deathly. To Alvin Sanoff Doctorow confided the despair that afflicted him before he found traction in the composition of *Ragtime.* To Bill Moyers Doctorow said, "I can't imagine ever giving [writing] up." In later interviews Doctorow has said of the process of writing that "you really live in those sentences."[2] My reading of the interviews has persuaded me of the utter sincerity of this conviction. Doctorow always impresses interviewers as a modest and reserved man who would be embarrassed to inject personal emotion into discussions of his work, but these comments on the existential importance of creativity seem so absolutely unequivocal as to make more understandable, by contrast, his more detached or

bemused interest in what comes afterwards—literary criticism and interviews.

For readers of this collection, the result is engagement with a mind that is
for the most part free from the defensiveness that in some form characterizes
writers like Salinger, Pynchon, or Frost. Instead, Doctorow welcomes the
opportunity to consider his works in the light of the varied agendas interviewers bring to the conversation; the only critical position to which he is hostile
is deconstruction. In fact, he has so distanced himself from debates surrounding his work as to make the extraordinary statement to Richard Marranca,
"It's probably a mistake to look for authority for critical interpretation to the
author of the book."

This reluctance to take sides in critical debates is also observable in discussions of his novels' political implications. Admittedly a man "of the left,"
Doctorow is sometimes prompted to situate his work in the intellectual context of European radicalism—the work of Emma Goldman, Wilhelm Reich,
Herbert Marcuse. However, while concepts from these and other writers appear in the novels, Doctorow is careful not to identify his own position with
theirs or those of other theorists. Instead, he says his political convictions
arise from a pre-theoretical intuition of injustice: "If I'm a leftist," he said,
"it's because, as I think of them, the Ten Commandments is a very left
dogma. What is just? What is unjust? That's where it all begins with me."

Despite such disclaimers, the political views of the writer and his work
form an important part of numerous interviews. Richard Trenner asked about
the "personal antecedents" of Doctorow's political philosophy and elicited a
response about his childhood observations of his father and grandfather.
Larry McCaffery pressed Doctorow to say whether his novels showed that
history was on the side of cooperation and compromise rather than radicalism; in responding, the author sought to distinguish his novels from universal
abstractions. When Michael Wutz asked Doctorow whether Walter Benjamin
was his "kindred spirit" in the critique of technocracy in the novels of the
seventies, Doctorow concluded his reply with the reflection, "Benjamin is a
philosopher of all of that. Novelists are not philosophers."

Of course, outside the novels, in his capacity as a citizen, Doctorow
doesn't hesitate to express his opinions on contemporary political issues, as
his interview with Bill Moyers attests. That interview is unusual in its near
exclusion of questions and answers about particular works. Instead, Doctorow laments the quietism and narrow focus of contemporary writing in
general; he warns of the injection of religious terminology into the media and

political debate. He concludes that Americans live according to premises which have not been critically examined in forty-five years. Certainly he emphasizes that writers are a part of a larger political process. To Moyers, as to Paul Levine, he says writers serve as "independent witnesses" to injustice. Nevertheless, when speaking of his novelistic practices, Doctorow again insists that his political ideas are only born and discovered, as it were, by the writing of the novels themselves, rather than existing beforehand and being imposed on the work from the outset. Thus Doctorow's final self-assessment to Bruce Weber is typical of many in this volume: "So if you ask am I a historical novelist, I say no. Am I a political novelist? No. Am I an ethnic novelist? No. I'm a novelist."

Doctorow's resistance to being categorized has not prevented interviewers from exploring specialized dimensions of his work. Liesl Schillinger asked whether his strong female characters meant that he held "explicit feminist views"; the question elicited Doctorow's unqualified endorsement of the goals of political feminism, together with a denial that he has "ever consciously written from an explicitly feminist point of view." And in his interview with me, Doctorow denied perpetuating the stereotype of the woman as white goddess. Nevertheless, assessment of the novels in terms of their depiction of women—especially women's voices in competition with men's— continues.[3] In a related context, Richard Trenner asked Doctorow whether his work reflected an ethnic or literary tradition of "radical Jewish humanism"; his reply—"I suppose so, though I don't think my kind of vision is *only* Jewish"—is characteristic in its acceptance of speculation and deflection of categorization. As in the case of gender themes, examination of Doctorow's affinities with contemporary American Jewish writing remains of interest to critics.[4]

Of the philosophical influences on his intellectual development, Doctorow singles out the existentialists, especially Sartre and Camus. "I trust the existentialist vision," he told Friedl and Schulz. "Like much metaphysics it is really a form of poetry." To Winnifred Farrant Bevilacqua he added that "existentialism is extremely important to me and has probably been important all through my work." Of literary influences the most frequently mentioned is Hawthorne, to whose idiosyncratic definition of and justification for the romance genre Doctorow frequently returns. But the index reveals Doctorow's easy familiarity with numerous canonized and contemporary American novelists; his protestation that he does not consider himself a "scholar" masks a formidable intellectual endowment.

Readers will note changes in emphasis in Doctorow's views over the years; of particular interest is his attitude toward film. In his 1975 interview with Jonathan Yardley, Doctorow refers to an "intra-media sense" which compels contemporary writers to acknowledge the effect of film on readers; he foresees a day when "people don't make a distinction between the book and the film." In his 1978 interview with Jared Lubarsky, Doctorow again notes the broad impact of film, though he now allows that he has certain "misgivings" about its potentially regressive nature. Doctorow's remarks to Larry McCaffery in 1983 seem on the whole positive: he speaks of the immense transformation of perception that film and television had wrought in him and his readers, and he justifies his novelistic techniques by analogy to film art. But by 1988 any initial enthusiasm for film has waned, and the misgivings voiced to Lubarksy become more pronounced. To Friedl and Schulz Doctorow actually vents anger at the medium, calling it "culturally regressive, non-verbal, simplistic, and a cause of rising illiteracy around the world."[5] So far as I am aware, critics have neither examined this shift in emphasis nor noticed any reflection of it in the novels.

Repetitions between or among these selections, inevitable for any frequently interviewed writer, will become quickly apparent to the reader. The most common include his undergraduate experiences at Kenyon College and the circumstances in which individual novels were written. On several occasions Doctorow gives an account of having invented a feature story for a high-school journalism class; this anecdote is used to illustrate the power of creativity. On a few others, he repeats the thesis of the Yale historian Robin Winks, whose study of the novels of Albert Payson Terhune shows, Doctorow argues, that even dog-stories can be political. This collection follows the general policy of the University Press of Mississippi, according to which interviews are published in their entirety, for the sake of their scholarly value, without regard to repetitions.

In what follows I give a brief overview of the collection by bringing together some of the scattered responses regarding each of Doctorow's novels and indicating some recurrent themes or overlooked remarks that may be promising for future study. Of course, these summaries are introductory and incomplete; the reader is referred to the index in order to find a full listing of references in this collection to each of Doctorow's works.

Several interviews recount the circumstances under which *Welcome to Hard Times* (1960) was written. While employed by Columbia Pictures as a reader of scripts, Doctorow was trying to write a novel about a boy in college, but the quality of what he read, especially the westerns, made him angry and ill. He became convinced that he could "lie better than the screenwriters I was reading." This resolve led to a short story, which later became the book's first chapter. There may be thematic interest in Doctorow's comment that the West is a place that "had to have been an experience for most people that betrayed them, an experience of promise and hope that defaulted in the actual living out of it." In terms of his artistic development, Doctorow claims that writing *Welcome to Hard Times* taught him two things: that he was *not* an autobiographical writer and that his writing could begin "as accident" or contingency.

It is no surprise that the novel given the least amount of attention in the interviews is *Big as Life* (1966). Doctorow said *Big as Life* was "the worst I've done" and compared it to Melville's *Mardi.* In a later interview he said he still liked two of the novel's images, the "bass player, Red Bloom, wheeling his bass through the streets of New York or indeed the aliens themselves who move in another space-time contimuum relative to their own size." Doctorow concedes the possibility that the book could be one day re-written but believes its weakness lay in his failure to follow out the darkest implications of its premise.

In his only comments about the experimental short fiction "The Songs of Billy Bathgate" (1968), Doctorow explains the circumstances of its composition and the coincidence of his choosing the same name for the hero of *Billy Bathgate* (1989). This response is one of several in which he acknowledges the existence of a "repertory company" of characters, images or settings that recur from work to work. Elsewhere Doctorow justifies this idiosyncrasy with an analogy to recurrent themes in musical works by the same composer. The critical implications of this comparison have yet to be fully addressed.

The Book of Daniel (1971), nominated for a National Book Award, brought Doctorow his first unambiguous critical acclaim, and questions about it have arisen in nearly all the interviews. Doctorow's account of writing 150 pages of manuscript, then tearing them up in despair before starting again, is repeated on several occasions; its immediate effect is to emphasize the creative importance of Doctorow's discovery of Daniel's voice. Also of interest is his reseach into the Rosenberg case: Doctorow freely concedes that his methods were "not systematic" but instead driven by the creative process. Of course, answers of this sort raise a question frequently asked by Doctorow's interviewers—the relation between his novels and the historical people and events they often represent. This aspect of the fiction has led interviewers to ask about Doctorow's relation to writers associated with the "nonfiction novels" of the 1960s, especially Truman Capote and Norman Mailer. Readers may also wish to consider this subject in the light of his more extended, philosophical treatment of the subject in the essay, "False Documents" (1977). Certainly the interviews, like the essay, give eloquent testimony to the artist's freedom to make use of all available texts in the process of rendering reality. In the case of *The Book of Daniel,* Doctorow claims his main interest in using the Rosenberg case was "in terms of what happens when all the antagonistic force of a society is brought to bear and focused on one or possibly two individuals."

In other remarks on the novel, he defends his eponymous hero from charges of sadism by explaining that his strength lies in his ability to survive by opening himself to perception in "however cold and frightening an embrace with the truth." Of the novel's discontinuous style, Doctorow comments that it is "constructed like [the sixties TV-comedy] *Laugh-In*"; its three endings are justified as "appropriate to Daniel" and part of Doctorow's interest in using postmodern technique in the service of pre-modern expectations of character in narrative.[6]

An even greater popular and critical success accompanied *Ragtime* (1975). In response to renewed questions about his use of history, Doctorow intensified his claim for the artist's freedom. "What's real and what isn't?" he rhetorically asks about the events in *Ragtime.* "I used to know but I've forgotten." Elsewhere he asserts that "everything I made up about Morgan and Ford is true, whether it happened or not." Questioned about the relation between fact and fiction in *Ragtime,* Doctorow responds with the even bolder claim that "there is really no fiction or nonfiction; there is only narrative." But while these statements may at first suggest a form of philosophical idealism, they are instead developed in an analysis of narrative voice and its distance from the characters. In separate interviews with Alvin Sanoff and Herwig Friedl, Doctorow called his view of history "phenomenological," but the complexity of these responses should caution critics against reflexive use of the label. In any case, the persistent return to the question of the "truth" of Doctorow's fiction leaves the impression that his interviewers may not be able to overcome a dichotomous view of the world or to entertain Doctorow's repeated call for a more sophisticated understanding of novelistic representation—one that may be both more capacious and more threatening to established ways of thinking.

As to local interpretive issues in *Ragtime,* Doctorow has frequently responded to questions concerning characters, especially Tateh and Emma Goldman. In these responses he has treated each character in a balanced way, thwarting suggestions that any can be considered wholly sympathetically.[7] He has addressed his *hommage* to Kleist in the character of Coalhouse Walker. In the Nieman Seminar he discussed a chapter he felt obliged to cut in which Houdini put on a show for the Archduke Franz Ferdinand. On the enigmatic subject of the narrator of the novel, Doctorow's most direct response was given to Michael Wutz: "The hidden narrator in *Ragtime* is probably the little boy in later times"; however, the full context of that remark—including his response to Wutz's expected "Why 'probably?' "— may leave the answer as ambiguous as ever. In other replies, Doctorow has commented on the novel's general style (imitative of the chronicle, in part owing again to the influence of Kleist), its mockery of nostalgia, and its adaptation into film.

Drinks Before Dinner (1979) is Doctorow's lone foray into the theatre. Catherine O'Neill's interview recounts some of the circumstances of the play's composition as well as Doctorow's response to the production process.[8] In this interview Doctorow compares the revisions that took place during the composition of a novel with those made necessary by the production of a play; in the latter Doctorow had to recognize that "the context of your inner authority is gone." No doubt this realization was one reason for his decision to abandon drama: "Like all the best decisions I've made it was instinctive and without sufficient thought, but it was the right one."

The story of Doctorow's inspiration for *Loon Lake* (1980)—he saw a sign with that name in the Adirondacks—is recounted in several interviews.[9] In many ways this anecdote exemplifies the lesson of another story Doctorow often repeats—Henry James's parable of the young woman who happens to pass by the open window of an army barracks, whereupon she is able to compose without any further observation a complete work of the imagination dealing with such otherwise foreign experience. The arbitrary or contingent spark of the imaginative process allegorized in James's story is a constant throughout Doctorow's reflections on his own work. Doctorow compares the effects of discontinuity in *Loon Lake* with those of *The Book of Daniel*; he concludes that readers will be able to understand the book, nonetheless, since "anyone who's ever watched a news broadcast on television knows all about discontinuity." In the same interview he calls attention to technical elements that are new for him: "A lot of broken line stuff in it—weighted lines." These have not as yet received much critical attention.[10] As to the vexed question of the novel's narrator, Doctorow explains that it is Joe "who does all the writing in the book, I think, and the computer language as I see it, is his computer mimicry which he practises ironically and perhaps even with a kind of self-disgust."[11] Of course, responses like this raise the overarching theoretical question, broached at the outset of this introduction, of the extent to which an author's interpretation of his or her own book can be privileged. Doctorow's qualified language here as well as his customary openness to the interpretation of his work suggest that debates concerning uncertain narrators may be interminable. In playful or enigmatic responses to questions, Doctorow acquiesces in such uncertainty; for example, in reply to a question as to why he gave Joe the Polish surname of Joseph Conrad, he offers, "Perhaps to confound the Ph.D.s" At points like these in the interviews the ultimate chasm between Doctorow's experience and the act of talking about his work may become evident. In such moments of passing from writer to reader, on the edge of the looking glass, as it were, the writer's adoption of a mask of inscrutability may be the most appropriate recourse. Certainly it betokens an interpretive dilemma—what the French call an *aporia*—that momentarily brings a halt to discourse.

Doctorow's collection of short stories and a novella, *The Lives of the Poets* (1984), revealed to critics yet another instance of the utter unpredictability of his works. Doctorow confessed to Michael Silverblatt that each of the pieces in the collection was the beginning of a novel that was never completed, though he developed the characters of "The Writer in the Family" in *World's Fair* and the enigma of "The Waterworks" in the later novel by that name. In terms of Doctorow's work to date, both the volume as a whole and the presumably independent works within it reflected new voices: the Poe-like mystery of "The Waterworks"; the bureaucratic/national security voice of "The Leather Man"; the European milieu of "Willi"; and (most puzzling) the self-indulgent, name-dropping, posturing Jonathan of "Lives of the Poets." With its problematic narrator and lack of continuity, the collection seems a synechdoche for Doctorow's works to this date. Two interviewers provoked intriguing comments on the collection. The writer Jay McInerney spoke of the book's theme of isolation or retreat into self, to which Doctorow replied that *Lives of the Poets* "can make a fair claim not only to describing the state of this artist's mind, but also to making him a representative of the artwork of our particular moment in history." To Bruce Weber, Doctorow confided that Jonathan's girlfriend, who is traveling around the world, should be understood as "the muse." (Of course, this is just the sort of authoritative interpretation that Doctorow elsewhere seems to disavow for himself; in the event, readers must decide whether alternative readings of the character and novella may be equally plausible.)

Liesl Schillinger's interview following the publication of *Lives of the Poets* brought up for the first time a speculation that other interviewers have pressed on Doctorow—the idea that taken together, his novels form a continuous examination of American history divided into rough periods of the late nineteenth-century (*Welcome to Hard Times*), the Gilded Age (*Ragtime*), the Great Depression (*Loon Lake*), the postwar-era (*The Book of Daniel*), and contemporary America (*Lives of the Poets*). But Doctorow's reply to this suggestion is that any such national history did not "come of any scheme or plan on my part." Speculation on this subject has continued, however, in the light of other Doctorow titles.

Doctorow called *World's Fair* (1985) his "bonus book," because he completed it in one year instead of his usual three-to-five year gestation period. This time the novel's germ was a phrase. After he had begun a story about a pre-adolescent, "one morning the words *world's fair* popped into my head. Why? Maybe because I realized that this child was born in 1931, that his life would intersect with the New York World's Fair of 1939. Then, somehow, I had what I needed to create the boyhood of someone who had gone on to become an artist of some kind." Because his protagonist's name is Edgar and so many of the novel's details match those of his childhood, Doctorow's comments on this book often directly confront the issue of autobiographical fiction. We've seen that in responses as early as those on *Welcome to Hard Times,* Doctorow repeatedly asserted that autobiographical allusions in his work are to be understood as subordinated to the larger artistic effects he wants to achieve. While conceding that from one perspective "all art is autobiographical," he consistently reminds readers that autobiographical details, like any others, are filtered through several prisms prior to their final incarnation in a text; this process makes such details interpretable on their own, within the created fiction, and effectively severs their original connection with the author. In Bruce Weber's "The Myth-Maker," Doctorow clearly distinguishes his interest in Edgar Altschuler from the autobiographical details deployed to characterize him. For Doctorow, an important theme of the novel was the morally complex life of a child. In Weber's interview, Doctorow explains how this and other themes are separable from the adapted details of his own life. In Alvin Sanoff's "Writing Is Often a Desperate Act," he reiterates the need to observe this separation in understanding *World's Fair.*

Doctorow believes his main intellectual challenge in *World's Fair* was to "write something with narrative advance that did not depend on plot, that is to say, that seemed to be life, not a story. To break down the distinction between formal fiction and the actual, palpable sense of life as it is lived, the way time passes, the way things are chronically dramatic . . . to assault fiction, assault the forms, destroy it so it can rise again." This is a remarkable statement, whose conclusion, below, also warrants study—by readers of all of Doctorow's work, not just *World's Fair.* What the author outlines here is an artistic act of simultaneous destruction and creation—a modernist poetics some critics have associated with the work of Joyce, Conrad, Lawrence, or Nabokov.[12] For such writers, art destroys history's epistemological and aesthetic illusions and replaces them with new creations now freed from the grip of the past. Of course, the artistic danger is that the destruction of illusions makes each new act of creation extremely difficult and risky, since there is so little left to the artist to compel or even solicit belief. Readers of this collection will soon learn that Doctorow's interview voice is almost always direct and discursive; however, the conspicuous rhetoric in the remainder of the passage from Weber's interview may indicate the excruciating experience of accepting such intellectual risk: "You let go of the tropes one by one. You get rid of the lights, you get rid of the music, you forego the drum roll, and finally you do the high-wire act without the wire." Consistent with the modernist poetics sketched out above, it should be noted that this is a trope which seems to arise from the destruction of tropes. It could stand as a miniature Doctorow novel. Some implications of the figure of the high-wire artist (and of other figures, such as the ventriloquist) for the understanding of *World's Fair* are suggested in Bruce Weber's interview and in my own. Exchanges like these continue to reveal that exceptional and admirable feature of Doctorow's approach to his own work—his ability to examine it from the outside, as it were, without defensiveness or overprotectiveness. It is as if once the creation has been completed, the author has become just another curious, polite reader.

World's Fair was followed by *Billy Bathgate* (1989), another unexpected change of genre; at the same time, Doctorow indicates that there may be a broad connection between the two: "In a very rough sense, Edgar is my Tom Sawyer and Billy is my Huck Finn." Given *Billy Bathgate's* acquiescence in and inheritance of the depravity of Dutch Schultz, this literary parallel cries out for critical investigation. Interviewers have mainly been drawn to the corruption of both Dutch Schultz and Billy. To Alvin Sanoff, Doctorow explained the "mirror system of morality in evil" represented in "mythic Schultz," which allows him to justify logically his depredations. Michelle Tokarczyk elicited an acknowledgment from Doctorow that in America such crime "—along with sports and the arts—is the instant way up from the lower depths." This link between the criminal and the artist, central to the work of Doctorow's namesake, Poe, as it is to the broader tradition of the romantic agony, seems an area open to further exploration in Doctorow studies.[13] Elsewhere, Doctorow linked *Billy Bathgate* with myth, especially "the American love of transgression and sociopathic behavior." This love, in turn, reflects the unsettling fact that our ostensibly law-abiding society was in fact born in acts of revolution and violence, and Billy Bathgate "dwells in that myth." Of course, the fundamental illegitimacy of state or corporate power had been a repeated refrain of the subversive meditations of Daniel Isaacson and Joe of Paterson; however, the impunity of Dutch Schultz's power and the collusion of law enforcement paint America's sociopathology as more egregiously, inescapably evil than ever before in Doctorow. In the world of *Billy Bathgate,* the only alternative to such ruthlessness is the marginalized character of Billy's mother, whose role Doctorow discusses on occasion. But the very tenuousness of that alternative may foreshadow the even grimmer scene of moral evil that is the focus of *The Waterworks* (1994).

That novel's corruption, Doctorow said, came of the nexus of "government, wealth, and science," an answer that allegorizes the characters of Boss Tweed, Augustus Pemberton, and Dr. Sartorius. It is interesting to note Doctorow's response to Michelle Tokarczyk, that he at first considered the use of narrative frame, in which McIlvaine would be telling the story of *The Waterworks* to a "captive audience," in the manner of Joseph Conrad. In any case, in the final monologue McIlvaine becomes as at least as complex a narrator as Marlow. Readers of *The Waterworks* may also wish to pursue an intriguing revelation Doctorow made to Richard Marranca—the fact that there are lines in the novel that overlap with those in his essay "The Nineteenth New York," collected in *Poets and Presidents.* That essay, published in *Architectural Digest,* evokes the spirit of the novel's historical era. The detail is interesting as a late instance of intertextuality—of Doctorow's borrowing or self-plagiarism from one work to another, a trait already noted in his interview-responses about the "repertory company" of characters he sometimes writes about. (Of course, *The Waterworks* is already Doctorow's most elaborate example of this practice, in its wholesale adaptation of the short story, "The Waterworks," from *Lives of the Poets*.) Doctorow's remarks to Marranca make clear that his essay was inspired by the novel, not vice-versa; such an emphasis on the way fact may be conditioned by fiction seems only the most recent example of Doctorow's career-long demonstration of the fluidity of the line separating the two and his challenge to readers to learn the difference.

Given the intertextuality between fiction and non-fiction, it should come as less of a surprise that Doctorow's interviews may also illuminate his essays. By comparing the dates of interviews with those of the essays (see chronology) and allowing for the delays between interview or composition and publication, students of Doctorow's work can gain a better idea of the development of his views on subjects ranging from Hemingway or Jack London to the Reagan administration and the Constitution. In what follows three examples will represent the numerous points of contact between interviews and essays.

In the first example, Doctorow worries that the assumption that the narrative of a single life can have universal implications may be breaking down under the pressure of the nuclear age. In a 1982 interview he tells Richard Trenner:

> The unsettling experience in writing fiction now may be in finding that the story of any given individual, and I don't care who it is, may not be able to sustain an implication for the collective fate. There's a loss of consequence, that's what I mean. The assumption that makes fiction possible, even Modernist fiction—the moral immensity of the single soul—is under question because of the bomb. To write fiction now as it has been written may be to misperceive or avoid the overriding condition of things, which is that we're in the countdown stages of a post-humanist society. On the other hand, if that's true, I wouldn't mean to imply that the problems of fiction aren't the least of our problems.

Two years later, Doctorow returned to this idea in the essay, "The Beliefs of Writers." He again argues that the assumption of the "moral immensity of a single soul" is endangered. It is no longer defined, as it was by the great modernists, in a "moving outward" against society. With few exceptions, the fiction and criticism of the eighties have abandoned public conflicts in "an act of withdrawal." Doctorow deplores the "timidity" of contemporary writing, its "stunned submission to political circumstances." The essay thus develops evidence in support of the interview response. Both provide one context for reading *The Lives of the Poets,* which for many critics narrates the moral cowardice and narcissism of art in the Reagan years.

A related argument concerns what Doctorow calls "the theme of a life." It appears in both an interview response to Alvin Sanoff and in a commencement address made at Brandeis in the same year (1989). Responding to Sanoff's question about the mixture of fact and fiction in his work, Doctorow adopts a new metaphor as justification for his practice:

> The way we respond to our experience creates the theme of our lives. That theme may be deviousness, innocence, failure, success or what have you. When I deal with characters who are historically verifiable, I am responding to the themes of their lives as they were worked out publicly. I can make judgments.

Here Doctorow amplifies on the assumption of the "moral immensity of a single life" by claiming that a writer has the capacity to understand the essence of actual people. Of course, this is an extension of his earlier claim that his treatment of J. P. Morgan was "more accurate to the soul of that man than his authorized biography." Both quotations are Emersonian in their aggrandisement to the author of divine powers of perception. In his commencement address Doctorow calls upon students to become readers of their own themes. He begins with a defense of the "impractical" nature of a liberal arts education, adopting as a premise the idea that he will speak to the students as the faculty, collectively might have wanted to:

> The presumption of your life here, the basic presumption, is that every life has a theme. It is a literary idea, the great root discovery of narrative literature: every life has a theme and there is human freedom to find it, to create it, to make it victorious. And so however you find your society as you walk out of here, you do not have to embrace its lies, or become complicitors to its cruelties. Perhaps that is what your faculty wanted to say to you.

The interview and address show Doctorow using the same metaphor ("the theme of a life") for both literary creation and real life, thereby suggesting the powerful hold of this Emersonian ideal. It continues Doctorow's concern for "the moral immensity of a single life" put in jeopardy by contemporary political life. Doubtless these are the representational assumptions that novelists *cannot* wholly contest, as first conditions of their work.

A final example concerns the Constitution and, more broadly, America. In his interview with Paul Levine in 1983, Doctorow makes the following claim:

> It seems to me we are, at least on paper, supposed to be different from, or better than, we are. And that kind of irritation confronts us all the time And has from the beginning. The Constitution was a precipitate of all the best Enlightenment thinking of Europe, and it's really quite a remarkable document. That we don't manage to live up to it is the source of all our self-analysis.

The idealistic argument sketched here is echoed in many interviews and comes to fruition in the essay "A Citizen Reads the Constitution" (1986). That essay's admiration for the discursive voice of the Constitution's sentences, as well as its consciousness of the construction of legitimacy out of an act of violent rebellion, makes the Constitution for Doctorow perhaps one of the few "true documents" amidst the welter of false documents—literary and other—in the American scene.

I'm very happy that this volume includes the first publication of two of Doctorow's interviews originally given on public radio (the Michael Silverblatt interviews) and the first publication of an interview given in Italy in 1989. It's a pleasure to acknowledge the assistance of E. L. Doctorow, who provided the leads to previously-unpublished interviews; to Professor Michelle Tokarczyk, for consulting her own research materials on my behalf; to my colleagues at Norwich University Ms. Deborah Ahlers, reference librarian, and Professors Kathleen Dana and David Ward for very helpful research assistance. For financial help in support of this project I am indebted to the Faculty Development Committee and Provost of Norwich University. I'm also indebted to Professor Andrew Knauf for thoughtful copy-editing and to Sharon Smith and Ursula Bensheimer for tireless secretarial assistance. Most of all I am grateful to my wife, Martha, my inspiration in all things, and to my sons, Jason and Daniel, to whom I dedicate this book, for the joy they bring to me.

Notes

The interviews and feature stories chosen for inclusion in this volume were those dealing primarily with Doctorow's fiction. The cost of permissions, contractual provisions or difficulties in determining copyright made it impossible to reprint the following: Hillary Mills, "Creators on Creating: E. L. Doctorow," *Saturday Review* 7

(October, 1980), 44–48; Carol E. Rinzler, "A Dialogue with Doctorow," *Cosmopolitan* 199 (November 1985), 66 +; Charles Ruas, "E. L. Doctorow," in Charles Ruas, editor, *Conversations with American Writers* (New York: Alfred A. Knopf, 1985), 197–212; George Plimpton, "The Art of Fiction," *The Paris Review* 28 (Winter 1986): 23–47; Elinor Wachtel, "E. L. Doctorow," in Elinor Wachtel, editor, *More Writers and Company* (Toronto: Alfred A. Knopf, Canada, 1996), 177–92; interview with Jackie Lyden on *All Things Considered,* August 28, 1994. A transcript of the last interview is available from National Public Radio. In the notes below, I indicate information in these interviews that is not duplicated in the contents of this volume; of course, readers should consult the originals.

A comprehensive listing of interviews with Doctorow is part of Michelle Tokarczyk's *E. L. Doctorow: An Annotated Bibliography* (New York: Garland, 1988); for the years after 1988, readers should consult the MLA Bibliography as well as online sources like Infotrak.

Like many best-selling authors, Doctorow has granted numerous promotional interviews in regional newspapers in connection with specific publications; an example is Tim Warren's "Doctorow's 'Waterworks' Shows Bad Old New York," *The Albany Times-Union* 12 June 1994. Recently there have been several interview/feature stories in connection with the Broadway musical version of *Ragtime.* Three examples are Rick Lyman, "Learning to Hear What Music Has to Say," *The New York Times* 11 December 1997, C1 +; "Doctorow Changes Tune about Musicals," *The New York Daily News* 8 January 1998; "Doctorow Discusses Musical *Ragtime,*" *The Seattle Times* 20 January 1998. As of this writing, the last two interviews were available at their sources' web-sites.

1. In *E. L. Doctorow* (New York, Continuum, 1991), John G. Parks devotes two pages to Doctorow's life. The other book-length studies—Paul Levine's *E. L. Doctorow* (New York: Methuen, 1985) and my *Models of Misrepresentation: On the Fiction of E. L. Doctorow* (Jackson: University Press of Mississippi, 1991)—are exclusively critical. For a review of the criticism that adopts the perspective of reception studies, see John Williams, *Fiction as False Document: The Reception of E. L. Doctorow in the Postmodern Age* (Columbia, SC: Camden House, 1996).

2. In the uncollected interview with Carol E. Rinzler, Doctorow makes a very direct expression of the importance of writing: "It's a passion for me; I wouldn't know how to live without it. It's the only thing I know how to do." *Cosmopolitan* 199 (1985), 66.

3. See Marshall Bruce Gentry's "Ventriloquists' Conversations: The Struggle for Gender Dialogue in E. L. Doctorow and Philip Roth," *Contemporary Literature* 34 (1993), 512–37.

4. Doctorow's response to Trenner was elicited in the context of John Clayton's article, "Radical Jewish Humanism: The Vision of E. L. Doctorow," in Richard Trenner, editor, *E. L. Doctorow: Essays and Conversations* (Princeton, Ontario Review Press, 1983), 109–19. Doctorow's position among contemporary American Jewish writers was later examined by Sam B. Girgus in *The New Covenant: Jewish Writers and the American Idea* (Chapel Hill: University of North Carolina Press,

1984), Chapter 9. For a continuation of this critical interest, see Minako Baba, "The Young Gangster as Mythic American Hero: E. L. Doctorow's *Billy Bathgate*," *Melus* 18 (1993), 33–46.

5. In his interview with Jackie Lyden on National Public Radio, Doctorow further condemns those readers who allow non-print media to take the place of reading.

6. Postmodern narrative technique in *The Book of Daniel* has been the subject of numerous critical articles. A recent example is T. V. Reed's "Genealogy/Narrative/ Power: Questions of Postmodernity in Doctorow's *The Book of Daniel*," *American Literary History* 4 (1992), 288–304.

7. Critics are divided on how to assess Tateh. In *Fiction and Historical Conscious-ness: The American Romance Tradition* (New Haven and London: Yale University Press, 1989), Emily Miller Budick argues that Tateh's shift from silhouette-making to movie-making is accomplished by a realization about art and history that also informs the novel as a whole. John G. Parks, in *E. L. Doctorow,* agrees, seeing the marriage of Tateh and Mother as the representation of "a new historical composition" and Tateh's films as a "regenerative and morally responsible" vision (69). On the other hand, Paul Levine, in *E. L. Doctorow* points to Tateh's "corrupted sensibility" in exploiting the myth of success (59). Arthur Saltzman, in "The Sylistic Energy of E. L. Doctorow," in Trenner's *E. L. Doctorow: Essays and Conversations* believes Tateh's success is satirized because it is so conspicuously the result of "blind luck" (94).

8. For further details concerning the genesis of *Drinks before Dinner,* see George Plimpton, "The Art of Fiction," *The Paris Review* 28 (Winter 1986), 45–46.

9. A second step in the composition of *Loon Lake* was the publication of the poem, "Loon Lake." See Hillary Mills, "Creators on Creating: E. L. Doctorow," *Saturday Review* 7 (October, 1980), 46.

10. In her review of *Loon Lake* in *Commonweal* 107 (December, 1980), Francine du Plessix Gray called attention to the novel's "rhapsodic, long-metered prose that is faintly reminiscent, in turn, of Walt Whitman [and] D. H. Lawrence" (696); Anthony Burgess noted that "whole patches of *recit* are presented as *vers libre*," *Saturday Review* 7 (September, 1980) 67. But later articles on the novel have ignored discussion of this aspect of its style.

11. See the interview conducted by Herwig Friedl and Dieter Schultz, p. 112. Doctorow may have made this statement as a clarification, in response to some early reviews. For example, in "Singing the Same Old Song," *Commentary* 70 (1980), Pearl K. Bell thought that the narration of Joe's adventures were "repeatedly inter-rupted by mysterious computer printouts" (72). In "Fiction Chronicle," *The Hudson Review* 34 (1981), Dean Flower suggested that "fat poet Warren Penfield wrote it" (106). On the other hand, Doctorow's "clarification" here is expressed in characteris-tically tentative or ambiguous phrases.

12. Whitney Balliett compares Doctorow and Joyce in "Through History with E. L. Doctorow," *The New Yorker* 56 (December 8, 1980), 233; Alan Nadel, in "Hero and Other in Doctorow's *Loon Lake*," *College Literature* 14 (1987), 136–45, com-pares Doctorow and Nabokov (143–45); George Stade, in "Types Defamiliarized," *The Nation* 231 (September 27, 1980) compares Doctorow and Conrad.

13. Of course, Billy Bathgate's artistry is his juggling, which captures the attention of Dutch Schultz. In "Doctorow's *The Book of Daniel* as *Kunstlerroman*: The Politics of Art," *Papers on Language and Literature* 18 (1982), 384–97, Susan Lorsch argues that for Doctorow's title character, art is the "only viable response to alienation." While Daniel is not a criminal in a juridical sense, Doctorow's epithet for him—"a criminal of perception"—may hint at a more general link between crime and art; another link might exist between Coalhouse Walker as both skilled artist and revolutionary.

Chronology

1931	Edgar Lawrence Doctorow born 6 January; son of David R. and Rose (Lenin) Doctorow in New York City.
1936–48	Attends public schools in New York City.
1952	Receives an A.B. degree in philosophy from Kenyon College, Gambier, Ohio. Studies under John Crowe Ransom.
1952–53	Graduate studies in drama at Columbia University, New York City.
1953–55	Serves in U.S. Army.
1954	Marries Helen Seltser, 20 August 1954; three children: Jenny (born in an army field hospital in Frankfurt, Germany), Caroline, and Richard.
1955–59	Works as a reservations clerk at LaGuardia Airport. Reads scripts for CBS Television and Columbia Picture Industries, Inc., New York City, senior editor.
1959–64	Editor with New American Library, New York City, senior editor.
1960	Publishes *Welcome to Hard Times*, Simon & Schuster.
1964–69	Editor in chief, Dial Press; vice president, 1968–69. Quits in 1969 to write full-time.
1966	Publishes *Big as Life*, Simon & Schuster.
1968	"The Songs of Billy Bathgate," *New American Review*.
1969–70	Writer in residence at University of California, Irvine.
1971	Publishes *The Book of Daniel*, Random House. Nominated for National Book Award.
1971–78	Regular faculty position at Sarah Lawrence College, Bronxville, New York.
1972	Guggenheim fellowship.

1973–74   Creative Artists Program Service fellow.

1974   "The Bomb Lives!" *Playboy*

1974–75   Creative Writing Fellow, Yale School of Drama.

1975   Visiting Professor, University of Utah.

1975   Publishes *Ragtime,* Random House. (Also Book-of-the-Month
           Club selection.)

1976   National Book Critics Award, Arts and Letters Award for *Rag-
           time.* Awarded L.H.D. by Kenyon College; "Writers and Politi-
           cians," *The New York Times;* "After the Nightmare," *Sports
           Illustrated.*

1977   "False Documents" in *New American Review* (Bantam); intro-
           duction to Barahemi's *The Crowned Cannibals* (Random House).

1978   Play, *Drinks before Dinner,* first produced off-Broadway at Public
           Theatre, November 22, 1978. "Living in the House of Fiction,"
           in *The Nation.*

1979   Play, *Drinks before Dinner,* published by Random House. "The
           Language of the Theatre" in *The Nation.* Honorary Litt.D.
           awarded by Hobart and William Smith College.

1980   Published *Loon Lake,* Random House. "Ronald Reagan," in *The
           Nation*; "Words into Rhinestones" in *The New York Times* and
           "Mother Jones Had Some Advice," in *The New York Times Book
           Review. Loon Lake* receives the National Book Critics Circle
           Award.

1980–81   Visiting Senior Fellow on the Council of the Humanities,
           Princeton University.

1981   Appears before House subcommittee re National Endowment for
           the Arts funding; remarks are included in "Art Funding for the
           Artist's Sake," in *The Nation.*

1982   Visiting professor of English, New York University. "Introduc-
           tion" to the Bantam Classics edition of Theodore Dreiser's *Sister
           Carrie.* Forward to an edition of Kleist's plays edited by Wealter
           Hinderer (Continuum). *American Anthem,* photographs by J. C.
           Suares and text by E. L. Doctorow (Stewart, Tabori and Chang).

1983   "The Novelist Who Was Born Old," in *The New York Times Book
           Review;* "On the Brink of 1984," in *Playboy.* Addresses the grad-

uating class of Sarah Lawrence College and publishes those remarks in "The Bomb Culture," in *The Nation.*

1984   Publishes *Lives of the Poets: Six Stories and a Novella,* Random
        House. "The Beliefs of Writers," the Hopwood Lecture delivered
        to graduating students of the Creative Writing Program at the Uni-
        versity of Michigan.

1985   Publishes *World's Fair,* Random House. "The Beliefs of Writers"
        appears in abridged form, under the title "The Passion of Their
        Calling," in *The New York Times Book Review,* and in its entirety
        in *The Michigan Quarterly Review.*

1986   "Braver Than We Thought," in *The New York Times Book Review.*
        "A Citizen Reads the Constitution" address given at Constitution
        Hall in Philadelphia under the auspices of the Pennsylvania Hu-
        manities Council. "Schultz and PEN" and "The State of Mind of
        the Union" in *The Nation.* "The Importance of Fiction, Ultimate
        Discourse" in *Esquire.* Wins American Book Award for *World's
        Fair.*

1987   "A Citizen Reads the Constitution" in *The Nation*; "Tap Dancing
        Among the Literati" and "Pumping Out Success," in *The Sunday
        New York Times.* Introduction to Frank Kafka's *Amerika*
        (Schocken).

1989   Publishes *Billy Bathgate,* Random House. Reviews Jack Lon-
        don's *Letters* and Clarice Stasz's *American Dreamers* in *The New
        York Times Book Review.* Delivers commencement address to the
        graduating class at Brandeis University; the address appears later
        in the year in *The Nation.* With Eric Fischl, publishes *Scenes and
        Sequences* (Peter Blum Edition).

1990   "Introduction" to Vintage Library of America edition of Jack
        London's *The Call of the Wild.* "James Wright at Kenyon" in *The
        Gettysburg Review.* "Two Waldens" delivered at the Walden
        Woods Project Press Conference in Boston, Massachusetts, 25
        April.

1991   "Standards" in *Harper's.* "Art vs. the Uniculture" in *The Nation.*
        "Open Letter to the President" in *The Nation.*

1992   "The Character of Presidents" in *The Nation.* "The Nineteenth
        New York" in *Architectural Digest.* "Unnatural Acts" in *Ameri-
        can Theatre*

1993   *Poets and Presidents* (collection of essays) published by Random House. With two partners, announces the creation of Booknet, a 24-hours-a-day, books-only cable TV service.

1994   *The Waterworks* published by Random House.

1995   "Mythologizing the Bomb" in *The Nation*

1996   "F. S. F., 1986–1996" in *The Nation*

1998   Introduction to Signet edition of Sinclair Lewis's *Arrowsmith*; "Comment: Has Starr Humiliated Us All?" *The New Yorker* 12 October 1998

Conversations with E. L. Doctorow

PW Interviews: E. L. Doctorow

John F. Baker / 1975

From *Publisher's Weekly* 207 (30 June 1975), 6–7. Used by permission.

E.L. Doctorow is already becoming accustomed to being asked about the characters, real and imaginary, in *Ragtime,* his extraordinary new novel out July 14 from Random House. And already he is becoming a little impatient with the questions: Did Harry K. Thaw, Stanford White's killer in the "crime of the century," really watch Harry Houdini stage an escape from the Tombs? Did Pierpont Morgan really have a conversation with Henry Ford about reincarnation in his famous library? Did liberated Emma Goldman really take society beauty Evelyn Nesbit under her wing?

These are only a few of the happenings in *Ragtime,* in which real people of the first decade of the 20th century in America interrelate with the cast of a fast-moving but entirely imaginary narrative. For Doctorow, such contemporary figures are "images of that time," with something of the power of myth attaching to them, and he is anxious not to spoil their mystery by being too literal-minded about them. "As a writer," he says quietly and thoughtfully (and Doctorow thinks carefully about everything he says, no matter how often he is asked it), "I have learned to trust myself in the act of writing. These people occurred to me—and specifically *these* people, Morgan, for instance, *not* Andrew Carnegie—because they carried for me the right overtones of the time."

As to whether they really did some of the things he attributes to them— what is real in his narrative, and what not—he is as near being playful as one suspects he ever gets, "What's real and what isn't? I used to know but I've forgotten. Let's just say that *Ragtime* is a mingling of fact and invention—a novelist's revenge on an age that celebrates nonfiction."

Doctorow himself lives in the 1906 house in New Rochelle (just outside New York) where the action of the book begins, and he recalls very specifically its genesis. Sitting in his study looking down at the street, he visualized, suddenly, the people who lived in the house at that time being visited by Harry Houdini—"I don't know why"—and the rest of the book is an elaborate expansion upon that moment, and that idea. He has worked very hard on the book for the past two years, but still looks back on it as a "happy, easy book to write—it didn't fight me."

Ragtime is much the most accessible book of the four Doctorow has written, and he is glad of it. "I've always wanted my work to be accessible. Literature, after all, is for people, not some secret society. It probably seems so accessible this time because I was very deliberately concentrating on the narrative element. I wanted a really relentless narrative, full of ongoing energy. I wanted to recover that really marvelous tool for a novelist, the sense of motion. Two or three hundred years ago it was much more common— Defoe had it, Cervantes, more recently Edgar Allan Poe. You have to make sacrifices for it, of course: you lose psychological complexity in your characters, you have to distance yourself from them, and that's an approach that hasn't been characteristic of recent fiction."

And for Doctorow, this dedication to narrative energy worked splendidly for his book. "Once I was under way it generated itself, made its own rules, its own demands, and by the last third of it, it had developed complete inevitability." There are plenty of indications that *Ragtime* is going to be a big success—a BOMC choice, movie rights sold, large printings—and Doctorow, who has previously enjoyed excellent reviews but not overwhelming sales, is delighted at the prospect.

"I shall feel very good if it's a success. It's funny, but all the time you're writing you don't think about that at all, beyond the book being published. Then once it is published, you don't think about anything else but the possibility of its success." But as one who doesn't even relish being interviewed, Doctorow hardly relishes the prospect of literary lionizing. "I don't think I could cope with that. In fact I hope to go right away very soon and get back to work."

Back to work in this case means the completion of a play commissioned by the Yale Repertory Theater, and which, says Doctorow, they hope to perform in the coming season. "Is that a realistic hope?" *PW* asks. Doctorow laughs delightedly. "I see you know a lot about writers? Let's hope it is." He also has a new novel in mind, but nothing is written yet.

Doctorow was in publishing himself for many years before he left five years ago to devote himself to writing (with occasional teaching, currently at Sarah Lawrence). He began as a reader for Columbia Pictures, where for three years "I read just about everything that was published." (His own first novel, *Welcome to Hard Times* was made into a movie.) Thence to New American Library, where he worked his way in five years to senior editor. Finally, in the mid-1960s, he went to Dial Press as editor-in-chief. In his early publishing days, "I just saw it as a means to survival while I continued writing," and he would put in 20-hour days between the office and his typewriter. "Then when I got to Dial I found it very interesting and creative, and I began to neglect my own work because editing and publishing was such fun. Finally I realized I just had to concentrate on my own work."

He looks back fondly on an "enormously satisfying time" at Dial. He was there in the first years after Dell's takeover allowed a great deal of expansion capital. "We were very busy and very ambitious, and it was an exciting period. For a little house we made a lot of noise." He recalls working with Norman Mailer, Vance Bourjaily, James Baldwin, Thomas Berger, Richard Condon, Ann Moody, Larry McMurtry—even one of Abbie Hoffman's first books. "We had a good bit of action with *Report From Iron Mountain*, if you remember that. And we were ahead of our time—do you know, we commissioned a multivolume Bicentennial history, back in 1966 or '67—and we did probably the first book on *The Great Comic Book Heroes*, with a terrific introduction by Jules Feiffer."

Although he feels narrative skills are being somewhat neglected by many contemporary novelists, Doctorow doesn't want to be dogmatic about it—or, in fact, about anything. "I don't want my interest in it to appear exclusionary. There's a lot of splendid writing going on. It's a very exciting time for fiction. Literature isn't a horse race after all, and I hate the idea that in this country of 200-million people there's room for only a few writers at a time."

As to whether, with *Ragtime,* he has launched a new genre of novel, "maybe we need some new definitions—and I leave that to the critics." He is not likely to be among their number, although he has been asked on occasion. "I think it was Cyril Connolly who said: 'Writers should avoid three things: tennis, sex and reviewing books.' I've accepted a third of this advice."

As a former publisher, Doctorow is overwhelmed at the treatment his new novel has received (Random, almost unprecedentedly, sent out a specially printed gift edition "to friends of the author and publisher" in advance of publication as a mark of its enthusiasm). "As an author, I am prepared to find fault, as a matter of principle, with anything a publisher does. But I must say Random has been tremendous."

In the end, despite all the prepublication praise the book has received, Doctorow appreciated as much as anything what his mother, to whom it is dedicated, said: "She said it was like having a piece of fine lace in your hands, and enjoying the intricacies of the design and pattern. Isn't that great?" He grinned. "Maybe we should print it on the jacket: 'The author's mother writes . . .' "

Novelist Syncopates History in *Ragtime*

Mel Gussow / 1975

From *The New York Times* 11 July 1975, 12. Copyright © 1975 by The New York Times. Reprinted by permission.

For a long time after finishing his novel *The Book of Daniel,* E. L. Doctorow sat at his desk in his home in New Rochelle, N.Y., contemplating what to write next. "I became aware of the room in which I was sitting, and I began the first line—'I live in a house built in 1906. Teddy Roosevelt was President.' "

That life eventually changed, but Mr. Doctorow was soon transported back in time. He imagined Harry Houdini stopping in front of his house in a Pope-Toledo Runabout. Gradually, Houdini, Emma Goldman, Evelyn Nesbit, J. P. Morgan, Henry Ford, Sigmund Freud and many other figures in history became characters in a novel, *Ragtime,* a "chronicle fiction" about America at the beginning of the 20th century.

This unusual book, Mr. Doctorow's fourth novel, is being acclaimed by reviewers and is sure of commercial as well as artistic success. Random House has already printed 60,000 copies. It is a Book-of-the-Month Club summer selection and is scheduled to be filmed by Robert Altman.

At 44, after years as an editor and teacher as well as novelist, Mr. Doctorow couldn't be happier about his success.

"I do want the book to be accessible," he said in an interview. "I want working-class people to read it, people who don't follow novels. Reading novels often requires an effort of the will. I want the reader to be as unaware of committing a cultural act as he is when he goes to the movies."

In pursuing that goal, Mr. Doctorow made *Ragtime,* unlike many other experimental novels, enormously readable. It tells a story, or rather a series of interlocking stories.

To the author's chagrin, "Storytelling has been appropriated by sociologists and psychologists. Books about physical fitness and diet tell stories—with villains. Fat-around-the-middle is a villain. There is conflict—and resolution. Even when they report the weather on television, they dramatize it; 'We'll have that story in a minute.' "

4

Where does that leave the novelist? "He is pushed into realm of personal experience—a very small preserve he is allowed to wander in.

Ragtime is an act of restoration, what Mr. Doctorow calls "a novelist's revenge."

"It defies facts," he says. "Give 'em all sorts of facts—made-up facts, distorted facts. I begin to think of *Ragtime* as fictive nonfiction. It's the reverse of Truman Capote. I see all those new journalists as guys on the other side."

The method, as he sees it, is at least as old as Daniel Defoe. "He claimed to be the 'editor' of *Robinson Crusoe,*" he says. "At the same time he relied on the public's knowledge of Alexander Selkirk"—the real-life model for Crusoe. "Selkirk's whole life was justified by 'giving' Defoe his life story."

"From the beginning, novelists have used strategies, have mixed up fact and fiction. That's the region where *Ragtime* is located—halfway between fiction and history."

"Kenneth Rexroth said that *Moll Flanders* is a false document because Defoe wrote in the voice of a prostitute. My book is a false document. A true document would be the Gulf of Tonkin resolution or the Watergate tapes. The basic false documents are dreams, which repeat things that didn't take place—and prophesy our lives."

The characters, real as well as imagined, began to have a life of their own. "Houdini kept coming back very insistently, whereas Freud was quite content to have a walk-on," he said. "I wanted to do more with Emma Goldman, but the book ended before I could."

One of the major characters is Coalhouse Walker, a ragtime pianist turned revolutionary (in one scene Booker T. Washington tries to talk him out of blowing up J. P. Morgan's library). Asked if this angry black man were a real person Mr. Doctorow said, "There are several hundreds of thousands of Coalhouse Walkers in this country."

Then he indicated that Coalhouse is actually a tribute to Heinrich von Kleist, one of whose stories is called "Michael Kohlhass," about "a German horse dealer during the time of Martin Luther who becomes an incendiary and revolutionary."

Sort of Resonance

The title of Mr. Doctorow's book changed many times in the course of the writing. "I became more aware of the possibility of the musical analogy and the form of the book," he said. "It is divided in four parts, as rag is. A title is something to use up as you write the book, to give it some sort of resonance."

With *Ragtime* published, Mr. Doctorow is anxious to get back to work, to finish the play he is writing for the Yale Repertory Theater under a fellowship from CBS television and to start his next novel.

But it will be difficult to leave *Ragtime* behind. Constantly he is besieged with questions: what is fact, what is fiction? He prefers to leave answers to the reader's imagination.

Pressed on specific incidents, he said, "The book is a series of meetings that never took place," and admitted that he "made up a lot of tricks for Houdini." On the other hand, "Freud and Jung's trip to America is well documented, as is the fact that they went to Coney Island."

But did Freud and Jung ride through the Tunnel of Love together, as they do in *Ragtime,* and when their group visited the Lower East Side did they all have "to enter a dairy restaurant and order sour cream and vegetables so that Freud could go to the bathroom"?

"Who's to say it didn't happen?" asked Mr. Doctorow.

Mr. Ragtime

Jonathan Yardley / 1975

From *The Miami Herald* 21 December 1975. Used by permission.

The hot ticket in Hollywood these days is *Ragtime,* the hugely successful novel by E. L. Doctorow which Robert Altman is now preparing to film. From Paul Newman to Mick Jagger to O. J. Simpson, the glittering names of pop-culture stardom are scrambling to win parts in what gives every promise of being a blockbuster movie.

But if Doctorow himself has any say in the matter, you may not recognize a single face on the screen once the film reaches the theaters. He is writing the screenplay himself, and he recognizes that a problem central to his task is the novel's intermingling of historically "real" and fictional characters. When all of them are played by actors, can the movie have the effect on the viewer that the novel does on the reader? "A possible answer," Doctorow says, "would be to do the whole movie with unknowns and make the people playing historically identifiable characters look as much like their known public appearances as possible—so that you get someone playing Freud who really looks like Freud and someone who is the image of Houdini."

Economics, Doctorow readily acknowledges, may make that impossible: to make a boxoffice success of the film, it may be necessary to hire a cast of certifiable box-office drawing cards. For now, in any event, Doctorow is far less concerned with questions of casting than he is with writing a screenplay that will be not merely "an illustration of the book, but a film that has some kind of integrity of its own."

It's not a task Doctorow invited. His original intention was to stay as far away from the film as possible. A "really bad" movie was made of his first novel, *Welcome to Hard Times,* and "I had determined not to have anything to do with *Ragtime*—not that I was asked, as I recall." But Joan Tewksbury, who had begun work on the adaptation—she did the screenplay of *Nashville* for Altman—withdrew from the assignment and Doctorow was then persuaded to take over.

Doctorow talked about *Ragtime* and a number of related subjects during a recent visit to Key Biscayne. He came there to show the flag at the annual sales conference of Bantam Books, which paid a record $1.85 million for paperback rights to the novel. "The interview is not my medium," he says. "My medium is a book." But he talked animatedly and forthrightly for an hour and a half before lunch, during lunch, and in an afternoon auto tour of the island and the erstwhile Nixon compound.

He is a short, stocky, energetic man who gives the impression that he misses nothing happening around him. He has alert, lively eyes, and he walks with an athlete's bounce—though a truncated bounce that day because of a minor leg injury suffered in an early morning tennis game. To a photographer who expressed surprise at finding a teacher of writing and literature relatively undemonstrative, he remarked: "I would be more physical, but I'm wounded. It's a mistake to play tennis early in the morning."

Doctorow talks carefully—not out of self-defense but to make certain that he expresses himself as precisely as possible—and confidently. Of nothing is he more confident than *Ragtime*. He feels he has created something unique, perhaps even precious, and he has been supported in this belief by the remarkable critical and popular reception the novel has earned.

It is, as some quarter-million purchasers already know (and you probably can multiply that by ten to make a guess at the number of people who have read it), a short, intense yet leisurely novel that begins in 1906 and ends with the coming of World War I. It involves three fictional families and a host of historical figures ranging from J. P. Morgan to Booker T. Washington to Harry Houdini to John J. McGraw to Emma Goldman, and it weaves their lives together so subtly and skillfully that fiction and history merge into an utterly persuasive and joyful whole.

The book has dazzled readers: Doctorow is somewhat dazzled himself. "The book seems to have somehow laid something down in the public consciousness in this country at this time that I haven't even begun to analyze," he says. "I'm not even sure I should. In some peculiar way something very crucial has been touched in the American nerve. I think the fifteen or twenty-year-old person who reads *Ragtime* immediately has more to say about that period than is in the book. Do you know what I mean? There's an awful lot of knowledge that exists in a person that can form up around something in a book—like magnetic filings. I think young people, even infants, must know a lot more about history than they're called upon to realize."

That the *Ragtime* phenomenon has occurred is something of an accident. When Doctorow sat down to write what would become his fourth novel—his third, *The Book of Daniel,* was his best-known up to then—he had nothing more in mind than the vague notion of a fictional treatment of Bishop Pike and the occult. But when he finally got a sentence into the typewriter, it read: "In 1902 Father built a house at the crest of the Broadview Avenue hill in New Rochelle, New York."

So much for Bishop Pike. The novel acquired a life of its own. Doctorow describes what happened:

"I started with a narrative presumption, that I had a story to tell and that I was going to. In a certain sense the book was an act of exploration, to find out what it itself was about, I did that with *Daniel,* too. The first two books I was very calculating, and I think that was a mistake. I learned to trust the act of writing and not to impose the degree of control that could kill whatever might happen. There are very few pages that I wrote less than a half-dozen times; nevertheless, my memory of the experience of writing the book is of a tremendous exhilaration and great ease. It took about two and a half years, possibly a bit more if you count the poking around.

"I became acutely aware of narrative as opposed to fiction. The most conscious technical idea I worked with as I proceeded was the idea of the rigorous narrative which, combined with a certain distance to the characters, allowed me to produce a kind of reality that I really liked, that exists somewhere between fiction and modern journalism or history, sort of an in between region, I found it, and I liked being there.

"I think the experiment I did is very much within very common, traditional motives of the writer. It's sometimes a fact that what appears to be new, and excites people very much, is really quite traditional. Defoe, for example, said there really was a Robinson Crusoe, that this was just a memoir, and that he, Defoe, was really just the editor. And Cervantes claimed that there was this historian whom he was just translating, and that's how we were able to read about Don Quixote. In *Ragtime,* the trickery I suppose is in saying that this book is so true, it's about real people you know to have existed. But that's really just another way of throwing up the knives and balls and juggling in the old marketplace."

If Doctorow pays tradition the respect it deserves, he is also very much aware of the changed conditions under which writers now work. A question about his reaction to having his work translated into film leads him into an extended comment on the relationship between books and the cinematic arts, and what it means for writers:

"One can take the traditional point of view, and refuse to sell the film rights, and I might be justified in that insofar as I found that first film such a dreadful experience. But I think what's happening is that a new kind of intra-media sense of a piece of literature is happening in this country. I think all sorts of things are happening to esthetic perceptions.

"For instance, I don't think a writer can ignore seventy years of optical technology when he sits down and writes a book. You can't ignore the fact that children grow up now and see a commercial which in thirty seconds or a minute has five or eight scenes and tells a whole story, with extraordinary visual values that carry a child through several emotions culminating in a desire to purchase.

"The rhythms of perception are shot. That's why the theater is in such difficulty today, because people watch actors standing on the stage for fifteen or twenty minutes doing exposition and they get very restless. We receive things faster, we don't want to have things explained to us, and our internal biorhythms are esthetically shot—totally shot. If that's so, then the writer probably has to foresee a time in which, if something's successful, people don't make a distinction between the book and the film.

"People understand things very rapidly today, and I really want to keep one step ahead of them. I find a lot of modern writing very static and self-indulgent. The novel has to constantly recreate itself by assaulting its own traditions, the form has to be abused somehow in order to be re-invented each time you write a book. The novel used to be a primary act of culture, and I think that in the last twenty or thirty years people have come not to believe in novels any more—at least not in any massive way. So if you're a writer of fiction, you've got to contend with that."

That may, in substantial measure, explain why both of Doctorow's most successful novels are extrapolations upon historical reality. *The Book of Daniel* is about the Rosenberg case and the lives of the two boys whose parents were executed; *Ragtime* not merely introduces historical figures into fictional narrative, it also concerns itself directly with political issues. Doctorow rapidly agrees that one is "right on target" in describing both novels as essentially political, but he finds nothing unusual in that:

"I think everyone writes political books, actually. If you write dog stories, that has some political value in some way, and as a matter of fact Albert

Payson Terhune's dog stories are highly political. Those are very white Anglo-Saxon Protestant dogs—they defend the property of the wealthy against the evil ethnic minorities. That was pointed up by a historian at Yale, Robin Winks.

"I don't see how it's possible for a novelist not to recognize the political implications of his work. If you write a book about your marriage, your own neurosis, your divorce, your affairs, the writer can derive a political universe from that and find the forces that reinforce a certain political point of view.

"I think what both *Daniel* and *Ragtime* suggest—*Ragtime* particularly—is what a part of the family radicalism in America has been, an integral part of our public experience. I think *Ragtime* by implication suggests that radicalism is a part of the picture, in the sense that we're all implicated in our relationship to the political extreme in our midst. Emma Goldman's radical position, for instance, on abortion, is the orthodoxy of today. I think the radical's roles in one generation suggest what becomes the orthodoxy in subsequent generations."

Doctorow's ability to speak so clinically and authoritatively about the writing of fiction doubtless reflects his current location within the academic world, but his personal background is broad enough to embrace many other interests. Born 44 years ago in New York City, he "had it in mind to write in about the third grade." He attended the Bronx High School of Science, a gathering place for many of the city's brightest young students, and then did a flip flop by attending Kenyon College in Ohio, a small institution famed at the time for the presence of the poet and critic John Crowe Ransom and as a center for the "New Criticism."

Midway through his college career, Doctorow switched from criticism to philosophy and also began to take up acting. That led him to Columbia, where he "took half an M.A. in theater and half in drama." He went into the Army and began writing plays at first. It was not until he was "about twenty-six or seven that I began writing my first novel" and it was—surprise—a Western.

"There was" Doctorow says, "a quality of circumstance and accident involved. I was working as a reader for a motion-picture firm. I sat behind some filing cabinets in the hall and was accursed to read things that were submitted to this company and write synopses of them. I had to suffer one lousy Western after another, and it occurred to me that I could lie about the West in a much more interesting way than any of these people were lying. I wrote a short story, and it subsequently became the first chapter of that novel."

Welcome to Hard Times was the result; it was followed by a second novel, *Big As Life*. Meantime, Doctorow had moved out of the movies and into publishing, first as an editor at New American Library and then in the same position at the Dial Press. He spent a year as a visiting lecturer at the University of California at Irvine, and four years ago he moved to Sarah Lawrence College in Bronxville, N.Y., "an amiable place and not a normal one—it has no departments, and as a result no departmental politics." He and his family, *Ragtime* readers will be interested to know, now live in New Rochelle.

Unlike many other celebrated American novelists, Doctorow has come relatively late to success. His slow passage toward the triumph that is *Ragtime* has given him qualities of self-awareness and self-deprecation that are valuable guards against the various temptations offered by instant celebrity. His answer to a question about how he is handling success is thoughtful and detailed:

"I don't know how I'm dealing with it. Some days I feel an enormous stress and other days . . . let me put it this way: I think if this kind of glory had occurred when I was in my twenties I would have had a terrible time. But I know myself too well now to be fooled about any of this in terms of the real emotional life that I have every day.

"The reality of that is that I have the same anxieties I've always had, the same failures of imagination, the same feeling that I don't know how to live, that I don't know about life and how to live any more than I ever did or than anybody I know does. Those are constants, so the success is something that exists around that. Somehow it has nothing to do with your sense of yourself as a very fallible human being with ridiculous needs and demands for gratification in outrageous portions. All that goes on and the success really doesn't touch it.

"What I have discovered is that there is a certain kind of pressure on me now that I thought would go away when the summer ended, but it hasn't—it's continuing. It has to do, for instance, with revving up and being larger than life to people I am called upon to meet—as, for instance, in an interview, or here when I'm asked to say a few words at a luncheon. I'm not really good at that. It's a different art, a kind of performing art that I'd just as soon do without. I'm a person who sits at a desk and writes. To the extent that there's pressure on me to turn this energy outward and to BEAM, to give experiences to other people who meet me—I resent that pressure."

Doctorow has paid his dues; that has a great deal to do with his ability to handle these pressures. Of no less importance, however, is his fundamental self-effacement; he is confident of the excellence of what he writes, and he does not embroil himself in the essence of his work. "There's something in me that identifies the writer not as a person who simply changed the names of the people in his life and wrote about them," he says. "I always liked inventing, and the stuff in my life is in my work only as an emotional topography. The psychic constructs are all there, but in terms of literal autobiography, I've never done that. That kind of person is how I allow myself to function. I'd be terribly bored if I felt I had to write a novel about my own life. I think my life, in its circumstances and in terms of personal history, is quite ordinary."

Were things continuing to be completely ordinary in Doctorow's life, he'd be working every morning on a new novel and teaching "half-time" in the afternoons. But Robert Altman calls, and Doctorow is making ready to take a leave during the spring semester in order to complete the screenplay. The job does not faze him.

"I've come around to the conclusion that a movie is just another means of distribution of my work and I would be crazy not to take the opportunity to have as much input into it as possible. Part of that has to do with trusting Altman and the people around him. I went up to Canada for a week to watch him work on a film called *Buffalo Bill and the Indians,* and actually took a small role in that film. It was very instructive. Then it appears there was a change in the plans for the writing of *Ragtime,* and I felt a bit more comfortable about doing it. I thought about it, and if I hadn't figured out a way to do it, I wouldn't have accepted."

It will be a while, probably sometime in 1977, before we see the results of his labors. It will be a while before we find out who plays whom. The battle is far from over: "Altman was in New York a few weeks ago getting his back fixed, and he was going around to Elaine's and every place making a joke about how so many people are hassling him about playing in this movie that he'd decided not to direct the movie but instead to write a book called *Casting Ragtime.*"

Doctorow pauses, shrugs, smiles: "It'll all work out."

Ragtime Revisited: A Seminar with E. L. Doctorow and Joseph Papaleo

Nieman Reports / 1977

From *Nieman Reports* 31 (Summer/Autumn, 1977), 3 +. Used by permission.

Editor's Note: Continuing our practice of taping Nieman seminars from time to time, we present the following transcript of a session with Joseph Papaleo, *chairman, Department of English, Sarah Lawrence College, and author; and* E.L. Doctorow, *author of* Ragtime *and* The Book of Daniel. James C. Thomson, Jr., *Curator of the Nieman Fellowships, introduced the speakers.*

James C. Thomson, Jr.: I first met Joe Papaleo some years ago on a tennis court—we are neighbors and friends on Cape Cod. Mr. Papaleo has many distinctions: he is Chairman of the English Department at Sarah Lawrence; he has authored a couple of novels that were published, some others that weren't perhaps—

Joseph Papaleo: Well, that's what I'm going to talk about—

Thomson: Joe Papaleo is at work on a novel, a fiction version of the Sacco-Vanzetti case, and he had the good sense, some years ago, to hire for Sarah Lawrence College a guy named Doctorow—

Papaleo: Who's been of no help—

Thomson: Does he ever show up for his classes?

Papaleo: Well, he showed up after I made the mistake—

Thomson: Anyway, I thought that since we had Ed Doctorow as well as Joe Papaleo, we would ask Ed Doctorow to respond to Joe's opening comment since Joe was his Department Chairman and hirer. And the question we'll begin with, as advertised on the menu, is "History as Fiction"—the creation of false documents.

Our two distinguished outsiders who are going to talk about literature or the problem of trying to write are willing to operate under what I call the "Polish formula" which is *liberum veto.* The reason why Poland never succeeded as a nation was that every man in the Polish Parliament had a veto on every proposition, and that's why Poland is barely alive.

Liberum veto means that we will have a transcript of these proceedings kept in a locked safe and we will distribute them to anyone who has raised their voice and is identified, and you can say, No—out! We will then publish in the most famous magazine in the country—beloved *Nieman Reports*—please subscribe—we love it—and we need you. End of spiel. Are we ready? Joe Papaleo, why are you here?

Papaleo: A couple of years ago I made the mistake of getting the idea of a piece of fiction based on the Sacco-Vanzetti case. I had written what my editor called ethnic fiction for a very long time, and I had hoped to write about two Italian radicals, turning to fiction. And I made the mistake of going to where they lived and to the Harvard Law Library where I kept finding facts which had not been known about Sacco-Vanzetti, and being energized by the facts, as if the facts would make fiction. I would then write a few chapters and my fiction editors would read the chapters and say, This is all facts. I was very confused as to what I was doing, and then slowly discovered that my imagination was being, in some way, cancelled out or depressed, and the confusion was that I was assuming that the energy of the new facts was the kind of energy that fiction writers get, that is like vibrations, to create fiction.

An example is that I met Rose Sacco's best friend, who told me that Mrs. Sacco was alive and was living in Watertown, and I could see her; and I was about to see her when I met Ed Doctorow who told me, Stop—you do too much and you're finished. He began to speak of his research and how he had a chance to meet, I think, a close friend of Emma Goldman—and he stopped himself. I think I had already done too much. I wish I had met him on the path earlier, but I hadn't.

So I've been thinking a great deal about that phenomenon which we all know, which is the imagination. How does one light it up, for fictional purposes, from historical information? This particular genre, which is getting popular and which has been popular for a long time, has been a stimulus for fiction for many, many hundreds of years and has a revival now, with Truman Capote, or with Norman Mailer. Fiction writers are trying to discover their identity in these ways. In the case of political figures, I borrow a statement from Ed Doctorow—we have in America an amnesia about a lot of our radicals. It was the discovery of the anarchists, the Italian anarchists, who were alive and were talking to me, right out here in Needham, that confused me in terms of the creation of fiction. So I begin by presenting the fact that I have a problem; and I've finally gone back to the oldest form of fiction—to letters.

Thomson: So this will be an epistolary presentation?

Papaleo: Partially an epistolary presentation—yes, and an attempt to base it on the character of Vanzetti and on all the study I've done—what we call research.

Thomson: Ed, would you like to try to elaborate on this problem you face?

E.L. Doctorow: It is true, I am guilty; I did say to Joe that it was danger-ous to know too much. The teaching of fiction-writing in American colleges usually includes the admonition to the student: "Write about what you know." What is implied is that you can only know things that you've experi-enced, that you have seen and witnessed. And of course, I don't think the writer of fiction is restricted by that. He can put himself in other skins, he can imagine what he has to know. He knows things in an intuitive manner. A fact doesn't mean that much to him, unless it's very beautiful in itself and resonates within him, in which case he can put it down, as he discovers it. But if it's not right, he can change it. This kind of thinking preceded scientific enlightenment and empiricism.

That is why I told my friend Joe Papaleo that it might be a mistake to see Mrs. Sacco. Just by thinking as a novelist, he could know everything she could tell him—possibly more. I would probably start, for the purpose of argument, by defining a journalist as a writer of fiction who doesn't acknowl-edge that he's making things up.

Someone asked me the other day if I'd ever done any journalism. And I suddenly remembered that I had a course in journalism at the Bronx High School of Science. And I sort of learned how to write a lead—is that what you call it? During the semester we got an assignment to do an interview and I took that assignment to heart and I turned in an interview with the stage doorman at Carnegie Hall. He was a lovable old man who, of course, had immense knowledge of musical literature and knew all the great artists, and he wore a blue serge double-breasted jacket and floppy brown pants and worn-down shoes, and he was a refugee from Hitler's Europe—and the teacher read my interview with the kindly old doorman whom all the artists knew and loved. She said, This is absolutely terrific. I think we ought to get a picture of him and run this in the school newspaper.

I said, Well, I didn't know how to take pictures.

And then she said, Well, I don't know if I can go down. It's a subway ride and I don't have the fare. And I hemmed and hawed and of course I had to confess that there was no such doorman—that I had made him up.

I suddenly realize I don't know why I'm telling this story. Only I suppose that my fate was decided at that point. If there wasn't a terrific old doorman at Carnegie Hall, there should have been. For all I know, there now is.

—But what were we talking about?

Diana Thomson: You were talking about the problem with using fact and fiction. We've had terrible trouble with that in *Ragtime*.

Doctorow: The truth of the matter is that to get a book going, you have to achieve a degree of irresponsibility that, once it comes upon you—and you're very lucky if it does—any such thing as truth in the factual sense is very destructive to your enterprise. But somewhere along the line, usually toward the end of the book, you realize that people are going to start asking questions and so you have these little discussions with yourself. You begin to defend your book and you begin to justify it and discover rationales for it— maybe if you're lucky—a whole aesthetic.

I had done that and a few people here heard it—Justin and Anne Kaplan have been through this before, but it's the proposition that there is really no fiction or non-fiction; there is only narrative; and that there are obviously ways to distinguish between the two—fiction and non-fiction—but certainly not in terms of verifiable truth; one mode of perception has no greater claim on truth than the other; that the difference has to do perhaps with distance— narrative distance—from the characters; it has to do with the kind of voice that is talking, but it certainly hasn't to do with the common distribution between fact and imagination. I believe everything in *Ragtime* is true.

Papaleo: I wanted to say, Ed is suggesting with *Ragtime,* a new kind of lying.

Doctorow: For a fiction writer, history simply is a source of imagery— images. He can organize these images and arrange them within the compositions that satisfy him.

On the other hand, if you think about it, historians do the same thing, only with a greater degree of distance toward their material. I wish Bernstein and Woodward had not stuck to the actual detections of investigative reporters. By doing that, it could be argued that they lent themselves for cover up. With the highest scruples of investigative reporting, they ran into the limits of the form. If they had taken off from what they knew they might have gotten a greater, more comprehensive understanding of exactly what happened.

Jack E. White, Jr.: Is it the case, though, that you were just having a good time when you were writing *Ragtime?* What you're coming up with now is all the stuff that you came up with to answer the questions that you thought people were going to put to you because you write about Harry

Houdini and Henry Ford and Sigmund Freud. And if that's the case, why are you repeating yourself? Why don't you tell us about what you were really thinking about when you wrote the book?

Doctorow: What I was really thinking about happens to be on the page. Of course I was having a good time. What kind of a puritanical society is this that a writer can't have a good time?

White: I was having a good time reading, that's why I'm asking you. I figured if you had all these things on your mind when you were writing a book, you probably would produce a rotten book and I don't think you did.

Doctorow: You know, you do all sorts of things to get your work done. For instance, you can see just how shaky a writer is and just how far over the edge of the cliff he is, but how much that title he keeps repeating is pulling him back; he says the title of the book he's doing to keep himself from falling. And so you use anything you can to get yourself through the day, and to get the book done. You can use the title, you can invent an aesthetic, you can write a manifesto, you can go to a bar and talk to other writers.

These are all ways you have of getting your work done, they're all justifiable in personal terms, if you finish the book.

Charles W. Bailey: We're dealing with a couple of continuums here, it seems to me. The one that has been suggested by Ed Doctorow anent journalists and historians has upset some people within my hearing, but there's also a continuum between non-journalists and novelists, and you've got a room full of people here tonight who have played around with different parts of that continuum.

Tony Lukas has written probably the best book about Watergate. Who's to say what's truth and fiction? Tony Lewis has written about Clarence Earl Gideon and the right to counsel; and it might have been a part in a novel about the military overthrow of the government; and who's to say that that's all fiction these days? I do think that you should be loose about where you're at on that continuum. It is one of the good things for writers in this period that the reader can't be sure where he is at. Don't sweat it. One of the nice things about *Ragtime* is that it ran the reader back and forth across that continuum. You were never sure what Mr. Doctorow was reporting and what he was making up. That is wise, after all. That's the end of my observation.

Dolph C. Simons, Jr.: Chuck, doesn't Capote—in *In Cold Blood*— purport to quote verbatim comments from the court or from the head of the Bureau of Investigation or the warden or scenes in Leavenworth which the reader is supposed to take as a verbatim conversation? Whereas in *Ragtime*, the way I read it, we're not supposed to assume that this is a specific quote of a specific person that can be checked against history.

Bailey: I think that Doctorow has an advantage that Capote didn't have here, in that Doctorow was dealing with something that happened 60 years ago.

Simons: But *Ragtime* makes no attempt to try to pass that stuff off as verbatim—

Bailey: Does *In Cold Blood?* You think that because it happened yesterday, it has to be verbatim?

Simons: I thought that Capote tried to indicate that this was indeed what was said and going on, as in Bernstein and Woodward—what the facts in the situation actually were.

Bailey: I think maybe Ed is a little unfair to Bernstein and Woodward, because I think that all they were trying to do was to capitalize on some work they had done for *The Washington Post* and make a lot of money out of it. There was nothing wrong with that—not a goddam thing is wrong with a reporter trying to get rich as long as he tells the truth. And later comes the chance to take off and to swing with it. They were doing some non-fictional things there that were very important, I think, and putting their stories together into a book.

Anthony Lewis: Well, I feel that it's almost intrusive to ask a novelist, unlike a journalist, what are the sources of his writings; why he wrote something—it's really none of our business in a way—but here we are. The thing that strikes me, not only about *Ragtime,* but about those other books—if I'm wrong I hope you will correct me—is their very political character. I wondered if you'll just say something about whether you feel—and I've already apologized for asking such a question but I'm driven to it—whether you have felt in all your novels that there is some general political theme or point of view—more so than many novelists—that you are expressing.

Doctorow: A novelist is thought to be a political novelist only when the politics of his novel are not the prevailing politics of his society. Then the politics stand out. We could discuss as a proposition the idea that all novels are political; all art is political, which seems to be endorsed in most countries of the world where the profession of novelist or artist is slightly more dangerous than that of high speed automobile racing. We have novelists who are put in insane asylums, who are tortured and put in cages, who are exiled. What does the rest of the world know that we don't know, about fiction and about art? I've often made the observation that this is one of the few countries in the history of western civilization in which artists are not seen to be a danger to the state.

There is a Yale historian, you'll forgive me for mentioning Yale, a man named Robbin Winks, I believe, who went back and read the dog stories of Albert Payson Terhune of a few years ago, and discovered something astonishing. Albert Terhune was a very popular author who produced a long string of books about dogs. *Bob, Son of Battle* was one of them. Do any of you remember *Bob, Son of Battle?* What Winks discovered is that all of these hero dogs were white, Anglo-Saxon Protestant dogs who defended the rather luxurious property of white, Anglo-Saxon Protestant homeowners. They heroically leaped at the throats of intruders, rapists, mad men, criminals and perverts, who were invariably black or Asiatic. Albert Payson Terhune is a highly political novelist. There's no question about that. But I didn't know that when I read *Bob, Son of Battle.*

There is an aestheticism in this country, which Saul Bellow talks about a little bit in *Humboldt's Gift,* I think,—a way of dealing with moral questions as if they were subject to aesthetic criteria. This is a point of view from which I dissociate myself, but it would define, for instance, the English department where Joseph Conrad is taught without reference to his highly conservative politics, or Dostoevsky without reference to his messianic conservatism, or James, or any of these highly political novelists. What the teachers talk about is the human condition, or the structure of the novel or stuff like that.

But there are writers around today who cannot be dealt with in strictly aesthetic terms, like this chap from Iran who was put in prison and tortured and is testifying wherever he can as a witness against the Shah's secret police, Savak. Or Solzhenitsyn, whom we regard critically as a bad writer, but who nevertheless has things to say about the Gulag Archipelago that more or less transcend these normal critical, aesthetic responses.

And I think I am a political novelist although I don't know exactly what my politics are—perhaps reformist Democratic with anarcho-socialist pretensions; but we have a peculiar way of containing our writers in this country, which is not to grant them any politics at all. So I guess what I'm saying is, thank you for recognizing me.

Monroe Engel: I was going to ask Mr. Doctorow whether he really wanted to go on making statements about the entire history of the novel or whether he wanted to talk about what he was doing himself. Because if he was going to stay on the entire history of the novel, I doubt that too much knowledge has been a disadvantage—I think that's at least arguable.

If he's going to talk about what I think is the much more interesting question of how he has found his own imagination can be energized, that's something different. I'm much more interested in having him talk about the second question than the first, and that's what I think Tony's question is about. If he wants to keep the historical context open to say that he really is talking about what has happened in the history of fiction, he can make that choice and I would like to know it.

Doctorow: Help.

Engel: Well, let me ask it more directly. Are you talking about Balzac or Dickens or—?

Thomson: Nobody talked about Defoe. I don't understand.

John E. Painter, Jr.: I have a question. Why did you decide to marry off an anarchist and a capitalist with a sort of unhappy and disaffected middle-aged housewife from New Rochelle?

Doctorow: Why not? It just worked out that way.

I appreciate the question about the kinds of things that energize my imagination. That's really a very astute question. I don't know. I think if I knew too well, it would be bad for me.

Painter: There was an incident in your book when the anarchist passed through New York and was going through New Rochelle and the little girl saw a little boy on the street, where you could have taken a different turn in your development and end up having the little girl marry the little boy, instead of the mother and the father.

Doctorow: Mailer would say on this imaginary shelf on either side of the novel as it is written, is the novel just to the left of it which could have been written, and the novel just to the right of it which could have been written.

Rodney Decker: I'd like to ask both gentlemen: it seems to me the work of both of you deals with judgments—judgments that we reach about people, about times, and about ages. Now, I'm suspicious of judgments where the person who judges doesn't somehow get down on his hands and knees, doesn't stoop into human detritus, and look at the facts that maybe are there, but ought not to have been there. And yet you reach rather specific judgments on these things—or it seems to me that you do—and could you comment on that please? Both of you.

Papaleo: I'm not quite sure what he's saying.

Decker: Are you talking about Sacco and Vanzetti? I should guess that the question is, did they do it? I should guess that that has to deal with facts that are facts.

Papaleo: The fictional part of Sacco-Vanzetti, which I haven't got yet, reminds me of what Ed was saying about Bernstein and Woodward. It's not the facts of what happened, it's the horribly bad taste of Richard Nixon, or the vulgarity of John Dean. Those aspects of character which resemble— forgive a word like hubris—that's what the fiction writer's looking for and in that, you get the truth, rather than the facts which, when they pile up too much, don't even make the truth, or obscure it, as Ed was suggesting in the case of Woodward and Bernstein.

Decker: It's exactly that suggestion that distresses me a bit. That some- how we're going to write about Sacco and Vanzetti and we hope we're going to write movingly. So that after the people have read it, they will say, It was this way or it was that way, and we should feel strongly about it. And yet we don't want to know the facts, somehow. If I were to talk to a judge or a jury who have had that attitude, or to a historian, I would be distressed. Why shouldn't I be distressed talking to a novelist?

Papaleo: Forgive me. I spent six months in the Harvard Law Library. I read all the letters, all the unpublished letters, all the six volumes of the case. I know so many facts. You don't mean that. That's not the—

Decker: Why, then, didn't you go talk to the lady?

Papaleo: Why didn't I talk to Mrs. Sacco?

Decker:—Because she would have had more facts—

Richard C. Wald: My question was along the same lines, but triggered by something that Mr. Doctorow said. I think I am one of those people on the continuum that Chuck Baily talked about who see the craft of the novelist as dealing with common matter with different tools. And my question would be, at what point is a fact intransigent; at what point is that there has to be a real archipelago or there has to be a prison camp? At what point is it that there has to have been a J. P. Morgan, and he wasn't black? Where is the point at which the fact needs to be revealed, as different from the point at which you can play with the pieces?

Doctorow: That's the key question. There are some facts as, for instance, the facts of what the Nazis did in Europe in the 1930s and 40s that have this intransigent quality that you speak of, in the face of which too facile a state- ment about the indistinguishability of fact from fiction is really appalling. But if the Nazis had won the war the facts of the death of six million Jews would now be construed quite differently. I think what I'm saying to Joe is—that it's possible that there's a certain kind of non-factual witness which doesn't destroy the facts or lie about them or change them, but in some peculiar way illuminates them. That's what we're talking about. It is the kind of muscle that novelists and poets develop, which in a—well, I think of what Henry James said about it. He said, If you have a young woman who has led a very sheltered life and she happens to walk past the army barracks and hear a fragment of conversation among the soldiers coming through the window, she can then, if she is a novelist, go home and write a novel about army life. And that's what I'm talking about. There are different sources of knowledge—one of a fact can be enough for a novelist to intuit an entire life.

Simons: Does that bother you?

Bailey: Yes, I'd like to ask you a technical question. What was the last thing or person that you took out of *Ragtime* before it was published? What was the last piece of whittling that you did—of editing you did—to remove an element from the story before it was in final version?

Doctorow: I remember very clearly a major bit of editing. It was a chapter in *Ragtime* in which Houdini put on his act for the Archduke Franz Ferdinand. After he flew the plane and landed, he was the invited to do a command performance in a hunting lodge in the Black Forest. Houdini did this performance and then warned the Archduke that his life was in danger, whereupon he was immediately wrestled to the floor by the Archduke's people, thrown into jail, and accused of being an anarchist. I really enjoyed writing that chapter.

Bailey: Why did you take it out?

Doctorow: I took it out because I couldn't—once that chapter was done—I couldn't then write past it. It was a good chapter, it pleased me, but it stopped me cold.

Bailey: Was that because you couldn't then get him out of jail?

Doctorow: Partially. Mostly it was that I had violated the voice of the book, or the narrative distance, that I had come in a little too close, that I had put myself in the position of having to plot, and that's not what this book was about. It did not have a plot. And so I took out that chapter; and saved some of the tricks for Houdini's appearance later in New Rochelle.

J. Anthony Lukas: Who is the hero of *Ragtime?* I ask because in another celebrated *Playboy* interview, Robert Altman says it is Tateh. Who do you think it was?

Doctorow: I don't know. I've never thought about it. Tateh becomes an American success story, but at the expense of his socialist principles. I don't know if that's heroism. He becomes a movie maker, which is what Bob Altman is. Maybe that's why Bob likes him.

Paul Solman: What you said about political journalism and all that business still disturbs me. The guy who comes around and testifies about the Shah of Iran's Savak, is it all right with you personally that when he bears witness about this situation, he makes it up—what the torture methods are and so forth?

Doctorow: I think what's critical here is the extent to which his art will propose to you that you are being tortured. Because if he just tells you what happened, of if he espouses political ideology, or shows you his scars, that would be a certain kind of truth. But if he writes so as to persuade you that you had gone through this with him, then what he has done is true.

Soloman: A lot depends on context, I grant. But if Baraheni says to me if he meets me in conversation, or at an event where he is describing what happened and what they do in Iran, isn't he making some kind of implicit pact with me that he is telling me as best he can what events actually transpired? Do you not see that as an important distinction?

Doctorow: I think we hear things all the time, from all sources, yet we live in states, most of us, of moral insensitivity. So the question of the writer, whether he is a journalist or writer of fiction or poet whatever, is: How am I going to get through to you what I know to be true? And no matter what he's experienced or what he's been through, he has no way of reaching you, paradoxically, unless he really knows how to write; and its true that that talent, that gift, can be *used* and this guy can be going around saying terribly mean, nasty things about the Shah of Iran.

Soloman: Well, I'm not really worried about the Shah. I'm worried about what happens, how he immobilizes people, if people then find out that what he said was not literally the case.

Doctorow: The point is if he's telling us something we didn't know before, we can act on it, we can verify it; but we won't unless we've really been moved by what he said.

Brenda Engel: I guess I'd say that perhaps a continuum is not from fact and fiction so much as from public to private knowledge, that fiction has always been based on people's lives, on things that are true, from Dickens to Balzac to Saul Bellow. Some of these characters happen not to have been publicly known, as Emma Goldman, for instance. But it doesn't mean that they weren't real. I find the two were rather confused in *Ragtime,* because my husband is a cousin of Harry Houdini. You know, a little fiction, a little fact, the private world and the public world are mixing. In the case of *In Cold Blood,* Truman Capote made private characters, who had perhaps some notoriety or some publicity, into well-known people. But I have a feeling that because we're in a meeting of journalists, these dichotomies are in the world that most of us know, in the world of public figures.

Marc Granetz: I have been very upset about the idea of trying to energize a writer by use of facts. R. V. Cassill, among others, has said that clearly the search of modern fiction is for subject matter. The historical novel, since perhaps *In Cold Blood,* is in a modern revival—providing that "matter." Defoe did, but he didn't do very much with it. This modern revival of historical facts (not knowing *too* much and then taking off on the facts) provides motivation for a writer or fodder for his fiction when he can't really work on pure imagination. You said you want to tell the truth as you know it. But do you need as a basis Sacco-Vanzetti, or something else actual to begin to tell the truth as you know it; actually, then, in fact as the modern public knows it? I see it as a little bit of failure of imagination. Maybe I'm completely wrong.

Doctorow: No, you may be right. That has occurred to me too; it's a pretty good point. I don't know, I resist any such thing as an aesthetic manifesto, for once you've done something, you claim, well, this is the way to do it, the only way to do it. Really, I think a novelist writes what he's capable of writing at any given moment; and this is the book I seem to have been able to do, so I did it. And it really is that physical a thing. You just press on and where it's possible to move forward, you do, and that's what turns into the book. If it's any good you will have broken somebody's rules. Of course *War and Peace* has Napoleon in it, which may be a failure of Tolstoy's imagination.

I'm coming to the conclusion that one of the reasons today's fiction writers are not read terribly widely is because we constrain ourselves. Writers of fiction come out of a very specific class in this society—the middle class. And we do not know what's happening anywhere in this country. We do not know what it feels like to mine coal or to be on welfare and most of us are recording our middle class marriages and failures and divorces as if somehow that's the whole world and that's what's happening. It may be a failure of imagination to begin to use history, or the materials of history, but at least I didn't write a book about growing up shy in the middle west.

Thomson: Or sharks—

Painter: Are you going to do a *Son of Ragtime?*

Papaleo: We're forgetting something—and forgive this textbookish sound—the truth, and the truth of *Ragtime* is the book—the book of fiction.

It's not really Harry Houdini or really anything. It's the metaphor it makes. In fiction it's the whole big metaphor it makes, which operates as a separate world from which we get another word about this present moment: the truth. And that is something which doesn't depend upon facts.

Bailey: No, that's absolutely right, though. You write something and somebody says to you afterwards, Wow, how did you figure that out? How did you know that was an important subject? And you're absolutely helpless because you can't say to them, Well, we thought it was a good story.

Comment: Right. But there were these intuitive sources that you referred to. . . .

Bailey: But you can't say that. That's not a respectable thing to say to a newspaper editor.

Painter: We have a short comment. There's a wonderful quote from Picasso that we artists lie in order to be able to tell the truth. And it seems to me that's what he's saying.

Thomson: Jimmy Carter says if you never lie, you'll never tell the truth.

Melvin Goo: Mr. Doctorow, to what extent, if any, would you care for a reporter writing for a daily metropolitan newspaper to move away from the seemingly pedestrian calling of just writing about the facts that he finds?

Doctorow: Oh, I would really love that. As a matter of fact, I have a fantasy about *The New York Times* and this is what it is: that on a day when Tony Lewis' column is not scheduled to appear, *The New York Times* is published—distributed to all of us—and I have written it all. If I could get Punch Sulzberger to agree to issue the paper as written in its entirety by me, on just one day, I would spend many, many years preparing that particular city edition. And I would consider it—it would be my life's work.

Bailey: But the question is, would you be willing to do it in the constraints of time and place, or whether you would get enough for me to do it with you in your way, so that it would have that immediacy and that truth of being the take-off on what happened.

Doctorow: It would be designed to blow us *Times* readers right off the street.

Thomson: Are you going to start at eight o'clock in the morning of the day when that happens?

If you do it, then what happens? Then you can't write it, you've got to be there. I want to know some day what writing fiction did for you, I mean seriously.

Doctorow: It puts my kids through college . . .

Engel: I want Mr. Doctorow to go on if he will with something he started talking about—that is, you said that all novels now are written by middle class writers, and that's true, but hasn't that always been true? And if it hasn't always been true, then I am wrong. But if it has always been true, what makes that different now?

Doctorow: It probably always has been true. But I find it hard to call Edgar Allen Poe a member of the middle class, or Herman Melville.

Robert Manning: Is that a personal difficulty, or a matter of fact?

Doctorow: It has probably always been true. But I live now, and that's the way I feel about things now: that we're all sort of doing this stuff that's fairly useless and there are a lot of people around the country who we don't know about and who are not educated and not college graduates, and who don't belong to the Book of the Month Club and own two cars, and so on.

I look at a guy like James T. Farrell, who really is terribly neglected by the Academy, by the critics for many, many years, a writer who lacks grace in the academic sense of the word, but he nevertheless reported about the lower and lower-middle classes in Chicago in the 1920s, or Dreiser, who talked about working girls and their rise and fall; or Richard Wright, who talked about the terrifying isolation of black people and their frustration, and the lower classes.

I don't really know who's around today who's doing that kind of recording. We all seem to be novelists for the Republican Party. That's why I'm feeling very happy that we have a new administration—I mean, just from a working writer's point of view, the national psychology is going to change over the next few years. I don't know what is going to happen, but it could lead to a different kind of novel.

Engel: I think that's right. Can you go on with that? But then what is the middle class novel supposed to do? I mean, we're not likely to get novels from anything other than middle class novelists. And that's why I want you to talk about the particular situation now. How is that material to come in? Where do you see it coming from?

Wald: It doesn't matter where the writers come from. If writers are novelists, and this pure young girl can walk by the barracks and intuit Army life, and write a novel about it, it doesn't matter where she comes from. It doesn't matter whether the novelist comes from the middle class; the middle class like everything else is right in the middle. But it matters what is the style or subject matter, what is the intention of intellect? And it seems to me that there *are* styles, there are Chicago schools, and there are Paris realists. What

you are talking about is how does politics set the style? How does a generation direct its mind? If you don't see the proletarian literature now produced
by the middle class, isn't it because people aren't paying attention to the
proletarians, not because there are no writers who are proletarians?

Doctorow: Yes, I agree with that. That's why I think that if Washington
begins to attend to some of our terrible built-in problems, there will be a
change probably in the kind of art that is being done, not just fiction, but the
other arts as well.

Question: Are you sure about that?

Doctorow: I think we are all highly subject to things like climates of
opinion or national psychological states.

Hennie van Deventer: I have a very stupid question to ask, but since we
have been carrying on at such a high intellectual level, I feel—

Thomson: Watch out! Watch out!

van Deventer: I don't even know if this is true of America, but surely it
is very true about the country where I come from—I mean South Africa—
that so many extremely good journalists turn out to be very rotten novelists,
and so very many extremely good novelists turn out to be extremely rotten
journalists. I would like to hear your comment on that observation.

Bailey: That's a long-range question.

Doctorow: I'll answer anything.

Thomson: Would you like to begin with Allen Drury?

Comment: Journalism destroys the imagination.

Doctorow: I'm not sure I agree.

Jose Antonio Martinez-Soler: Fiction is a kind of censorship. Well, I
come from Spain—

Papaleo: Where the reverse is always true. Journalism distorts the sense.

Doctorow: I think that there used to be a tradition in this country of the
novelist coming out of the journalist. It doesn't really exist any more. Maybe
there is some connection today with what we were talking about, the middle
class novelist, who knows about the middle class life, and the fact that so
many novelists today teach in universities and do not come out of newspaper
work. It occurred to me before, during the dinner, that novelists are no longer
the culture heroes they once were—except to journalists.

Tony Castro: The other day I was talking with some one who was saying
that for a long time in the history of American literature there has been this
great expectation of when are we going to get the great American novel, and
he said it is all based on the premise that the novel has to be the form of any

great literature in our day. That may not be the pace that James Agee set, as Agee's letters to Father Flye were better than even his novel, and maybe even his book on the sharecroppers. Are you not also suggesting that it may be the case that the loss of the cool, cool status, that the novelist might have had, may have been a false kind of thing—that the American novelist has been living in the past with European novelists, Russian novelists?

Doctorow: Yes, except that if you examine the history of novelists, you discover that the novel has never quite been the primary act of culture that it is supposed to be. And that novelists have always lied about themselves and what they were doing in an attempt to get a kind of authority for their work. From the very beginning, as I often say, Daniel Defoe pretended to be the editor of *Robinson Crusoe*. He claimed it was really a memoir—that he had only sort of fixed up the punctuation, which is approximately what Richard Nixon said about the Watergate case.—He took the same position. A really interesting thing about Nixon, I think, is that he was trying to make a composition and he almost did it, through all those months, and our fascination was that of people watching an artist at work. Fortunately, his novel failed terribly.

Justin Kaplan: Well, I have a combination—a question and a comment here. Ed Doctorow and I have been over some of this ground before. Of course, the question has to do with a piece of very shaky information I have, and that is, How would it bother your reading of Albert Payson Terhune as a political novelist if it were true that Terhune grossly mistreated his dogs? Which, I believe, was true.

Doctorow: I recognize the intentional fallacy.

Kaplan: All right, call it what you will.

You and Joe, in talking about Sacco and Vanzetti, may have come to grips with the real thing. I think that, reduced to a very simple statement, it means a helluvalot to me whether Auschwitz actually happened or was simply imagined by someone. I think that once you begin forgetting that distinction, you're in terrible trouble, or I am, anyway.

Doctorow: That's of course, exactly the point. But would you grant me the right to write about Auschwitz, even though I had never been there?

Kaplan: I think you're sidestepping your question.

I think it has to do not with your credibility or credentials as an eyewitness but with the literal, historical existence of the circumstances, which are not dependent upon whether you were there or not.

Doctorow: Nothing can be written that hasn't happened—if it hasn't happened, it will. Emerson, I think, said anything that can be thought can be written. If I imagine Auschwitz, then someone else can. Hitler imagined Auschwitz and look what happened. The imagination, the human mind, intrudes on life and composes experience all the time. It kills and makes history.

Bailey: Can I ask what may be a clarifying question? Are you suggesting that by fictionalizing something like Auschwitz, you diminish the perception of its reality?

Kaplan: Not really, but what I was suggesting is once you fictionalize actual circumstances, you begin to turn to the realm of pure invention. Then I think you undermine a terribly important reality. I'm not quarreling of course with anyone's right to write fiction.

Bailey: I think you are answering my question. Yes, though.

Kaplan: I wasn't aware of it.

Bailey: I'm not arguing with the fictionalizing, if by fictionalizing J. P. Morgan or Auschwitz, or Harry Houdini, or whatever, you undermine the perception of the reality of the real thing.

Kaplan: You don't though. You don't necessarily.

Simons: Undermine the reality, or the truth?

Lewis: I have a different question. Mr. Doctorow, I thought I heard you say a moment ago—or maybe I might have just got it wrong—that fiction would become more radical, or socially challenging, with a more socially-challenging administration taking office. You said something like that, didn't you?—We're going to have to have a change in administration and maybe fiction will follow. That strikes me as a rather amazing notion, since I thought it was the other way around—that during reactionary periods in politics it was the writers of fiction who challenged the assumptions, whether it was Dickens, or Orwell or whoever.

Doctorow: Why do you think we have a new administration?

Thomson: We have one real live American historian present, Frank Freidel, who has not been heard from, does he want to say something?

Frank Freidel: I'm counting journalists as historians tonight.

Thomson: No, you're not historians. You're journalists.

Diana Thomson: I have a possible difference. The way *Ragtime* deals with reality is different from the way Joe is trying to deal with reality with Sacco and Vanzetti. Because Sacco and Vanzetti is a whole, continuous, real narrative, and his problem is how to use which parts of it properly so it still stays real but is sufficiently interesting. Whereas *Ragtime* doesn't pretend to be a whole, coherent fictional reality. It's really made up of a character here, and a character here, and a character here, and they're sort of put together which may be the most exciting thing about it—to read about characters who have been exciting your imagination for years, suddenly in there together, working together. And really, *Ragtime* is a lot more imaginative, I think, than you are giving it credit for. You're assuming it's a piece of journalism that's been fictionalized and I think that it is something a lot more creative and a lot more different than that.

Freidel: I would say one thing. I think you gave Joe very bad advice, because you've got facts, facts, facts, and if you get to Sacco's widow, you will get feeling, which could stimulate his imagination.

I have never written a piece of fiction in my life, or at least I've never published a piece of fiction, but I do have a feeling that there would be great stimulus in terms of the emotions—feelings—because what I find as an historian, and after all I'm trying to recreate also, is that often through talking to people one gets totally a different perception.

Take Herbert Hoover, for example, notorious for his very dry as dust speeches. One didn't get that feeling when one talked to Hoover, the feeling there was one of dealing with somebody who had been a simple country boy in Iowa, because he had an Iowa idiom. That never came through in anything he wrote, and yet it came through in his conversations.

So when you talk to people who are involved in the times, it can be a marvelous stimulus to the imagination, more so than some times just simply reading through books and newspaper files.

Doctorow: You mustn't take Joe Papaleo's professions too seriously. What he's going to do now, and he's quite serious about this, is the kind of torture we go through. I used to be an editor and whenever I said to a novelist, How's it going? and he said, It's terrific! Just great! I knew we were in for bad times. But the novelist who really complains a lot and says he doesn't know what he's doing and worries and bites his nails and does socially impermissible things, then I think we have a chance for a really good book.

Of course, there's an immense literature about Sacco and Vanzetti but nobody, still nobody knows; and what the novelist often discovers in dealing with famous cases is that some kind of transcendent question occurs, having nothing to do with guilt or innocence.

Lukas: First I want to say I spent the weekend with Joe McGinnis who says to tell you that he is editing the *Playboy* interview you taped last summer and he is struggling to bring fictional truth out of prosaic reality. Second—

Doctorow: I never said I lusted in my heart. . . .

Lukas: The second question I have, though, is in a sense more a statement, I suppose, than a question, but I would be interested in your reaction
to the statement. The fact, I think, is that there are a lot of people in this room
who have been struggling with the question of fact and reality in the kind of
journalism that they do. Since Capote, since the "new journalism" there are
lot of journalists today who realize that the separation is not as simple-
minded, I think, as we might have believed some decade or two decades ago.
And I do believe, therefore, that somewhere between having our newspapers
written on wire service tradition and having Ed Doctorow write our newspapers, there is a mean that a lot of us are struggling to find. I'd rather read Ed
Doctorow's *New York Times,* but I want to read that between hard covers,
and I'll pay—it'll probably cost $17.50 at that point.

But I always felt when I worked for the *Times* that what my editors were
telling me was that objectivity meant that I should write within *their* definition of, within their unquestioned assumptions about, reality. And my problem with working at the *Times* ultimately—after ten years—became that I
wanted the freedom to write within *my* assumptions about reality, not their
assumptions; and that became a problem and so I left.

But I think that's a problem that a lot of the Niemans who are in this room,
and who have come to hear you tonight, are struggling with at their newspapers. And I think really what you said tonight has a lot of implications, serious implications, to them and the journalism that they are trying to do.
Whether they do it ultimately for their newspapers, or they start sending their
manuscripts to Bob Manning, or whether ultimately they start trying to do it
between hard covers, but I think that it has real implications for journalism
today, too. I would be curious as to see whether Doctorow had any reaction.

Doctorow: I've always thought that the most objective, accurate kind of
reality in newspapers is on the sports pages. The ball game is a very discrete
event, and the account is usually backed up with statistics. If you read an
account of a baseball game or a football game, it's really incredibly true. But,
nevertheless, you never read in a newspaper account of a baseball game what
it feels like to run under a fly ball in center field on warm summer afternoon.

Comment: You don't read *The Boston Globe.*

Granetz: I just wanted to say that I don't see anything but bad implications in what Mr. Lukas has said because—

Thomson: So much for you, Tony—

Granetz: I am extremely offended by the idea that authors should have gone beyond what they did and come up with some kind of transcendent reality.

Woodward and Bernstein discussed sources—we have three sources: we have four sources, we have seven sources: can you question the authority of our book? And I think they would have been offended if you would have thought that they should have written something other than they did. I can't see anything but improvement in literature's integrity as fiction tries to separate itself from journalism, stopping the production of the type of novel that needs the impetus of history and misinforms a lot of the reading public. I think it is not on very steady ground as far as literature's theory goes, whatever that's worth. There is a movement to join the two; I think both of them would be better off separate. I see a lot of journalists try to write fiction and I see a lot of fiction writers trying to write journalism and both results are surprisingly miserable.

Lukas: May I reply? It was the wine getting to me undoubtedly which meant that I was evidently not expressing myself well. I don't at all mean that journalists ought to be writing fiction, but I think that there is a serious question about what reality is. There were, in the 60s, let me tell you, real differences between people on American papers about what reality was. We did not go to Chicago trying to write fiction, or Vietnam trying to write fiction. But you know that Charlie Mohr got in a great deal of trouble with *Time* magazine and he had to quit *Time* magazine because his editors accused him of writing fiction. I think you're being glib when you suggest that the issue is merely reporters trying to do Ed Doctorow's business. It's reporters struggling with what reality is.

Bailey: Let me interrupt and follow that. If you read what Ward Just wrote in a book called *To What End* about Vietnam, which is fact, you will think it is fiction. I don't know where you are on that continuum when you read that. Nobody who reads it is going to know and people who were there aren't going to know. But it is fact.

Zvi Dor-Ner: I think it's a very comfortable notion that was introduced: the continuum between fact and fiction, and I think we are working with it for such a long time because it is so comfortable. But I suspect that it is totally irrelevant. The continuum is between good and bad, and the things move along this kind of continuum; and the better it is, I think we have different standards for it, or we don't know how to put standards to it. So if somebody writes a lousy fact and it's judged as fiction, it doesn't matter. If the opposite happens, it doesn't matter.

Cassandra Tate: Do you see anything—this is to Doctorow—that makes you feel uncomfortable about what nearly everyone seems to agree is a growing tendency to merge history, fiction, and journalism? Does that make you uneasy at all?

Doctorow: I just wonder why people are so alarmed at this? Politicians, journalists, and historians have always made up history. I should think the right of composition would extend to novelists as well.

Thomson: All right, may I make the following important statement. First of all, the Nieman tradition has been violated by seven minutes—it's seven minutes past ten. Second of all, we are deeply grateful for everyone who was here and who even spoke. Third of all, there is a story that I always tell—my wife tells me that I tell it wrong—but it's appropriate to this evening, and it is about Alice B. Toklas going to Gertrude Stein after some incredible seance she had set up. Alice had been able to call forth as several people have tonight, at great length and with enormous group interest—

Diana Thomson: Not Alice, Gertrude—

Thomson: There, she was right, I was wrong. Gertrude had held forth and Alice said to Gertrude after the event, "Gertrude, you've said things tonight that it will take you years to understand." And in that vein, I would like to thank Joe Papaleo and Ed Doctorow and everyone else.

History and the Forms of Fiction: An Interview with E. L. Doctorow

Jared Lubarsky / 1978

From *Eigo Seinen* 124 (1978), 150–52. Used by permission.

Lubarsky: Mr. Doctorow, I wonder if we could talk to begin with about the editorial process, as it affects the way American literature emerges. We can think, for example, of Malcolm Cowley: if he had not done the *Viking Portable Faulkner,* what would Faulkner's career have looked like? If Max Perkins had not been the kind of editor that he was, the careers of people like Hemingway and Fitzgerald and Thomas Wolfe might have had a very different shape. You've worked both sides of the street, as it were, and I wonder if you have any observation to make about the relationship between editor and author in modern American literature.

Doctorow: Well, it's usually a lot closer, of course, than it is in other countries. I think the value of the years I spent as an editor, apart from the friendships I made and writers I got to work with, was in becoming aware of the formal necessities of a book, the principles of composition—being always involved with the aspects of it that are invisible when the book is finished. I think that this has helped me enormously in my own work.

Lubarsky: What do you mean exactly by the elements that are invisible?

Doctorow: Those elements of composition which determine the flow of a book: knowing when a scene should end; or how to cut away what is superfluous and bring out what is essential; or how to make the narrative connections or transitions—just a general sense of the beat or the form of what you're doing, finding the form, and helping to realize it. This is probably the same effort that's made by a composer or a painter.

Lubarsky: So it's the ability to keep one part of your mind as an editor as you are composing that really makes things work?

Doctorow: I think so. Composition is very mysterious; creativity is very mysterious. I think when you're writing at your best, you don't work from calculation, you're not illustrating a preconception. You trust to the act of writing. You let it discover what it is you're doing, but once you have the

35

pages down, then the editorial mind in you takes over and you begin to cut and to prune and to shape.

Lubarsky: Could we move to a question about the relationship of history and fiction? I'm intrigued by a comment that you've made, that our American past is one of the very few things that gives us as a society a sense of community, a sense of being held together. Your own book *Ragtime* has appealed to a lot of people because of the enormous detail of its invocations of the past, as it were. And we can see in American society now a lot of fondness for bygone eras. I'm wondering, though, if this isn't the kind of nostalgia in which we are finally false to ourselves. I think of Southern fiction, which has really wrestled with the past in a very serious way, insisting that in order to live in the present and project oneself into the future one has to come to terms with the past. History is not something that you approach sentimentally.

Doctorow: I would agree that nostalgia is an inadequate self-deluding emotion. Usually you feel nostalgic for what you never experienced or for what you only have the illusion of having experienced. It is the disposition for nostalgia that *Ragtime* mocks. But I take exception to the idea that there is an objective or real history that perhaps a regional novelist could discover and a writer who's using historical materials more generally or more nationally could not. I think a good deal of what we think of as Southern regional writing is as nostalgic, in the sense of being inauthentic, as the more recognizable forms of nostalgia.

History is created by all of us, and perhaps least of all by the historians. I think the important point is that the uses of history are not only various in our country and necessary but widespread. The novelist is always recognized to be inventing history; the others—the historians, social scientists, journalists—are not. We seem to have been isolated as the one profession that lies and is forced to admit that it lies. Perhaps that's the reason to trust us all the more.

Lubarsky: The lies are all out front. We know where we stand with literature.

Doctorow: It seems to me we all make compositions of the life that we have, and who we are, and what we are, and what we are doing. A good deal of that work involves connection with the past. . . . I don't think the need for history should be minimized. We have so little, we need every bit of it. Fiction assumes that the sources of history are more various than the historian supposes.

Lubarsky: I'd love to have you talk about the actual processes of research and background that went into *Ragtime*. It's such a marvelously thick book for those kinds of historical details.

Doctorow: The book began accidentally, as all good things do. I happen to live in a house that was built in that period, and one desperate day, when the work was not going well, I found myself staring at the wall. I decided to write about the wall. And then about the house the wall was attached to, and then the street the house was on—and one thing led to another.

At that time, 1906, Teddy Roosevelt was President. The middle classes tended to wear white clothing in summer. There were images that came to my mind of the technology of the era, the early motor cars, the trolley cars, and so on. In very short order I had a set of images that in fact proposed the book to me, and the writing of it was in effect an attempt to find out why I had put these things down precisely in the way I did.

Once I began working in earnest I looked at enormous numbers of photographs of the period. It happens to be a very well-photographed era. We think of photography as a very recent medium, but there were photographers in those days for the wealthy and photographers for the poor; there were outdoor photographers and indoor photographers . . . an enormous pictorial documentation.

I also read a little bit, but I wouldn't dignify the process with the word "research"—which to me implies exhaustiveness, systematic attention to everything. There were some things that I happened to learn about and use and others that I looked over which didn't interest me. The process of selection was totally idiosyncratic and irrational. There were many, many people of that era who were fascinating, such as Eugene Debs or Andrew Carnegie, who aroused no resonant response in me, and so they did not appear in the book.

Lubarsky: By the time you finished the book I take it you had answered your own question, about why you started with those images. What ultimately turned out to be the appeal of that particular era in American history?

Doctorow: It was sufficiently in our past to have a certain innocence. One of the reasons we are intrigued by the past is our sense of the innocence of the dead—the innocence of their ambition and their vanity and even their murderousness.

I suppose, apart from that, that it seemed as I went along to be a useful way to describe us as we are now. Because that of course is what writing about the past is all about: you are really writing about the present. The Italian philosopher Croce said that all history is written for the needs of the present, the purpose of the present. I think that is true of fiction that deals with historical materials as well.

Lubarsky: I had the feeling in that book that there were a lot of characters who, perhaps without knowing it consciously themselves, were somehow aware that they were about to lose their innocence. There is the theme of escape, of being born again; there are characters like Father, terribly convinced of impending disaster. This was America somehow poised on a threshold of radical, disastrous changes in its society. . . .

Doctorow: This was not something I planned, though I think you can find it if you look. I was conscious of planning or wanting only a few things. I wanted to write a very rigorous narrative. I wanted, for example, to write something that was absolutely relentless, and I realized in doing so that I had to sacrifice a good deal of the wisdom of the modern novel, which is its ability to psychologically explore the interior lives of its characters. Once you commit yourself to this relentless narrative and the distance from the characters which it necessitates, you have to give up a kind of interior dimension. Characters become recognizable as having the kind of being characters enjoyed before literature became modern.

I realized as I went along that the model for this book, in terms of its narrative distance, was the chronicle fiction of the German master Heinrich von Kleist. His novella "Michael Kohlhaas" was very much in my mind when I found the black man Coalhouse Walker, driving up the hill in his Ford. . . .

Lubarsky: Critics are always discovering influences and parallels that never existed in the author's mind, but one that suggested itself strongly to me, and I think other readers have discovered it, too, is Dos Passos' *U.S.A.* . . .

Doctorow: I read Dos Passos when I was very young, and admired him. I think now he was a rather sloppy writer, often sentimental, and that there is a kind of openness of form to *U.S.A.*—with the fiction and the history separated—that does not appeal to me.

Lubarsky: What about *Welcome to Hard Times?* We talked about the appeal of the period in *Ragtime*; this earlier work of yours is a book about the end of the frontier era in American history. What kinds of things were you discovering in the contemplation of that time and place?

Doctorow: I don't think that book would have come into being if I hadn't been working for a film company and reading bad screen plays about the West. At a certain point I decided that I could lie better than the screenwriters I was reading. I had never been West at the time; I had never thought about it; I hadn't even liked cowboys when I was a kid. So I thought those were all good credentials for writing a novel about the West. I started it, and it seemed to me that the West had to have been an experience for most people that betrayed them, an experience of promise and hope that defaulted in the actual living out of it. And this somehow came to focus in the character of the central villain of the piece.

Lubarsky: The Bad Man from Bodie?

Doctorow: The Bad Man from Bodie. But again the book would never have been written if I hadn't worked for a motion picture firm. It's hard to understand, that something organized and composed can begin in such a compost heap of the mind, but that really is the way it happens. It is true that things get a start as arbitrarily and accidentally as life itself.

Lubarsky: You used the word "betrayal" a moment ago. The level of society in *Welcome to Hard Times* struck me as very thin, compared to your other works—that is, the stage on which these betrayals and self-betrayals take place is almost an allegorical one. If Blue, the central character, betrays himself it is really very much in personal terms. But one thing about *The Book of Daniel* and also about *Ragtime* is that betrayal is inseparable from the issue of one's relationship to society. Just to take *Ragtime* itself: the characters who maintain a special sense of integrity and wholeness in that book are all in rebellion, betraying their society or their own particular class in that society; and the characters who are the most deluded, the most self-betrayed, are the defenders of society. . . .

Doctorow: I could argue that to a certain extent, but it is true that I seem to be fond of people who offer some kind of resistance. My eye and feelings go out to someone who is not in harmony with society but somehow in conflict with it. I don't know why that is. I haven't analyzed it particularly. It may be only that it makes for better drama.

Lubarsky: The character who is in harmony with his society can't really be written about, can he?

Doctorow: There used to be a time when writing was done for the edification and instruction of people, and the heroes of stories, for instance Beo-

wulf, were heroes of conformity. Heroes were people who did things
properly. Beowulf was not only personally brave, but when he had booty he
knew how to share it and distribute it according to the rules. He expressed
the right respect for his elders. He was a model of social behavior. I think
modern literature does not usually produce that kind of heroism. The hero, if
he exists, is a hero of impropriety . . . the critic of society, the man or woman
whose life is lived and defined in terms of its opposition to the prevailing
values.

Lubarsky: How does that come about? What you are speaking about was
really the prevailing attitude in literature well into the 18th and maybe the
19th century. The thrust of *Tom Jones* is to get the hero into his proper niche
in the society, for example. And yet now we are in a world where to write
literature is really to write about the conflict between the individual and the
society.

Doctorow: I don't know the answer to that. . . . I suppose it all has to do
with the onset of the industrial world, the alienation of people from their
work and their dislocation from their pasts. But, you know, these are such
large, general, vague prescriptions. . . . The central things about fiction, of
course, is that it deals in specific images, specific sensations and events.

Lubarsky: Could we talk about film and how it ties in with the world of
literature? You've had one of your novels made into a film and now *Ragtime*
is going to be adapted for the screen. I'm curious about the pull of that
potential on the writer as he writes. . . .

Doctorow: Of course, I don't think any writer can work today without
being aware of the last seventy years of optical technology, and I admit to
learning a lot of things from films: the use of the cut, for instance, the use of
entirely visual images to create emotion, the use of repetition. There are
many, many ways in which we have all been affected by film: certainly in
the rhythms of prose, the shortened attention span of the reader. . . . At the
same time, I have misgivings about film. I think it involves regression somehow. After building up language and refining the art of linguistic symbol for
thousands of years, our use of film suggests a regression to literalism. If I
want it to rain in my book I use the word "rain," and I can make that word
work in infinite ways. If the film-maker wants rain, he has to go out and bring
all sorts of machinery to bear and spend tens of thousands of dollars to show
you the rain, and that's got to be going backwards somehow.

The Writer as Independent Witness

Paul Levine / 1978

From: *E. L. Doctorow: Essays and Conversations* (Princeton: Ontario Review Press, 1983), 57–69. Used by permission.

Interviewer: In your novel *Ragtime,* Freud says to his disciple Jones at one point that "America is a mistake, a gigantic mistake." Do you agree with Freud's judgement?

Doctorow: Freud actually said that, and I think in the context of the passage, it becomes very funny. I think it's funny to speak of anything that gigantic as "a mistake." And, of course, considering the sort of cosmic pratfalls of our history, in that sense, yes, we've done everything wrong. To someone of refined taste and culture, we must have appeared in those days really as monstrous. We probably still do appear that way. But I don't agree, of course, any more than I agree that any other nation is a mistake. They're all mistakes. Human life is a mistake.

Interviewer: There are a number of American writers who have treated America in various eras as a gigantic mistake. One thinks of Melville's *Moby Dick,* of the Pequod as a ship of state on an errand which is a gigantic mistake. One thinks of Twain—*Pudd'nhead Wilson*—who writes: "October 12. It was wonderful to discover America. It would have been even more wonderful to have missed it." There's a kind of unrequited love affair in American literature between writers and the country. Do you feel this is a particularly American tradition? Is it a tradition you've been conscious of as you've been writing your particularly *American* novels?

Doctorow: I don't know. It seems to me we are, at least on paper, supposed to be different from, or better than, we are. And that kind of irritation confronts us all the time and has from the very beginning. The Constitution was a precipitate of all the best Enlightenment thinking of Europe, and it's really quite a remarkable document. That we don't manage to live up to it is the source of all our self-analysis. But I think that all writers and all nations operate as children do of families whom they love and hate and try to distinguish themselves from and somehow reform at the same time. And I would put a nation's artists in that category—as loving and tortured children.

41

Interviewer: And yet there is something curious about this relationship between American writers and American society or American culture. It's a problem of definition. There is a sense in which American writers are constantly writing about American identity, as if it were something that was yet to be discovered. In Europe, for instance, the national identity of a Dane or a German or a Russian or a Frenchman is a given. It's not something to discover, it's *there*. And the literature, therefore, seems to begin at a different point (if you understand what I mean) from American literature.

Doctorow: Well, of course, this is a very young country, and it is a polyglot mixture that is still forming itself through waves of immigration, most recently Hispanic, and now, it seems, a small Vietnamese immigration. This is a constant of American history. And nothing has really disappeared yet into the mists of ancient history. We're very derivative. We derive enormously, of course, from Europe, and that's part of what *Ragtime* is about: the means by which we began literally, physically to lift European art and architecture and bring it over here. So that we had architects like Stanford White who could copy (to take an uncharitable view) any European style whatsoever on command. That's sort of our curse and our blessing at the same time. Not having fixed, narrowed or focused into a real, true national identity, we can have the illusion about ourselves that we are still in the process of becoming. It's a kind of fascinating suspense to see the ways in which all these strains—ethnic, social strains—clash with technology and industrialism and the effect of one on another, and the effect of both on the simple possibility of surviving. We don't have much of a history—that's the simple, statistical fact of it.

Interviewer: In the last ten or fifteen years, history seems to have become a major subject in American fiction. In the 1960's, one had a series of novels that revisioned history, such as John Barth's *The Sotweed Factor*. Thomas Berger wrote a novel called *Little Big Man* about the only survivor of Little Big Horn, General Custer's massacre. He invented a character. This was the beginning of an attempt to take history as it had been portrayed by the historians and to revise it—not simply to give us a new history but to transform it into something else, perhaps into myth—I don't know. What do you think caused this movement back to—to coin a phrase—"roots"?

Doctorow: Well, first of all, history as written by historians is clearly insufficient. And the historians are the first to express skepticism over this "objectivity" of the discipline. A lot of people discovered after World War II and in the fifties that much of what was taken by the younger generations as history was highly interpreted history. And just as through the guidance and wisdom of magazines like *Time,* we were able to laugh at the Russians' manipulation of their own history—in which they claimed credit for technological advances that had clearly originated in other countries, and in which leaders who had fallen out of favor were suddenly absent from their texts— just around that time, we began to wonder about our own history texts and our own school books. And it turned out that there were not only individuals but whole peoples whom we had simply written out of our history—black people, Chinese people, Indians. At the same time, there is so little a country this size has in the way of cohesive, identifying marks that we can all refer to and recognize each other from. It turns out that history, as insufficient and poorly accommodated as it may be, is one of the few things we have in common here. I happen to think that there's enormous pressure on us all to become as faceless and peculiarly indistinct and compliant as possible. In that case, you see, the need to find color or definition becomes very, very strong. For all of us to read about what happened to us fifty or a hundred years ago suddenly becomes an act of community. And the person who represented what happened fifty or a hundred years ago has a chance to begin to say things about us now. I think that has something to do with the discovery of writers that this is possible. At the same time this has been going on, I think there has been the drop in what used to be known as the "regional" novel. It seems to me that books published by Southerners aren't quite the "Southern" novels they were some generations ago. And there doesn't seem to be any other region in the country that finds itself in contemporary ways with strong cultural marks that everyone can relate to. So it's almost as if we're finding in *time* the sort of identification we've been losing in other ways—in space, in ethnic coloration, and so on.

Interviewer: When those novels began to appear (and I'm thinking of novels like *The Sotweed Factor* and *Little Big Man*), and shortly after, we began to get a series of novels that dealt with contemporary reality that was somewhere between journalism and fiction (I'm thinking of a book such as *In Cold Blood* by Truman Capote, which he called a "nonfiction novel"). The early works that I'm referring to here seemed not to have any overt political content. But in more recent works, such as Norman Mailer's *The Armies of the Night*—which is divided into two sections, "The Novel as History" and "History as the Novel"—in Thomas Pynchon's work, and particularly in your own work, there seems to be a very conscious attempt to revise history in such a way that we can begin to understand American society politically. Do you think that this movement that I'm trying to describe has been some kind of conscious effort to come to grips with American society on the part of writers?

Doctorow: Well, I think that's the great chore, task, or challenge our fiction writers have always dealt with. It's such an immense place and almost—in all its great, whirling, self-destruction—impossible to make a metaphor of. In fact, I think it's getting more and more impossible to do that. But this is the challenge, and our writers have always been extremely political. I think Dreiser is a political writer. Jack London. All through our history, our writers have been extremely political. I think their treatment in the universities has been anti-political. It's only recently that I've come to realize there's an enormous Marxist interpretation possible, or critical literature, about *Moby Dick*. I don't see this as anything new at all. I think it's impossible to do a book and not be political. If you do a book about a boy and his dog, you're making a political statement. I think the politics of novels become visible when they happen to differ from the prevailing political complacencies around them. And so books like *Daniel* or *Ragtime* would strike some people as being essentially political efforts. It's hard to think of a writer who cannot be given a very rigorous political interpretation. Certainly Henry James. Fitzgerald. Writers of the thirties, of course, were explicitly committed, many of them, to propagandize from a specific political point of view. And that leads to the interesting question of to what degree a writer can understand or know that he is political in order to get his work done. There's some kind of death that creeps into prose when you're trying to illustrate a principle, no matter how worthy. And this is quickly recognized by all critics in this country. But on the basis of that, of course, to declare that art should not have political intent—or can't afford to—that's not justified. One thinks of the intentions of writers, like Dostoyevsky, who simply and modestly wanted to change the world. That didn't seem, somehow, to limit his capacity to express truth. So I guess my answer is, I don't think this is anything new at all. If I were a better literary historian, I could come up with a lot of impressive names and citations, but certainly the careers of Dreiser and Jack London should stand for the novelist who is political.

Interviewer: And yet Dreiser and London (and I think you are right about the universities) stand outside what one would think of as the mainstream.

But even a writer who *is* overtly political, like John Dos Passos, is also, in a sense, outside of the mainstream. One can see a shelfful of books on Faulkner or Fitzgerald or Hemingway, and there really isn't a comprehensive critical analysis of Dos Passos' work. And yet one could say there is a whole group of novelists who could be interpreted in a political way, but that's different from someone who chooses an explicitly political theme. Let's talk about one of your novels for a minute—*The Book of Daniel.*

The Book of Daniel begins, or so it seems to me, with one of the major political events of the post-war period, and that was the execution of Julius and Ethel Rosenberg. Now it would be very difficult to begin a novel at that point and not have its overt, rather than its latent, content as political. This is rather different from Capote's *Other Voices, Other Rooms* or Salinger's *Catcher in the Rye.* This is a novel that begins in the bowels of American politics and seems in fact to deal with what Christopher Lasch calls "the agony of the American left." How did you come to write this novel?

Doctorow: I don't really know. In the late sixties I found myself thinking about the Rosenberg case, and it seemed to me that the more I found myself thinking about it, I saw that it was something I could write. And not knowing why or how or what conclusions I was going to come to, I started to write that book and discovered I could hang an awful lot on it—not only the explicit and particular story of two people who were trapped in this way, but also the story of the American left in general and the generally sacrificial role it has played in our history. The specific dramatic interest I had was solely in terms of what happens when al the antagonistic force of a society is brought to bear and focused on one or possibly two individuals. What kind of anthropological ritual is that? It is an explicitly political novel in that it deals with politics and political people, but, peculiarly enough, I have never thought of myself as a terribly political person. In fact, it was only after *Ragtime* was published that I was informed (not having realized it) that I tended to write about historical subjects. That hadn't occurred to me either. There's a certain way in which, in order to get our work done, we really have to be ignorant. We can't know too well what we're doing. If you know too well what you're doing, then writing simply becomes a matter of filling in. At its best, you write to find out what it is you're writing. I suppose this must be a disappointing answer, but my original *conscious* interest in that subject was a technical interest and discovered itself to have some moral basis.

Interviewer: Was your original interest with the children of the Isaacsons (as you call them in the novel), the children that you made up—or with the parents that you found? That is, it seems to me it's a book about an inheritance.

Doctorow: It's hard for me to isolate my own motives and feelings. I can tell you that I started to write the book in the third person, more or less as a standard, past tense, third person novel, very chronologically scrupulous. And after one hundred fifty pages I was terribly bored. That was a moment of great despair in my life, because I thought that if I could really destroy a momentous subject like this, then I had no right to be a writer. That moment, when I threw out those pages and hit bottom, was when I became reckless enough to find the voice of the book, which was Daniel. I sat down and put a piece of paper in the typewriter and started to write with a certain freedom and irresponsibility, and it turned out Daniel was talking, and he was sitting in the library at Columbia, and I had my book. I don't know why that happened or how that happened, but that is the experience I had in composing the book. I don't know if it's possible for a writer really, truthfully to describe as a conscious decision a process that is really mysterious to him and largely irrational.

Interviewer: Did you have to do much research on the Rosenberg case or the history of the Cold War or America in the 1940's and '50's for that book?

Doctorow: Once I got going, I found myself looking things up, but not in any systematic way. At a certain point, I think, when your mind is organized and you're attuned to whatever your subconscious is doing, you become a kind of magnet for your own experiences and reading, and things in the air become relevant. On the basis of that, you're led from one thing to another. You see a picture in a newspaper, or you're walking through some stacks in a library and you see a title of a book, and in some peculiar, mystical way, things just happen to come up when you need them. Someone will tell you a story at a dinner party or you'll catch sight of a scene on a street corner, and it will become appropriate to the book. The ongoing book or the creative process, I think, generates a certain kind of energy in the writer which makes him a kind of selective magnet for things in his environment. That's what I would call research.

Interviewer: The book is a remarkable imaginative recreation not simply of an event but, really, of an era. And it was the first novel about the Rosenberg case but not the last. This year Robert Coover has published a book called *The Public Burning,* and we've seen on American television in the last two years a three-hour dramatized documentary about the career of Joseph

McCarthy. There seems to be now an attempt to understand what happened to America in the years of the Cold War, between the end of World War II (when we supposedly lost a China that was never ours to lose) and the beginning of *détente*. There seems to be a surfacing of that history now, as if we've now got to come to terms with what was buried so deeply in the age that was supposed to be the age of the *end* of ideology. Do you have any explanation as to why *now* we've become so obsessed with this?

Doctorow: No, I don't. I don't know anything that everybody else doesn't know. If I have any specific capabilities as a thinker, they only come out in the context of the work I'm doing.

I think there's a natural lag between a trauma such as war and the country's ability to deal with it psychically. I think approximately fifteen years passed before there was any flow of literature in this country about the Nazis. As I recall, the first popular book on the Third Reich was William Shirer's, which was published probably around 1960. And then, of course, the gates opened. Perhaps there is already a large literature about Vietnam, and that's an exception to the rule.

Interviewer: Nothing about Korea.

Doctorow: Nobody seems to want to hear about it. But it's possible that each of these traumatic experiences and the communal attempt to deal with them lifts up the general perception a degree or two, and so the response can be a little faster next time. That would be the only explanation for the fact that we're already trying to deal with Vietnam. We were trying to deal with it as it was going on, and I think we have a lot more work to do. But it leads to interesting questions. For instance, the general supposition now is that what's happening in the seventies is a general retreat from political and social awareness: children in school all back to their studies and quietly intent on getting good grades so they can get jobs; the well-known abandonment of political language for mystical-religious sensation; the development of the great variety of sensitivity trainings; the appearance of one guru after another; and the defection of some of the political leaders of the students to these movements. The common wisdom is that there has been a retreat from a certain kind of political development or communal education. I'm not sure that's true. If you think of the early Wilhelm Reich, for instance, as a man who tried somehow to accommodate or bridge Freudian insight to Marxist sociology, then this is a very clear part of the process. Reich came to believe that there is no hope for political progress until people can be freed from their neurotic character structures. If you're a Reichian, you could make the claim, shaky as it might be, that people's streaming into various kinds of meditation and degrees of self-awareness are simply preparing themselves for a return to political life without some of the hang-ups they had first time around.

Interviewer: Are you a Reichian?

Doctorow: No, I don't think so, although there are things about his early work that really fascinate me. I don't know enough about Reich to be a Reichian.

Interviewer: Certainly that attempt to marry the insights of Freud with the insights of Marx seems to be the main intellectual burden of the late 1960's and the '70's. One thinks of people like Marcuse and Norman O. Brown and some of the people working in Europe now who have been trying to marry those insights.

Doctorow: It's extremely important and, of course, a fiercely argued point. Reich himself was excommunicated by both the Marxists and the Freudians as a result of his insights. He was driven right out of Europe because of that direction in his work. But surely the sense we have to have now of twentieth-century political alternatives is the kind of exhaustion of them all. The only one to my mind that stands out clean and shining—because it has never really been tested in any serious way—is a philosophical position of anarchism, which at this point seems to be so totally utopian in character as not to be seriously attainable. But certainly everything else has been totally discredited: capitalism, communism, socialism. None of it seems to work. No system, whether it's religious or anti-religious or economic or materialistic, seems to be invulnerable to human venery and greed and insanity. So it seems to me that anyone who likes to think about these things seriously in an effort to find some mediation between individual psychology and large social movements has to be going in the right direction.

Interviewer: I remember in *The Armies of the Night* that Norman Mailer calls himself a left conservative. He "liked to think in the categories of Marx to achieve some of the ends of Edmund Burke," he said. An interesting attempt to bring together these two aspects that you're talking about.

Doctorow: I think that political awareness in this country is very primitive generally. In terms of dealing with the issues and coming to terms with them in a rational way, we're terribly behind everyone else. We're doing things and saying things, the meanings of which we don't even know. Certainly, intellectually speaking, there are very few Marxists who have access to universities in this country, to journals except their own. And certainly the political dialogue in the media is rudimentary, and permissible opinion goes from a little bit to the left of center to very far to the right. And all the great political contests in this country are between the middle right and the far right. There's a lot we have to learn, it seems to me.

Interviewer: How do you account for that? It seems clear that the political dialogue in the United States does not move from right to left, as you say. It moves perhaps from right to center—that is, if one thinks in terms of the Western world. The Conservative Party in England starts roughly where the left wing of the Democratic Party starts—with an acceptance, for instance, of the welfare state as a reality, a non-negotiable reality. Is there another country that's industrialized that does not have socialized medicine? So the political discussion in the country is polarized in a completely different way from the political discussions in other countries, including Canada, where there is a social democratic party called the New Democrats. How does one account for the fact that in the twentieth century America has managed to turn its back on the great political dialogues that are going on in the rest of the world?

Doctorow: That's an interesting question. I think essentially it's our pragmatism that either protects us or damages us. We started off from the point of view of property, including slaves, and by means of the use of capital—as it discovered technology and was invested in technology—worked our way into a rather generous, prosperous society that was able to ignore the terrible decimation of working people and of minorities in order for it to achieve what it achieved. A kind of social and political blindness came along.

Whenever we have a problem, we tend to try to solve it technologically. Take pollution. The discussion about poisoning the environment or using up our resources is entirely in terms of how, on a technological basis, we can stop doing that. Discussion doesn't come around to why that is being done and who is profiting from it—in any serious way. So the solution to foul air is not any broad reconstruction of industrial power; it's simply to find an engine that will take those soots and hellish gases and make them harmless. We're tinkerers and pragmatists, and our technology is in the hands of those elements of us who have the money to use it and to exploit it for their own protection. And, of course, the media are owned by privileged members of our group and reflect that kind of faith in technology and the ability of the tinkerers. The interesting thing about pollution, of course, is that while it affects people who work in factories, for instance, vinyl chloride factories or asbestos factories, prominently—and they are members of the lower socio-economic class—it also affects people who live in suburbs but who breathe the same crap. I'm interested to see the extent to which the middle class in this country, which imagines itself the enormous beneficiary of our system, discovers that it, too, is expendable, just as the lower class is. As resources become less and less available, they will be allocated to fewer and fewer people, and at that point those of us who are in the middle class and feel that our lives can't be improved will wake up. But to get back to the question, I think we're a peculiarly pragmatic country, and so far the technology has made it work.

The other major thought I would have about this is what happened to the working class in this country in the 1930's. The more radical historians and critics feel that the American worker had an enormous opportunity in the 1930's which he blew by settling for a wage contract, at which point the structure of American labor was set and the leadership of the unions became, in effect, watchdogs of management.

Interviewer: The historian Christopher Lasch has also argued that an indigenous socialist movement in this country was, in a sense, sabotaged after the Russian Revolution, when American socialists began to look outside of the country rather than inside, and that the last indigenous movement would have been something like the Wobblies, the I.W.W. I wonder if that was something you thought about in terms of *Ragtime* as well as *The Book of Daniel,* since both books in different ways deal with the history of the American left. Emma Goldman is an important character in *Ragtime.* And it's clear in your version of the Rosenberg case (as one character says at one point in *The Book of Daniel*) that the two victims are victimized both by the F.B.I. and the Communist Party, that they're being set up, in a sense, by both groups, crucified by both. Do you have a sense that there was a golden moment in American history where it *could* have all been different?

Doctorow: Oh, no, no, I don't feel that way at all. I think the beginnings and ends and moments are artificial constructions. It's possible to cut and slice history really any way you want to, so that something is seen to be beginning or ending. That's probably why history belongs more to the novelists and the poets than it does to the social scientists. At least we admit that we lie.

Interviewer: You're the only honest liars around?

Doctorow: Exactly. But in retrospect, I suppose (speaking of *Ragtime* and *The Book of Daniel*) there is some kind of disposition—and no more than that—to propose that all our radicals (and we've had an astonishing number of them) and our labor leaders and our Wobblies and our anarchists and so on, have really been intimate members of the family—black sheep, as it were, whom no one likes to talk about. And I suppose one could make a case for my disposition to suggest that they are indeed related, that they are part of the family, and that they've had an important effect on the rest of us.

There's one other point to be made—that it's so much easier for the right to command mass support, because it does not attempt to reform. It does not attempt to answer the needs of people, alleviate their miseries and their terrors. All it has to do is confirm them in their fear and their hysteria. And it's therefore much easier in this country for the political right to maintain its position. The hard question and the difficulties—including the difficulty of communicating with people in a massive way—are the occupational hazards of the left in this country. It's much easier to terrify people and confirm them in their rigidity than to say—look, there are other ways we can do this. And I think that shows up in American history. The left, the radicals, have always been easily isolated and made objects of terror and have often been complicitors in their own destruction in some peculiar way. But what happens, sometimes, is that those proposals that the radical has made in one generation become the liberal or even the conservative dogma of the next. And so the very things the radicals were destroyed for come to pass. A clear example is Emma Goldman's feminist stand on abortion and contraception, which was too monstrous to even think about in 1910 and was strongly part of the reason for her deportation, I think—as much as her anarchism. Or Debs's endorsement of the radical idea of social security, which Roosevelt picked up twenty-five years later. So if that hazard for the left exists—the inability to compete with what is easy and fearful and neurotic—nevertheless, somehow every once in a while, an idea does come through.

Interviewer: If the writers are the only honest liars, and they usurp the traditional position of the historians, it means that, in a sense, a tremendous burden is put on novelists to explain, describe, invent, create the reality, unify the reality, of their time. Is this a problem that you feel as a fiction writer as being an extraordinary burden? Do you feel that writers today suffer under an extraordinary burden because of this role?

Doctorow: I think it's very hard to write novels. But I think novelists have always felt that way. I don't feel it as a moral burden, if that's what you mean.

Interviewer: No, I didn't mean it as a moral burden.

Doctorow: I don't take a vow to be responsible. I'm under the illusion that all of my inventions are quite true. For instance, in *Ragtime,* I'm satisfied that everything I made up about Morgan and Ford is true, whether it happened or not. Perhaps truer because it didn't happen. And I don't make any distinction any more—and can't even remember—what of the events and circumstances in *Ragtime* are historically verifiable and what are not. But I suppose that if you were to say to me, there's a danger in this sort of thing, I would have to agree. There is absolutely a danger. Except that writers are independent witnesses and, theoretically at least, not connected to the defense of any institution, whether it be the family or the Pentagon or God. If there are enough of us, somehow a common wisdom will come through the community and pick and choose what it needs in order to survive and go on. I certainly would much rather trust as a source of truth the variousness of literature, and its width and its breadth, than, for instance, a press release from a government agency, or even a sermon. It seems to me what must be maintained is the absolute multiplicity of us all, the numbers of us who color the palette from which the society draws its own portrait.

The Music in Doctorow's Head

Catherine O'Neill / 1979

From *The Chronicle of Higher Education* 28 September 1979, 5 +.
Used by permission.

In E. L. Doctorow's play *Drinks Before Dinner,* the cocktail hour before a fashionable dinner party is interrupted when a character named Edgar produces a gun and proceeds to hold the other guests hostage.

"For a while the joke among my friends was that I couldn't have thought of a better way to avoid invitations," says Mr. Doctorow, a quiet-voiced, bearded man whose eyebrows move eloquently, punctuating his sentences. This fall, he will deliver the manuscript of his first novel since *Ragtime* to Random House; in the meantime, his play has appeared, bound in a dust jacket bearing an ominous close-up portrait of a man glowering over the rim of a cocktail glass.

Drinks Before Dinner (Random House, 52 pages, $8.95) is no conventional drawing-room comedy; rather, it addresses various contemporary (and anxiety-provoking) issues; the effects of cars and cities on our lives, the falseness of social relationships, the meaning of guns, the existence of bad writers, the duplicity of politicians, and the imminent end of the world.

The play had a limited run of six weeks at Joseph Papp's New York Shakespeare Festival last fall, under the direction of Mike Nichols, with Christopher Plummer as Edgar. The production was "rather controversial," Mr. Doctorow says—emphasizing the "rather."

"It got a bad press from the newspaper critics, whom I don't regard as critics so much as customs inspectors. They weren't prepared to admit my play into the impoverished little kingdom."

Mr. Doctorow's opinion of the world of American theater in general is rather low, as it happens. He feels that the critical failure of *Drinks Before Dinner* was due to its "relentlessly verbal" effect, something for which neither audiences nor critics were prepared.

"I happen to think that theater today, in this country, is terribly insubstantial. What is regarded as an evening in the theater is so shockingly meager, insufficient, and boring that people will go crazy over a piece that has fewer ideas and less substance than you find in an ordinary short story. That's not my idea of what theater should be doing. Maybe it shouldn't be doing what I do in this play, but it should be doing something other than what it's doing."

Drinks Before Dinner, Mr. Doctorow believes, takes great risks because it represents a theater of ideas rather than action. "The people in my play take their identity from their positions in an argument, and of course the argument is a matter of life and death. The ideas that they hold, they hold passionately."

The play began as a kind of voice in Mr. Doctorow's head, and its language, he writes in the introduction, is cast in a "frankly rhetorical mode."

After discovering that voice, and writing several thousand words, Mr. Doctorow had occasion to read the work-in-progress aloud at several colleges around the country. "I gradually understood I had composed a monologue, that someone was speaking and that he had a lot on his mind. . . ."

From that point on, Mr. Doctorow recalls, he simply began responding to the remarks of the monologist. He named him Edgar after his own first name because "I thought it only fair to give the malcontent, the sorehead, my own name. It was only just. He is a glowing bundle of total dissatisfaction, and I've had days like that." He soon found that the piece of writing was taking the shape of a play.

"I got very excited about the idea of writing a play. Watching it go into rehearsal and watching it change was fascinating. And the social experience of a production is appealing. When you write a novel you sit alone in a room for three years or more, so the idea of a socially operative fantasy—a community effort—was thrilling. Of course, it has its drawbacks. When people join you in your fantasy, they have things to say and very strong opinions. So what you finally discover, when you're dealing with a stage, lighting, a set, costumes, actors, a director, and, finally, an audience—which of course from night to night can actually change the character of a play—is that you finally have more variables than can be dealt with sanely and rationally.

"Theater is extremely volatile. You never know whether you're making an adjustment because you're dealing with the actual expedient of a living human being who has a certain tone to his voice, or a certain level of talent and perception about the role, or whether it is your words that need changing. So the very nature of your critical understanding is itself under extreme pressure. When I'm reading a page very quietly and at leisure, I'm the absolute arbiter of what I see; I have an imperial authority over those words, and great confidence in what I'm doing. But when you're dealing with all these other elements simultaneously, the context for your own inner authority is gone."

Working on the production of *Drinks Before Dinner* was not Mr. Doctorow's first experience with the theater. In 1948 he went off to Kenyon College, which happened to be the alma mater of actor Paul Newman. Already possessed by a tremendous urge to write, Mr. Doctorow originally went to Kenyon to study with the poet John Crowe Ransom. While there, he also found himself doing a lot of theater. "After Paul Newman left Kenyon, I got all the parts," he says, laughing.

In addition to acting, he wrote a play, which he now insists is best forgotten. "It was about some guy who has dying sheep on his farm. It was a pastoral sort of a thing. A little later, at the time that I was writing *Welcome to Hard Times,* I came to the conclusion that you had to be suicidal to commit yourself as an unknown to writing plays, because you not only had to write them, you had to get people to read them. A book, on the other hand, was finished when you were finished; all you had to do then was deal with the publisher.

"So I gave up playwriting. And like all the best decisions I've made it was instinctive and without sufficient thought, but it was the right one."

He pauses for a long moment, then says: "In a sense, doing *Drinks Before Dinner* was recalling myself to the beginning. And I like the idea of beginnings very much—it's a sort of a Zen idea. Keeping yourself in that state of mind is extremely important. It's the way to stay alive as a writer."

Mr. Doctorow became a writer very early, as he tells it. "My older brother, who's eight years older than I, was always a model for me. When I was still at the Bronx High School of Science, he was in World War II. So he was sort of the family hero. After the war, as a veteran, he took a writing course at City College, and I used to watch him writing a novel, when I was about 14 or 15. That meant a lot—to see him doing that gave writing a sort of imprimatur. From the time I was in the third grade I had thought of myself as a writer, although I didn't feel I had to deliver on that—I just knew. And then when I saw him doing it, I thought that this was really a practical possibility."

Mr. Doctorow's first novel, *Welcome to Hard Times,* may seem an unlikely one for a young man who grew up in New York City. The book, set in the West and peopled by whores, silver miners, and bartenders, is about the destruction of a small frontier town in a single day by a villainous character called "The Man from Bodie."

He concedes that the book made an idiosyncratic beginning. At the time he began it, he says with a self-deprecating gesture, he was writing "a novel about a young man who goes off to college," and was supporting himself by working as a reader for a film company, writing synopses of the unsolicited screenplays that arrived at the studio. "An awful lot of them at the time—the late 1950s—were westerns, and I found them oppressive. They made me ill. So I thought to myself, *I* know more about the true West than these people do, even though at the time I hadn't been west of Ohio."

So the young New Yorker went home and wrote a story, which turned into the first chapter of *Welcome to Hard Times.* "I showed it to a friend of mine, and he told me I ought to make a novel of it. So I went back home and put another page in the typewriter, typed in 'Chapter Two,' and simply continued the story. I wrote that book in Jackson Heights, Queens, and it wasn't until after it was published that I ever got out West."

His Easterner's conception of the great West did not go entirely unchallenged. A letter arrived from an elderly woman in Texas, taking issue with a scene that described a man relishing a meal of roasted haunch of prairie dog. "She wrote, 'Young man, you've obviously never been out here, because if you had you'd know that the haunch of a prairie dog wouldn't fill a teaspoon.' So I did the only thing I could do. I wrote back, 'Ma'am, that's true of prairie dogs today, but in the 19th century they were much bigger.' "

The most important thing he gained from his research for *Welcome to Hard Times,* Mr. Doctorow says, was confirmation of the idea he instinctively had that there were no trees in the Great Plains. "That concept was very meaningful—it became a creative image for me. Basically the book turned on two ideas—one, the barrenness of the landscape, and two, the fact that most of the people who went out there and developed the West, and moved the frontier westward, were losers, people who were defeated by the experience."

The notion of finding some sort of compelling idea—such as the barrenness of the Great Plains—seems central to Mr. Doctorow's method. His second novel, *Big as Life,* he deems a failure and has kept out of print. But for his third, *The Book of Daniel,* the compelling force turned out to be—as it was later for *Drinks Before Dinner*—the discovery of a voice. The novel is about a young man whose parents (the characters bear a resemblance to Julius and Ethel Rosenberg) were executed for conspiring to steal atomic secrets.

"I possess a sort of irresponsible openness to words and whatever sort of music they can make. It's probably a dirty little secret that most writers have, that their seriousness is contingent upon whatever voice they confine. From book to book it can change. With *The Book of Daniel* it was Daniel's voice that allowed me to write. When I had written about 150 pages, and it was not working out, I was very upset. In fact, I was desolate, and when I had just about given up, I sat down at the typewriter recklessly and irresponsibly, full of rage and frustration, just to do something. And I had my book. I was talking in Daniel's voice. It sounds obvious, on the face of it—I had to go through that kind of emotional upheaval to discover who Daniel was.

"I think that's what Samuel Clemens meant when he said 'I never write a book that doesn't write itself.' Once you find some sort of propelling image, everything falls into place."

For *Ragtime,* his novel interweaving fictional families with historical figures like Henry Ford, Emma Goldman, and J. P. Morgan, Mr. Doctorow found several "propelling" images. Some of them appear in the first chapter and serve to establish the novel's turn-of-the-century ambiance: a dormered house in New Rochelle; a Charles Dana Gibson drawing of Evelyn Nesbit, mistress of the architect Stanford White; a shiny, black, 45-horsepower Pope-Toledo Runabout driven by escape artist Harry Houdini.

"*Ragtime* was a book that gave me great pleasure to write," he says. "That is, I remember the experience as pleasure, but in fact I had to write every page five or six times to keep that certain narrative distance from the characters. Everything you do depends originally on this line, or that image, or that voice, on even the vaguest sense of possible music.

"But people don't like to hear that," he adds. "This is a scientific age, and people like the idea of planning and calculation. But you can't write that way."

Modern novelists often must undergo what can be a traumatic experience: the transformation of their books into films. *Ragtime* is currently undergoing such a process, at the hands of Milos Forman, director of *Hair* and *One Flew Over the Cuckoo's Nest.* Mr. Doctorow worked with the director on an outline of the movie, but is not writing the screenplay, although he does expect to be consulted.

"I'm very fond of Milos and I'm very happy with what he's been doing. I think he knows how to make films," Mr. Doctorow says, but he admits that the prospect of seeing his book on screen is a bit daunting.

"A very bad film was made of *Welcome to Hard Times.* I had high hopes for the film, and was very disappointed with it. It probably ought to be redone someday, maybe in sepia color with everyone very scruffy and full of pockmarks.

"When I sat down to see that film, which I had had nothing to do with, my sense of outrage and violation flared within the first 10 seconds. Somebody came on the screen from the left, and I had always imagined him coming on from the right. So you see, they tamper in secret, personal ways with images, with an internal sense of things that you're not even aware you have until you see how it has been violated. That's basically why I think no author can ever be satisfied. What happens is a kind of literalization of the book that's in your head."

He remains hopeful about *Ragtime,* however. "If a good film is made, there's the possibility of a fascinating thing occuring. The audience's perception becomes a projection of the book, coming out of the left brain; the film is seen with the right brain, and a third entity is created, by some sort of stereo vision, of the book / film. That's really the best possible thing that could occur, and with a little luck, I think I can hope for that with *Ragtime.*"

One subject E. L. Doctorow does not feel argumentative about, although he warns that this may simply be due to a good mood resulting from a successful morning's work on his novel, is the art of American fiction, which he feels is in much healthier condition than contemporary dramaturgy.

"I think there's a lot of good, interesting work being done, and I also think we're on the verge of something even better. So I'm holding in my head opposite sides of the same question, which I'm told is O.K. But while I like a lot of what's going on, I have this feeling that we're still to flower, those of us who are writing today, in some great historical way. But don't ask me how, or when, or through whom."

Whether or not his own new book will contribute to the renaissance is a question Mr. Doctorow declines to address. Nor will he reveal the novel's subject—"not for any reason except that I always work that way. I find that I cannot sensibly talk about a book I'm working on."

Then the old Kenyon College actor in him smiles: "My impulse, when someone asks me about it, is to read it out loud in its entirety. So if we had several hours, I'd recite it happily."

E. L. Doctorow: I Saw a Sign

Victor Navasky / 1980

From *The New York Times Book Review,* 28 September 1980, 44–45.
Copyright © 1980 by The New York Times. Reprinted by permission.

The first time I heard of E. L. Doctorow was in 1964 when a friend of mine, then working at the Dial Press, told me they had hired a new editor in chief who had written a novel, a Western that was made into a movie with Henry Fonda.

The new editor was E. L. Doctorow, the novel was *Welcome to Hard Times,* which turned out to be not so much a Western as a play against the genre. "When you use a genre you are playing against the music already in the reader's head," Mr. Doctorow explains, "and you can get some nice effects that way." The movie, he says, "is the second worst movie ever made." (If you ask, he'll tell you that the worst is *Swamp Fire,* with Johnny Weissmuller.)

His second novel, *Big as Life,* played against the science fiction genre and, Mr. Doctorow is quick to concede, lost. "That wasn't as good music," he says. "There are some good things in that book, but it didn't work. Norman Mailer [whom he served as editor while at Dial] once told me I didn't go far enough in that book, and I think he's right. I overcontrolled it." That, at least, is what Mr. Doctorow says now. At the time, he was enough of a writer to believe in his book and enough of an editor to see that his publisher, Simon & Schuster, didn't, which led him to change publishers.

Working as a Dial editor by day and a Random House author by night, he spent the next six months writing 150 pages of the first version of what became *The Book of Daniel,* the novel inspired by what happened to Julius and Ethel Rosenberg. The trouble was he didn't like what he had written, which was a straight chronological narrative, and began to wonder whether he was a writer at all.

"I was desolate. I was finished. I actually gave up," he says. "I sat down at the typewriter recklessly and irresponsibly, full of rage and frustration and despair, and just to do something, almost in mockery of the pretense of writing, I began to type something. I didn't even know what it was. What it was of course was the book I had been looking for, struggling for. I was writing in a voice that I subsequently realized was the voice of Daniel, the couple's son. To do the book from his point of view rather than my own—that was the discovery that came out of my despair. Not I, but Daniel, would write this book. And the act of writing would be part of the story."

After *Daniel* came the best-selling *Ragtime,* and again, to hear Mr. Doctorow tell it, he was sitting at his typewriter in his house in New Rochelle, which was built in 1906, staring at either the wall or the blank page when inspiration struck. "I live in a house built in 1906," he wrote, and while that did not stay the first line in the novel, he was off and typing.

Comes now *Loon Lake.* When interviewers ask Mr. Doctorow where he got the idea for the novel he says, with a straight face, that he was driving one Sunday in the Adirondacks and saw a sign which said *Loon Lake,* and that was it. "You've got to let things happen to you to write."

Recently, he addressed a group of librarians and confidentially shared with them one of his favorite stories—an experience in his journalism class at the Bronx High School of Science that he claimed was "crucial" to his development as a writer.

"The journalism teacher gave us the assignment of doing an interview. I was a conscientious boy, so I turned in an interview with the stage doorman at Carnegie Hall—and he had a really interesting life history. He was a refugee, an old man who had gotten out of Germany just ahead of Hitler. And he wore this old blue serge jacket and brown baggy pants, and he spoke with a strong accent. He lived alone on very little money, and he brought his lunch to work in a paper bag with a thermos of tea. His life had been shattered, but he had spirit, and as it turned out he was very knowledgeable about music. He knew the entire classical repertory. He knew all the musicians who played at Carnegie and over the years had become a fixture in the place, and all the great recitalists, Horowitz, Rubinstein, Jascha Heifetz, knew him and called him by his first name, Carl. And the journalism teacher said, 'This is the best interview I've ever read in all my years teaching this class. I want to run it in the school paper. What we'll do is send one of the photography kids downtown to take a picture of this guy.' And I squirmed around a bit and finally had to confess that it couldn't be done. He wouldn't let his picture be taken. 'What do you mean?' the teacher said. 'I mean there is no Carl the doorman,' I said. 'I made him up.'"

Personally I don't believe a word of it. Mr. Doctorow's account of his life as a journalism student sounds like a metaphor to me, whose truth is intended to be poetic rather than literal. And his description of the genesis of his books has the sound of the apple which fell on Newton's head—nice mythology but of limited value as a guide to the complexities of the creative process, especially one which has yielded such carefully designed works as *Daniel, Ragtime* and now *Loon Lake.*

My own theory is that Mr. Doctorow talks about his books the way he does partly to disabuse those who praise *Daniel* for dramatizing the impact of a historically momentous episode or who believe that the distinctive contribution of *Ragtime* was to introduce historically verifiable characters into fiction. "The principle which interests me," he says, "is that reality isn't something outside. It's something we compose every moment. The presumption of the interpenetration of fact and fiction is that it is what everybody does—lawyers, social scientists, policemen. So why should it be denied to novelists?" His point is well taken, but it does not diminish my own suspicion that he brings to his interviews (even with friends like me) and lectures on his own writing habits the same presumptions that he brings to his novels, namely that a mix of fact and fiction, the objective and the subjective, is the best way for us all to discover what we have to say.

Another clue to Mr. Doctorow's vocabulary may be found in his undergraduate years at Kenyon College, a bastion of the new criticism (he studied with the poet/critic John Crowe Ransom), which holds that the text rather than the author's intention is the proper focus of the serious literary critic. Thus when he talks of the themes in *Loon Lake* he is careful to introduce or close his comments with such phrases as "anyway, that's my theory" or "as I see it." Mr. Doctorow makes it quite clear that, as far as he is concerned, his theories about his books are no more qualified than anyone else's. He is, in the words of a mutual friend, a walking refutation of the intentional fallacy.

It is therefore ironic that unsympathetic critics accuse Mr. Doctorow of writing "political" novels. "It seems to me more of a comment on our time than on anything I have written that a novel that contains concern for our society is seen to be unusual," he says. "*Moby Dick* is a political novel. *The Scarlet Letter* is a political novel. Dostoyevsky and Conrad wrote political novels, although when they are taught, little attention is paid to, say, Conrad's conservative politics. But to think that I'm writing to advance a political program misses the point. To call a novel political today is to label it, and to label it is to refuse to deal with what it does. My premise is that the language of politics can't accommodate the complexity of fiction, which as a mode of thought is intuitive, metaphysical, mythic.

"Joe Heller wrote *Catch-22,* and when it was published some critics said

it's an unfair view of the war—World War II wasn't like that, we were fighting the fascists. Then along came Vietnam, which turned out to be the war
he was writing about. Those who would judge a novel by its alleged politics
want to set up a Commissar in the Republic of Letters. They are members of
what I call the love-it-or-leave-it school of criticism, making political judgments in the guise of esthetic objectivity."

One critic recently made the mistake of automatically attributing to author
Doctorow a particular political perception of narrator Daniel. As it happens,
the politics of author Doctorow, at least as he describes them, consist of a
fairly primitive sense of outrage against injustice, and one of the injustices
he probably has a right to be outraged by is precisely this sort of confusion,
given his highly tuned sensitivity to the uses of narrative voice. "What was
new about *Ragtime*," he insists, "was not that it used historically verifiable
people. To me the unusual thing was to have narrative distance. To create
something not as intimate as fiction nor as remote as history, but a voice that
was mock historical—pedantic."

"In *Daniel*," Mr. Doctorow says, "the narrator declares himself at the
outset. In *Loon Lake* the narrator throws his voice, and the reader has to
figure out who and what he is. The convention of the consistent, identifiable
narrative is one of the last conventions that can be assaulted, and I think it
has now been torpedoed. For the first time, I've made something work without the basic compact between narrator and reader, and technically I'm
pleased at being able to maintain a conventional story despite giving up that
security."

When *Ragtime* first appeared, Mr. Doctorow was quoted as saying that he
wanted his work to be accessible to vast new constituencies, he wanted gas
station attendants to read it. Now that he has written a novel that intentionally
lacks conventional narrative exposition, how does he square this with the
aspiration that led one British journalist to dub him "the Balzac of the petrol
tanks"?

"There's always someone around to tell you what you shouldn't be doing.
You shouldn't be using historical characters. You shouldn't focus on the child
labor laws. You shouldn't shift voices. In *Daniel* the narrator jumped around
in time and tense. Here you don't know who's talking so that's one more
convention out the window. That gives me pleasure, and I think it might give
pleasure to readers, too. Don't underestimate them. People are smart, and
they are not strangers to discontinuity. There's an immense amount of energy
attached to breaking up your narrative and leaping into different voices,

times, skins, and making the book happen and then letting the reader take care of himself. It's a kind of narrative akin to television—discontinuous and mind-blowing."

What, I asked, would have happened if instead of passing a sign which said Loon Lake, you passed a sign which said Lake Placid?

"I did pass the sign," he said, "but I didn't notice it."

Politics and the Mode of Fiction

Richard Trenner / 1982

From *The Ontario Review* 16 (1982), 5–16. Used by permission.

Interviewer: I'd like to talk with you about your political beliefs and activities, both because they interest me and because I think they deeply inform your writing. I see in your work an explicit political rhetoric and an insistent concern with how political and social forces help shape the lives of your characters.

A timely way into this subject might be your recent testimony before a subcommittee of the House Appropriations Committee. As I understand it, P.E.N. asked you to testify against the cuts the Reagan Administration planned for the budget of the National Endowment for the Arts. Your testimony—and the testimony of other advocates of federal funding for the arts—very likely kept the cuts from being as drastic as the President would have liked. And your remarks received a lot of publicity. You spoke memorably and forcefully *for* public support for individual artists and *against* the vast increases in military spending Reagan successfully sought. I think of the almost passionate language and the self-acknowledged sense of futility of your going to Washington to testify. This leads to my first question, which concerns the forms a writer's engagement in the work of political and social change can or should take.

What *should* a writer do who wants to be politically effective in these days of growing militarism and social divisiveness throughout the United States and other parts of the world?

Doctorow: That is a question that you struggle with every day. It's an infernal question—the degree of engagement. We're all pretty well educated in the dangers to one's writing of ideological piety, of a fixed political position. Every writer knows how dangerous it can be in terms of doing something good. But I'm rethinking the whole thing. In view of the emergency—I think that it *is* an emergency—is some kind of new aesthetic possible that does not undermine aesthetic rigor? A poetics of engagement.

Interviewer: I'm not sure why you can't have a very powerful political work that is also aesthetically excellent.

Doctorow: You can. But it would usually end up acknowledging, by its very nature, the ambiguities of what it's talking about. The works that have been destroyed by ideological commitment are, by and large, obscure today, like a lot of the novels of the Thirties. Political sentimentality is as bad as any other kind.

The failure arises from diction. What very often happens is that the novelist or the poet assumes the diction of politics, which, by its very nature, tends to be incapable of illumination. If you use political diction, you're not reformulating anything. You're telling people what they already know. Your rationale is your own language, and the danger of explicit politics in a book is in giving that up.

Interviewer: Yes, but I see *The Book of Daniel,* for instance, as more than a political book. It's a deeper book, not only in its subject matter but in the sense of the characters' dire spiritual and psychological predicaments. The rhetoric of the novel is political, and yet it's certainly not the sort of sterile and deceptive language that you see in straight political writing. So maybe you have already managed to combine something that is aesthetically good with a strong political statement.

Doctorow: Maybe so. But one has to invent each time a way to do that. For instance, when I was in Peru recently, someone asked me an extraordinary question at a lecture I gave. All the questions had been very literary— informed, thoughtful. There were writers there, and academics. It was a civilized audience with elegant manners. And this guy piped up and said, "When are you going to write about the neutron bomb?" Everyone was embarrassed. But it was a good question. "I've been writing about the neutron bomb all my life," I told him. And in one way I have. But what he was talking about was, What are you going to do *now*? How can you feel (and I don't, of course) that anyone's written anything since it's still there? It's your bomb! When are you going to write about it?

I've been thinking about the question ever since it was asked. It's the only one of the evening I remember.

Interviewer: Isn't the novel insufficiently active and direct for the kind of threat that the neutron bomb represents? Maybe what's called for is a lot more direct political action, or at least much more direct rhetoric.

Doctorow: I don't know what's called for. I think it was Robert Jay Lifton who discovered that anyone who talks about nuclear bombs has twenty minutes. You can talk about these things for twenty minutes before people numb out. I don't know if it's even *that* long.

Interviewer: On the other hand, what is the alternative to writing about the neutron bomb—about the ever more dominant militarism of our time? What more important subject is there right now?

Doctorow: Let me talk about this from the inside of the novelist's mind. In here it's not a subject at all, not to be formulated in moral or ethical terms. In here, as I think about it, the bomb loses its political character entirely. The unsettling experience in writing fiction now may be in finding that the story of any given individual, and I don't care who it is, may not be able to sustain an implication for the collective fate. There's a loss of consequence, that's what I mean. The assumption that makes fiction possible, even Modernist fiction—the moral immensity of the single soul—is under question because of the bomb. To write fiction now as it has been written may be to misperceive or avoid the overriding condition of things, which is that we're in the countdown stages of a post-humanist society. On the other hand, if that's true, I wouldn't mean to imply that the problems of writers of fiction aren't the least of our problems.

Interviewer: Have you been politically active outside of your writing? Or have you used your writing as the main way in which you respond to hard political and social facts?

Doctorow: I have generally stayed away from any kind of consistent political activity. I have given benefit readings. I have given my name to various groups and ad hoc committees and causes of one kind or another—peace, trade unionism, civil liberties, getting foreign writers out of prison, and so on. They are all quite specific. And I don't go out and look for them. They are available to me all the time. I'm actually quite selfish. I do relatively little. Going down to Washington to testify on behalf of the National Endowment is, I suppose, an example of direct political action. Or testifying for P.E.N. on the issue of conglomeration in the book industry—the heavy commerce that is coming into the book industry, the effect of that in First Amendment terms. But I'm not a well-organized person and I don't write efficiently. I need a great deal of time in order to get my day's work done—which is a very small number of words—probably between five and six hundred words a day. I have to give myself six or seven hours. It might all happen in fifteen minutes, but not until the end of the sixth hour. You never know. So I'm always very conflicted about doing public things. Sometimes this shows up as bad spirit, a reluctance to be interviewed. Or I will feel I have made a mistake and that in this particular situation I'm being exploited. Or I will think that what I am doing is quixotic and of no real value or consequence at all. I was very much for that writers' congress held recently in New York and lent my name from the beginning to promote and publicize it, but I participated rather marginally on one panel, and then with great reluctance. I'm personally disposed to privacy and a low profile and constantly have to deal with issues of publicity as if I've never dealt with them before. I always feel ill-equipped when someone calls up and says, "Will you do this? Will you speak? Will you give an interview?" I don't learn. It's as if I've never had an experience of this sort before. I can never really adjust to it or think of myself as a forum for any social ideas that I have.

Interviewer: I must say, your interview with Paul Levine has a clear and useful political content. You talk at length about your political views and your sense of history. So sometimes giving an interview works. It's just very hard to predict when one will.

Doctorow: I always have the feeling that my mind has no distinction, except possibly in the book I'm writing. In other words, whatever I have to offer only emerges or is realized through the act of writing. My political opinions are quite ordinary. Fiction is really a different mode, an illuminated way of thinking. And every time I give an interview or write or deliver a speech or do anything like that outside of my work, I think I'm hurting myself. I'm not being in myself, I'm being out of myself. And this shows up in the conflicted feelings I have. It's so easy to become an expert in this country. There's such a sucking thirst for expertise and authority. So if you sit down and think for a couple of days and write something about the National Endowment, then you get dozens of requests because you're an expert, you're a voice of authority on money to artists. But whatever you knew, you've said. And you've only been able to say it because you could sit quietly in your room and work it out.

Interviewer: I appreciate that your truest work, politically, is as a writer. I believe that. I've seen it in your books.

Doctorow: And yet, if you asked me, "What *are* your politics?"—I'd have a tough time.

Interviewer: Well, let's start with the obvious. You're on the left.

Doctorow: I would say I'm a leftist. But of the pragmatic, social democratic left—the humanist left that's wary of ideological fervor. It's a very exhausting place to be. I think the clear, definitive ideologies have all discredited themselves by their adherents.

Interviewer: What is the genealogy of your politics? Are your political values largely the result of personal experience, or what you've seen in the streets, or of your reading over the years? A combination of all three?

Doctorow: Victor Navasky wrote about me that I have a kind of primitive politics, almost a primitive sense of what's fair and what's not fair, what justice is and what injustice is. There's something true about that. So to go on to answer your question, in one sense I don't think of my ideas as political because they're so basic, the perceptions so fundamental and indisputable—like the most glaring sort of prophecy. It's at the level of "Don't do this. This is wrong. God is going to punish you." It's that simple-minded. All the analysis is built on it: Stealing is wrong. Therefore tax laws which favor the wealthy are wrong. Murder and torture are wrong. Therefore the foreign policy which funds and supplies murderous torturing dictators is insupportable. I've been called an idealist and naive and a pseudo-Marxist. But in this country the reference has to be the Constitution; and the political analysis, Marxist or otherwise, will have to develop from just such elemental biblical perception, from what we are in our mythic being, not from what Europe is.

Interviewer: As a preface to my next question, let me tell you something about myself. I grew up in a prosperous Republican family in a prosperous Republican town, but my politics, which are not very articulate, are strongly different from the politics of most of the members of my family and the people of my hometown. Why? Difficult to say, but I like to think they are different because I've had glimpses into the lives of both the rich and the poor, and I've had a couple of years during which I was supporting myself and making a bad job of it. And I think I began to connect with what it means not to be protected and supported by money, class, and school affiliations. I wonder, what are the personal antecedents of your political philosophy, however unevolved, in a beautiful theoretical sense, that philosophy may be?

Doctorow: I immediately think of my grandfather and my father. Mine was not an experience like yours. I grew up in a lower-middle-class environment of generally enlightened, socialist sensibility. My grandfather was a printer, an intellectual, a chess player, an atheist, and a socialist. His was a kind of socialism that represented progress, the coming into the light from centuries of darkness. He had emigrated from Russia as a very young man.

He learned the English language and read Ingersoll and Spencer and Jack London. It was a very Jewish thing, somehow. Humanist, radical, Jewish. The sense of possibility. All the solutions were to be found right here on earth, and the supernatural was not taken seriously. I remember my grandfather giving me Tom Paine's critique of fundamentalism, *The Age of Reason,* when I was ten or eleven. And this continued with my father. My father was a romantic, a dreamer. He was born in New York and lived there all his life, but loved best the real downtown, the docks, the import-export firms, the ship chandlers. He liked to bring home exotic foods. He never traveled but I think he must have dreamed about the sea. He was a midshipman in training in World War I. Toward the end of his life, he routinely read every newspaper, magazine, and journal from every corner of the left.

Interviewer: Did your grandfather and father work in politics?

Doctorow: No. My grandfather was a printer and, by the time I played chess with him, he was retired and quite elderly. My father owned a record and radio and musical instrument store in the 1930's and lost the store later in the Depression. He then became a salesman for a jobber in the same industry—home appliances and, later on, *tv* sets and stereo equipment. His politics were expressed through the papers he read at the kitchen table, the lectures he attended, and the sentiments he expressed when the news was read over the radio. I think he belonged to some sort of fraternal Jewish socialist organization that had a very good insurance program, burial benefit.

Interviewer: John Clayton's essay is entitled "Radical Jewish Humanism: The Vision of E. L. Doctorow." Is there something deeply Jewish about your political convictions?

Doctorow: I suppose so, though I don't think my kind of vision is *only* Jewish. Historically, there's been a kind of tradition among Jews—often very embarrassing to mainline, establishment Jewish thinking. Emma Goldman is a perfect example of that tradition. Her father was a rabbi. Somehow what she did—when she got over her bomber phase, at a relatively early age—had a Jewish-prophet character to it. Think of the terribly unpopular and personally dangerous positions she got into all her life. The connection between one's precarious position in society and the desire for some analysis that would change society is not exclusively Jewish, but it runs all through modern Jewish history. Yet there's more to it than that. In *Prophets Without Honor,* his book about the renaissance of German-speaking Jews in the thirty or forty years before Hitler, Frederic Grunfeld shows this tradition at work.

It's in Freud. It's in Kafka, Schoenberg, in some of the poets killed by Hitler, in the critic Walter Benjamin. Whether they were that radical or not, there was some sort of system to thought—a humanist critique, a social or political skepticism, whatever you want to call it—that had to come from their inability to be complacent or self-congratulatory.

Interviewer: Aside from whatever anti-Semitic impulses at work in some people on the far right, there may be the fearful recognition that radical Jewish humanism is very dangerous to their position.

Doctorow: The Nazis used that. The Jews they went after—the Jews who most enraged them—were the assimilated Jews, the families who had lived in Germany or Austria for hundreds of years. Einstein, for instance, infuriated the Nazis. Einstein was coming up with a universe in which nothing stayed the same very long. Things kept transforming and there was no space without time, and energy became mass and mass became energy. They saw all this relativism as a great threat to their psychic security and a typically Jewish maneuver to undercut and destroy the Aryan race. It was not the pious, practicing Jews who kept to themselves who so much enraged the Nazis at the beginning. It was the Jewish professors and composers (like Mahler) and scientists, all of whom had assimilated to one degree or another. The number of poets, novelists, critics, painters, and musicians whom they destroyed. Migod. That's the other connection you make between art and social criticism.

To get back to the idea of a radical Jewish humanist tradition, if I was not in that tradition, I would certainly want to apply for membership. Years ago in New Rochelle, I gave a talk at a Conservative synagogue. This was at a breakfast meeting of a men's club or something like that. The title of my talk was "Other Jews." And it was just this I was talking about: the expression of Jewish rectitude in humanist political terms. I mentioned Emma Goldman. And I mentioned Allen Ginsberg, this buddhist, homosexual, Beat poet. Ginsberg is right smack in the middle of that tradition. I thought a suburban synagogue was a good place to talk about it.

Interviewer: To move away from the especially Jewish quality of your vision, how would you summarize abstractly your social ideals?

Doctorow: There is a presumption of universality to the ideal of justice—social justice, economic justice. It cannot exist for a part or class of society; it must exist for all. And it's a Platonic ideal, too—that everyone be able to live as he or she is endowed to live; that if a person is in his genes a poet, he be able to practice his poetry. Plato defined justice as the fulfillment of a person's truest self. That's good for starters.

Interviewer: To bring that about would, of course, require a tremendous reorganization of the social and economic structure of our society. Would you say that we'd have to have a socialist reorganization to make possible the kind of justice you describe?

Doctorow: Probably, yes. But it would come up out of us, our best illusions about ourselves. It would be pragmatic and honest and plain-spoken. We would build on what we already have, we would go out in the barn (which is the Constitution) and tinker. And it's the failure to recognize *that* which has always brought programmatic radicals up short in this country. You want to achieve some degree of genuine enlightened social control of production and services—but without creating a bureaucracy that turns oppressive, and without relinquishing any of the political freedoms that exist now.

Interviewer: Do you think the shift in the opposite direction that Reagan represents is a temporary aberration? Or is it (coming from some deep impulse in the American political character) likely to endure?

Doctorow: The great political contests in this country since Franklin Roosevelt have been between the center and the right. So in that sense Reagan is not an aberration. On the other hand, there is something new about him: the abandonment of the liberal rhetoric by which we've always disguised our grubby actions from ourselves. This president is saying the conflict between our democratic ideals and our real political self-interest is over; that the conflict between our constitutional obligations and the expediencies of economic capital reality is over; the crackling contradiction between our national ideals and our repeated historical abuse of those ideals is over. It turns out after all we were not supposed to be a just nation, but a confederacy of stupid murderous gluttons. So there's a terrible loss of the energy you get from self-contradiction, from the battle with yourself. If there was a way of taking a national EEG, you'd find that the brain waves have gone flat. That's new. The religious fundamentalists and the political right have made explosive contact, and in the light of their conjunction it says Armageddon.

A Spirit of Transgression

Larry McCaffery / 1983

From *Anything Can Happen: Interviews with Contemporary Novelists*
Tom Le Clair and Larry McCaffery, editors (Urbana: University of
Illinois Press, 1983). Used by permission.

On April 3, 1980, as I drove up the hill on Broadview Avenue in New Rochelle, New York, towards E. L. Doctorow's beautiful turn-of-the-century
house, I sensed that something about the drive seemed familiar. But it was
only after Doctorow had greeted me and was making us some coffee that I
realized I was sitting in the house described in the opening lines of *Ragtime:*

> In 1902 Father built a house at the crest of the Broadview Avenue hill in New
> Rochelle, New York. It was a three-story brown shingle with dormers, bay win-
> dows and a screened porch. Striped awnings shaded the windows. The family
> took possession of this stout manse on a sunny day in June and it seemed for
> years thereafter that all their days would be warm and fair. . . .

My realization gave me sensations familiar to millions of *Ragtime*'s readers, who are repeatedly asked to examine the thin line which separates fact
from fiction, history from storytelling. The street I had driven on is the same
street that Harry Houdini cruises along in his black 45-horsepower Pope-
Toledo Runabout in one of *Ragtime*'s opening scenes. It is also the street that
Coalhouse Walker travels on to see Sarah—before his fancy motorcar is ru-
ined, Sarah is killed, and he sets out to take his tragic revenge. And here I
was, sipping coffee and eating breakfast rolls in Father's very own
kitchen. . . .

E. L. Doctorow is a handsome man in his early fifties. As we drank coffee
(we shifted to beer during the interview) and made small-talk before beginning the interview, he put me at ease with his humor and utter lack of preten-
tiousness. The telephone rang repeatedly during the several hours I was there:
prepublication activities concerning *Loon Lake,* his novel which was to be
issued that summer. But Doctorow managed easily to shift several times between his telephone and my tape-recorder.

Interviewer: You spent the first few years of your professional life as an
editor, first with the New American Library and then with the Dial Press.
What was the background of this involvement with editing?

Doctorow: I knew from a very early age that I wanted to write, and the question was, how was I going to support myself? Somehow, I stumbled onto the profession of reader. There was a demand for expert readers on the part of television and film companies in New York during the 1950's. You'd read a novel and write a synopsis of it and tack on a critique in which you said whether you thought this story or novel should be adapted for film or television. I immediately declared myself an expert reader, did a couple of books on a tryout basis to establish my credentials, and I was off and running. I had myself a fairly active career.

Interviewer: How active is "fairly active"?

Doctorow: I was reading a book a day, seven days a week, and writing synopses of them. I suppose each synopsis was no less than 1,200 words. I was getting an average of ten or twelve dollars a book, so I was making pretty good money—anywhere between seventy and one hundred dollars a week.

Interviewer: This sounds pretty intense.

Doctorow: Yes, it was. No time to do my own work! But then I was offered a staff job as an inside reader for a film company. An inside reader drew a salary, so this job paid me the same amount of money no matter how much work I did.

Interviewer: Did this staff job lead you directly to editing?

Doctorow: Well, I hacked away at it for a year, or a year and a half. Then one day we found out about a book that had a good advance word. There's great competition among film companies, you know, to get an early look at these things. What my boss, the story editor, discovered was that there was a set of galleys over at a paperback house called NAL—the New American Library. So I went over there and quickly read the thing. The editor-in-chief, Victor Weybright, had said, "When you're through, come tell me what you think." I did, and eighteen months later he called up and asked if I'd like a job. I began as an associate editor at NAL, became a senior editor, and stayed there for five years. It was a great life, publishing good books in big printings—and, in those days—selling them for pocket change. You could feel good about the way you made your living—reprinting a first novel that nobody knew about, working on everything from Ian Fleming to Shakespeare to books on astronomy and every other damned thing, and seeing those books go out with price tags of fifty or seventy-five cents. I felt very good.

Interviewer: Why did you change houses?

Doctorow: Mostly because the owners of this wonderful paperback house sold their company to the Times Mirror Corporation of Los Angeles. Within the year it became quite clear that things were not the same, not as much fun. Publishing is a business of personal enthusiasms, hunches, instincts. The Times Mirror brought in their business consultants and personnel people who had no sympathy for this kind of work. The soul went out of the place. Along about then, a man named Richard Baron, who was part-owner of the Dial Press with Dell Publishing Company, started to talk to me about coming to work at Dial. Eventually I took that job as editor-in-chief, which I held for five years. I got to be vice-president and then publisher before I quit to write full-time.

Interviewer: As an editor, did you find yourself favoring a certain type of book—championing the non-traditional approaches that you yourself were developing during this period, for example?

Doctorow: No, not at all. The publishing mentality, ideally, is generous, expansive, catholic in taste. You have to be receptive to lots of things, to know the value of different things. This might mean loving a book because it's highly and seriously accomplished or because it's a good trashy novel with no literary pretensions whatsoever. Or to think up an idea for a book and find just the right writer to do it. The point is that you don't have a set of rules or preconceptions to restrict your availability to what comes along; you just have to be as open to as much as possible and pick and choose from what flows by.

Interviewer: What sort of effect did your experiences as an editor have on your own writing?

Doctorow: I don't imagine I would have written *Welcome to Hard Times* if I'd not been working at that film company and reading lousy screenplays week after week. I had no affinity for the genre—I'd never even been west of Ohio. I thought Ohio *was* the West. Oh, as a kid I'd liked Tom Mix radio programs and maybe I went to see a few movies; but, really, I had no feeling for Westerns. But from reading all these screenplays and being forced to think about the use of Western myth, I developed a kind of contrapuntal idea of what the West must really have been like. Finally one day I thought, "*I* can lie better than these people." So I wrote a story and showed it to the story editor, Albert Johnson, who was by now a friend, and he said, "This is good. Why don't you turn it into a novel?" And so I did.

Interviewer: Was this your first try at a novel?

Doctorow: No. I had been trying to write a book about a boy in college. I was actually working on that book when I took up this other project. *Welcome to Hard Times* was crucial for me for a couple of reasons. First, because it showed me my strength, which was *not* autobiographical writing. Somehow I was the kind of writer who had to put myself through prisms to find the right light—I had to filter myself from my imagination in order to write. The second thing I learned was that all writing begins as accident. Eventually it will come around to who you are, it will find some essence, but the *start* of a book is necessarily contingent; you can't plan it. If I had not worked as a reader and gotten angry at what I was reading, I would not have written that particular novel.

Interviewer: You've said somewhere that *Ragtime* began as a set of images that were related to this house we're sitting in. Is this the sort of accident you're talking about that gets you going on a novel?

Doctorow: Yes, that's exactly the kind of thing. In the case of *Ragtime,* the creative accident occurred one day as I was staring at the wall. I started to write about the wall. This house was built in 1906. And I was off.

The other element for me in this kind of creative accident is my own desperation. I've learned that, each time around, I have to reach a truly desperate moment. I need to really feel very keenly a crisis of despair in order to find the level of recklessness or freedom that allows me to write the book. This has happened time and again. In the case of *The Book of Daniel,* I knew the subject, it interested me, and I thought I could hang an awful lot on it. I spent about six-months initial work on it—about 150 pages. And those pages were terrible, awful. At this point I thought that if I could ruin a momentous subject like this, then I had no business writing. I threw away the pages and in a state of reckless, irresponsible, almost *manic* despair, I sat down at the typewriter and started writing what turned out to be *The Book of Daniel.* The point is that it had to be done in Daniel's voice, not my own. And I had to really hit bottom to come to this realization. This terrible moment happens with every book, sometimes earlier and sometimes later. In the case of the book I just finished, *Loon Lake,* it happened fairly late, while the book was in its third draft.

Interviewer: You mentioned earlier that you knew very early on that you wanted to be a writer, and yet you studied philosophy at Kenyon College as an undergraduate. How did these two things jibe?

Doctorow: I went to Kenyon to study with John Crowe Ransom. He was a wonderful teacher but also an Olympian presence. As much as I learned from him—I studied prosody with him, for instance—somehow I was inclined to a different kind of mental life. And I found it, I thought, in philosophy. I had a mind for philosophy and although I kept taking English courses, it was never with the same excitement I felt for my philosophy work. The philosophy department there was very small and I had some very fine teachers, but the man I responded to most was Philip Blair Rice, a brilliant philosopher and also the associate editor of the *Kenyon Review*—Ransom being the editor. I studied metaphysics and aesthetics with Rice and ethics and logic with his colleague, Virgil Aldridge. I loved it. During that four-year period, I did relatively little writing and had little interest in the established English Department requirements. Instead, I did philosophy and got into theater as a student actor. I had no plan, I just did what interested me. I was erratic, totally without discipline, full of longings, feelings of power, and not knowing what to attach them to. When I graduated, Rice said to me, "Doctorow, you're one of the five best students I've ever had. And of the five, you're the least informed."

Interviewer: What made you turn away from pursuing an academic career in philosophy?

Doctorow: I don't think I ever intended to pursue it. On graduation day, Ransom introduced me to Robert Penn Warren, who was getting an honorary degree, and who happened at that time to be teaching playwriting at the Yale Drama School. I had written a play at Kenyon and had acted in several. In my senior year I'd decided that I wanted to be a playwright. Ransom said, "Red, I think this young man ought to go to Yale," and Warren said, "All right, Pappy." What a beautiful day in June! But this was during the Korean War and my draft board told me I would have only one year for graduate studies before I'd get packed off—and the Yale M.F.A. program was a three-year program. So I ended up going to Columbia for one year, studying English drama and acting and directing, and then I was drafted, just as they had promised. And I never went to Yale. But it's almost as good that Ransom spoke for me on my graduation day.

Interviewer: *Welcome to Hard Times* and *Big As Life* both obviously lie pretty far outside the realm of traditional, realistic fiction. Did you have any sense, when you were starting out as a writer, of reacting against a certain type of fiction, of trying to create your own niche as a writer? I ask this because your early books are so startlingly different from the kinds of books that most other serious writers were producing during that period.

Doctorow: I think I've already almost answered that question by suggesting the accident of my involvement with *Welcome to Hard Times*. What happens is that you do something and only then do you figure out what it is. You write to find out what you're writing. It was only after I had written those first two books, for example, that I developed a rationale for the approaches I had taken—that I liked the idea of using disreputable genre materials and doing something serious with them. I liked invention. I liked myth.

Interviewer: I take it, then, that you were hardly under the spell of any particular writers at the time—that you weren't relating, either positively or negatively, to the sort of thing you were seeing every day on your desk as an editor.

Doctorow: As an editor, I spent a lot of time taking books and making them work. Structuring them. Cracking them open and putting them back together. Getting their authors to do more—or to do less. I liked doing that and I suppose my own books have gained from the practice. But I've never related to my contemporaries on a competitive basis. Mailer, for instance, was a long-established writer when I started writing; I had read his first book in high school. That whole generation of writers—Mailer, Styron—they're not ten years older than I am, but they've been around a long time. They all flashed pretty early and got the hang of literary combativeness. I think this might have something to do with their going through World War II. When people fight in a war, it takes them a while—and society a while—to wind down afterwards, if at all. The war keeps on after the war is over. Different generations imprint differently, of course. It's the fate of my generation that we've never shared a monumental experience. We think of ourselves as loners.

Interviewer: So you've never seen yourself as part of a literary movement which reacted against the type of fiction being written in the 1940's and '50's?

Doctorow: I don't think the real life of a writer has anything to do with literary movements. To the extent that it does, the writer may be in trouble. You're just singing, you're just doing what you can, discovering what you can, living and trying to do something that is sound and good.

Interviewer: One of the criticisms leveled against a lot of fiction written in the past twenty years—but not against yours very often—is that it is "too academic," too directly responsive to the analytic, critical mind. Do you think this type of thinking is actively harmful to the creative process?

Doctorow: I did a lot of criticism as an undergraduate. I know what that analytic faculty of mind is. I saw it working in true splendor in Ransom, who had as nice a mind as I've seen. But I think this faculty works against you unless it's in balance with everything else. I like to affect a kind of ignorance about my work that might be a sham, an affectation. On the other hand, I'm really wary of being too critically informed.

Interviewer: It can't be just an accident that *Big As Life* is rarely mentioned on your dust-jacket biographies.

Doctorow: Sometimes it's mentioned, sometimes not. Unquestionably, it's the worst I've done. I think about going back and re-doing it some day, but the whole experience was so unhappy, both the writing and the publishing of it, that maybe I never will. It's my *Mardi*—you know, Melville's *Mardi*?

Interviewer: Sure.

Doctorow: *Big As Life* is mine.

Interviewer: Except for *Big As Life,* all of your books have used the past to explore not only the past but certain parallel tendencies in the present. In *Welcome to Hard Times,* one of your characters expresses this idea as, "We can never start new." In *The Book of Daniel* it goes, "Everything that came before is all the same." Could you discuss this inability of the present to escape from the errors of the past?

Doctorow: Those lines came out of those particular books and I'm uncomfortable talking about things in the abstract. I would say that the fact that they're similar and express similar sentiments should not suggest that I started the books because of those ideas. In each case, it came as a discovery to me as I was writing through the personality of the narrative voice I was using.

Interviewer: Obviously, then, you don't begin a work with a specific point to make or a thesis to illustrate. It sounds like you regard your work more as a kind of personal exploration rather than a vehicle consciously devised to develop a theme.

Doctorow: I like to quote a remark of Marcel Duchamp. He appeared to have given up painting. Someone said, "Marcel, why have you stopped painting?" He said, "Because too much of it was 'filling in.' " That's a wonderful line. Anybody who finds himself in the situation of writing to a prescribed notion or to illustrate or fill in what he already knows should stop writing. A writer has got to trust the act of writing to scan all his ideas, passions, and convictions for these to emerge *from* the work, be *of* it. I think that's standard wisdom, at least among American writers.

Interviewer: Since all of your works, in one way or another, seem passionately committed to examining major social and political issues, I would assume you would take issue with, say, William Gass's claim about art's "disconnection" from ordinary reality.

Doctorow: Yes, I'm opposed to that view. I think art and life make each other. Henry Miller said, "We should give literature back to life." I believe that. I believe more than that.

Interviewer: When you're intensely at work on a project, do you find yourself usually focusing on a specific aspect of writing—the plot movement, the language, the character development, the fleshing out of your own ideas?

Doctorow: I think it varies with the book. In *Ragtime* it was the historical imagery and the mock-historical tone which most interested me. And the idea of composition at a fixed narrative distance to the subject, neither as remote as history writing—which is very, very distant from what is being described—nor as close as modern fiction, which is very intimate with the subject. I was aiming for the narrative distance of the historical chronicle that you find, for instance, in Kleist who, of course, was very important in the composition of that book.

In the case of *Daniel,* it was a far different feeling. It was the characters and their complexity that moved me—the historical intersection of social and personal agony, history moving in Daniel, shaping his own pathology—all this had an enormous meaning and interest for me. So did his relationship to his sister and the parents' relationship to each other, and Daniel's relationship to himself as he sits in that library and does these historical essays and descriptions of himself in the third person, breaking down his own voice and transforming his own being to produce this work. Daniel breaks himself down constantly to reconcile himself to what is happening and what has happened to him. This kind of act that the book is—*Daniel's* book—is the central force that I felt in the writing of it.

With *Welcome to Hard Times,* it was just a sense of a place which moved me tremendously. It was the landscape. I loved writing about it, imagining it. I had never been West. Halfway through the book, it occurred to me that maybe I ought to make sure it really was a possible terrain. I went to the library and read a geography book by Walter Prescott Webb—a marvelous book called *The Great Plains.* Webb said what I wanted to hear: no trees out

there. Jesus, that was beautiful. I could spin the whole book out of one image.
And I did.

Interviewer: What about your new book, *Loon Lake?*

Doctorow: It is more like *Daniel* in being a discontinuous narrative, with
deferred resolutions, and in the throwing of multiple voices that turn out to
be the work of one narrator. So there are similarities with *Daniel,* but the
subject is far different and the tone is also different. It takes place in the
Depression, a sort of Depression *Bildungsroman.* But not with that form's
characteristic accumulation of data. I have a lot of broken-line stuff in it—
weighted lines. That's new for me. In *Loon Lake* the sound the words make
is important—the sound in the words and their rhythm. I think a good many
parts of it are better read aloud.

Interviewer: Was there an accident involved in your getting started with
Loon Lake, as there was with the others?

Doctorow: I was driving through the Adirondacks a couple of years ago. I
found myself incredibly responsive to everything I saw and heard and
smelled. The Adirondacks are very beautiful—but more than that, a palpably
mysterious wilderness, a place full of dark secrets, history rotting in the for-
ests. At least that was my sense of things. I saw a road sign: "Loon Lake."
Everything I felt came to a point in those words. I liked their sound. I imagined a private railroad train going through the forest. The train was taking a
party of gangsters to the mountain retreat of a powerful man of great wealth.
So there it was: a feeling for a place, an image or two, and I was off in pursuit
of my book.

Interviewer: You tend to develop rather peculiar narrative structures that
several critics have labeled "cinematic." Did the cinema or television affect
your notion of structure?

Doctorow: I don't know how anyone can write today without accommo-
dating eighty or ninety years of film technology. Films and the perception of
films and of television are enormously important factors in the way people
read today. Beginning with *Daniel,* I gave up trying to write with the concern
for transition characteristic of the nineteenth-century novel. Other writers
may be able to, but I can't accept the conventions of realism any more. It
doesn't interest me as I write. I'm not speaking now of a manifesto—but of
the experience of the writer, or at least this writer. You do what works. Obviously, the rhythms of perception in me, as in most people who read today,
have been transformed immensely by films and televisions.

I don't think, however, that this issue is primarily a matter of writing visually as opposed to not writing visually. I don't know what non-visual writing is. I think all writing puts pictures in people's heads—pictures of different things, but always pictures of the moral state of the characters being written about. Good fiction is interested in the moral fate of its people. Who they are or how they look or what they do or how they live—these are judgments of character, finally. A poem, too, tries to define someone's moral existence. And that comes off the images. Poets are not alone in using imagery. So when someone says my prose is visual, I don't really know what that means. No, what we've learned from film is quite specific. We've learned that we don't have to explain things. We don't have to explain how our man can be in the bedroom one moment and walking in the street the next. How he can be twenty years old one moment and eighty years old a moment later. We've learned that if we just make the book happen, the reader can take care of himself. You remember that television show *Laugh-In?* That was the big hit on television while I was writing *Daniel*. I told people when *Daniel* was published that it was constructed like *Laugh-In*. They thought I was not serious. But the idea of discontinuity and black-outs and running changes on voice and character—it was that kind of nerve energy I was looking for. *Loon Lake,* too, is powered by discontinuity, switches in scene, tense, voice, the mystery of who's talking. Will people be able to understand it? I think they will. Anyone who's ever watched a news broadcast on television knows all about discontinuity.

Interviewer: Daniel says something about life not being as "well plotted" as we would like it to be. Is this one of your problems with the conventions of realism?

Doctorow: Life may have been better plotted at one time.

Interviewer: That's an interesting idea. Philip Roth suggested back in the early 1960's that it's more difficult for contemporary writers to create realistic fiction because "reality" is less realistic, more extravagant than any world the writer can hope to create. In fact, your character Harry Houdini in *Ragtime* seems to be an artist-figure who has a difficult time in making his art more wondrous than that of the world. Do you share this sense of a world outstripping your ability as an artist to produce wonders?

Doctorow: Certainly the clatter, the accelerated rate of crisis, the sense of diffusion of character, the disintegration of belief or social assumptions are reflected in the novelists who find the novel itself no longer convincing and who write anti-mimetic novels essentially about how it's impossible to write. That view explains a lot of stuff that's been done in the last twenty years, but it doesn't explain Roth, does it? Fortunately, he keeps trying. Whatever the difficulties are, the obstacles, that's the nature of the game.

I enjoy problems and I enjoy adversity, at least professionally, and if life as represented in the headlines of the paper makes the act of writing absurd, I accept that and I'll try to deal with it. That's the condition under which I'll do my work. And I may fail, probably will, probably have, probably always will fail, but that's a kind of occupational hazard—it's built into the trade. I can imagine Cervantes sitting there in jail tearing his hair out while he wrote *Don Quixote*.

Interviewer: When *Ragtime* came out, several critics expressed their surprise about the use of historical figures. Obviously, though, real people and events appear in your earlier book, *Daniel*—sometimes disguised but sometimes not. What do you find so intriguing about the use of real facts and real historical people in your work?

Doctorow: As my answer to the last question suggests, if you do this kind of work, you can't finally accept the distinction between reality and books. In fact, no fiction writer has ever stood still for that distinction and that's why Defoe pretended that *Robinson Crusoe* was really written by Crusoe. I don't want to understand that distinction between art and everything else, so I don't. This is not merely an aesthetic position, you understand. I get impatient with people who are moralistic about this issue. Someone said to me, "Don't you think it shows a lack of imagination to use historical characters?" And I said, "Yes, it does. Of course, it was a terrible lack of imagination on Tolstoy's part, too, when he made a character out of Napoleon." In fact, he even made a character out of Napoleon's General Doctorow, an ancestor of mine. Someone said another time, "What would *Daniel* be if there hadn't been a Rosenberg case?" I said, "You're absolutely right. And where would *The Red Badge of Courage* be without the Civil War?" What I think has happened is that people used to know what fiction was and now they've forgotten. It comes as a surprise when they're reading a novel and they find Harry Houdini saying things and carrying on. It could be that there's been such a total disintegration into specialist thinking on the part of all of us in our trades and jargons that no one remembers what the whole life is. What is imagined and what is experienced? The imagination obviously imposes itself on the world, composes a world which, in turn, affects what is imagined.

That's true even in science. Indisputable. I suppose this leans towards a kind
of philosophical idealist's position, although it isn't really that exactly. I
mean, I know that when I kick the rock, I refute Berkeley. But I also know
that a book can affect consciousness—affect the way people think and therefore the way they act. Books create constituencies that have their own effect
on history, and that's been proven time and again. So I don't see that distinction between facts and art. If you read a good social scientist, an anthropolo-
gist, a sociologist, I think you'll find they do everything we fiction writers
do. These people who write sociology create composite characters. Anyone
who represents a class or a kind of ethnic or economic group is dealing in
characterization. That's what I do.

Interviewer: Gass has a line about Plato's soul being one of the greatest
literary characters of all time.
Doctorow: Well, why not? And if you read the newspapers, you see the
creativity involved. Just deciding what to look at and write about is an immensely creative decision. As a newsman, you're deciding what will exist
and what won't exist.

Interviewer: I was intrigued by another remark you made once: "When
you write about imaginary events in the lives of undisguised people, you are
proposing that history has ended and mythology has begun." What were you
trying to suggest in your distinction between history and mythology?
Doctorow: Just what we've been talking about. All history is composed.
A professional historian won't make the claims for the objectivity of his
discipline that the lay person grants him. He knows how creative he is. It
turned out that American historians had written, for the most part, as an
establishment. They had written out of existence the history of black people
and women and Indians and Chinese people in this country. What could be
more apparent than the creativity of that? That's part of what I meant when
I said of the little boy in *Ragtime* that "it was evident to him that the world
composed and re-composed itself constantly in an endless process of dissatisfaction."

Interviewer: As you've acknowledged on several occasions, the figure of
Coalhouse Walker is based on Kleist's Michael Kohlhass. What was the background of your decision to use this earlier fictional character in your own
book?
Doctorow: Several years ago my wife related a true story she'd heard

about a housemaid in our neighborhood who bore a child and then buried it
in a garden. I knew when I heard this I'd use it someday. I found myself
using it in *Ragtime,* where I never knew in advance what was going to happen. Suddenly there was Mother discovering the little brown newborn in the
flower bed. There was Sarah coming to live in the house with this baby.
Obviously, she would have tried to kill her child only from some overwhelming despair or sense of betrayal. So there had to be a father. I had introduced
Houdini driving up Broadview Avenue hill in his car and that was the way I
decided to introduce the child's father. He came along in his shining Ford, an
older man, and he said, "I'm looking for a young woman of color." Where
had he been? I decided he was a musician, a man who lived on the road,
going where he found work. Now he was back to make amends. He starts to
court Sarah and when she refuses to see him, he plays the piano for the
family in their parlor. And that's how I found the central image of the book.
Then I began to think about the implications of a black man owning his own
car in the early 1900's. I knew Sarah would forgive him and they would be
reconciled. But that car: What would happen to that lovely car of his is what
happened to Michael Kohlhaas's horses. I had always wanted to rework the
circumstances of Kleist's story. I felt the premise was obviously relevant,
appropriate—the idea of a man who cannot find justice from a society that
claims to be just. So there it was—I'd finally found the use for that legend
I'd hoped to find—but not until the moment I needed it.

Interviewer: Both Coalhouse and Younger Brother die in the pursuit of
their radical ideas. And, of course, the Isaacsons are framed and eventually
electrocuted. You seem to be opting for the view that history is on the side
of compromise and cooperation—that idealism is rarely rewarded in our
country.
   Doctorow: I believe it's more complicated than that. The radical ideas of
one generation make up the orthodoxy of subsequent generations, so the
radical role is to be sacrificial. Certainly in the history of this country, the
radical is often sacrificed and his ideas are picked up after he himself has
been destroyed. I believe Eugene Debs came up with the idea of social security and he really suffered for that. And among Emma Goldman's outrageous,
radical ideas, for which she was deported, was that of a woman's right to her
own body, her right to have an abortion if she chooses. Hideous radicalism
at the time, yet it's the law of the land, although there is some challenge to it
right now.

Interviewer: Tateh is allowed to become a financial success even though he sells out his moral beliefs. Were you tempted to condemn him for abandoning his working-class ideals?

Doctorow: No, I love that character, but also understand him. I was making an observation in my treatment of him, that very often a man who begins as a radical somehow—with all his energy and spirit and intelligence and wit—by a slight change of course can use these gifts to succeed under the very system he's criticizing. Very often this happens without his losing his sense of himself as a radical. You can often find among the wealthy a conviction that they are unrestructured radicals. They give a lot of money to political causes of the left, and so forth.

Interviewer: Tateh's presence in *Ragtime* seems to me to undercut some of the criticism your book received for being blindly sympathetic to its leftist characters.

Doctorow: Yes, when people claim that I have this sentimental, simplistic approach to the characters on the left, they're not reading carefully. As compassionate as we feel for Tateh and as much as we love him, here's a man who has betrayed his principles and sympathies and gotten ahead that way. After all, he has gotten to enjoy his life by abandoning his commitment to the working class. So that's hardly an uncomplicated, simplistic view of one of the book's leftists. I think I also portray Emma Goldman as a person who stomps all over people's feelings, who just wreaks havoc with people's personal lives wherever she goes. This sort of thing is true of the radical idealist personality, though it's hardly a simplistic portrayal of her.

Interviewer: Do you recall what initially interested you in the Rosenberg case as a possible source for a novel?

Doctorow: When I started thinking about the case, the Rosenbergs had been dead fourteen or fifteen years. I think I was in the Army serving in Germany when they were executed, and maybe that's why at the time it was a more remote horror to me than to many others. I was fully sensitive to the McCarthy period generally. But the case didn't propose itself to me as a subject for a novel until we were all going through Vietnam. Here was the New Left, the anti-war movement, an amplification by a later generation of the torment of the 1950's. At any rate, it seemed to me that I could write about the case, that my imagination could find its corporeal being in those circumstances. I would not write a documentary novel but quite clearly and deliberately use what had happened to the Rosenbergs as *occasion* for the book. I don't mean this as a comparison, only as an example: Defoe knew Alexander Selkirk had been a castaway and that the idea of the castaway was very important and alive in London. And that's all he needed to do *Robinson Crusoe*—the real phenomenon of the castaway.

I felt people would know about the Rosenbergs and that was all I needed to write a book about Paul and Rochelle Isaacson. Although I was perhaps a little older than Daniel, I was of an age where I could respond, symbolically or metaphorically, as a person of his era. So a lot of things came together around this idea. The relationship between radical movements of one generation and another. The idea of a radical family—all the paradoxes and contradictions of that family against whom the entire antagonistic force of society is directed. So I wondered, what is the nature of that experience? What happens to people under such circumstances? How does it feel? I found that I had a proprietary sense of recognition for the subject. Also, I was angry. It seems to me certainly a message of the twentieth century that people have a great deal to fear from their own governments. That's an inescapable worldwide fact. Daniel has a line about every citizen being the enemy of his own country. It is the nature of the governing mind to treat as adversary the people being governed.

Interviewer: Given your personal sympathies, were you ever tempted to make Daniel a thoroughly sympathetic character, rather than giving him sadistic, at times almost monstrous, qualities?

Doctorow: Suffering doesn't make people virtuous, at least in my experience. But I see his "sadism," as you call it, in a slightly different way. I see the scene where he abuses his wife, for instance, as the same kind as the scene in which he throws his son up in the air. The act has existential dimensions. Daniel is over-tuned to the world. He doesn't miss a thing. He's a hero—or a criminal—of perception. When he delivers his eulogy of his sister Susan, he says there has been a failure of analysis: Susan could only survive by limiting the amount of reality in the situation insofar as her parents were concerned. She had to come to a very strict, defensive judgment, and eventually it broke her. But Daniel gives himself to the act of perception and opens himself to it—much as all writers must—and he survives that way, survives by however cold and frightening an embrace with the truth. That is perhaps his only strength. Of course, it would take a tremendous act of the will to accept the very idea of a family after this kind of thing has happened to you as a child. Daniel recognizes this, and in acting out the terrible conflicts within himself between giving in and not giving in (his sister chose not to go on and he's trying to go on), he is enduring—by letting in as much truth about himself and his life as he can.

Interviewer: As you've implied, this openness to perception seems to make Daniel an especially interesting example of *any* artist.

Doctorow: Maybe the nature of fiction is that, unlike reporting for *The New York Times,* it has to admit everything—all aspects and forms of thought and behavior and feeling, no matter how awful they may be. Fiction has no borders, everything is open. You have a limitless possibility of knowing the truth. But there are always people telling you what you can't do, where you mustn't go. Every time you write a book, someone says, "Oh, you shouldn't have done this or you shouldn't have done that." There's always a commissar who wants to tell you what the rules are. Yet when I'm writing out of a spirit of transgression, I'm probably doing my best work.

Author, Author: An Interview with Doctorow

James McInerney / 1984

From *Vogue* 174 (1984), 152–55. Copyright © 1984 by E. L. Doctorow and James McInerney. Reprinted by permission of International Creative Management, Inc.

"Writing is like driving at night," says novelist E. L. Doctorow. "You can see only as far as the headlights, but you can make the whole trip that way."

Doctorow's journey began of necessity at night. After graduating from Kenyon College in 1952, he spent his days working as an editor at New American Library, and later as editor-in-chief at the Dial Press. He worked on his own novels at night. Doctorow took a leave of absence to finish the critically acclaimed *Book of Daniel*—which many readers took to be a fictional meditation on the case of Julius and Ethel Rosenberg—and never returned to publishing. Since then, he has been a morning writer. "If you get up and write first thing," he says, "then you know that's what you are— you're a writer."

With the publication of *Ragtime,* in 1975, Doctorow acquired both critical acclaim and a popular audience. The book won the National Book Critics Circle award, became a best seller, and commanded a record-breaking paperback advance. *Ragtime* was subsequently made into a motion picture, about which Doctorow says, "People think that movies can do anything. But they are limited by being strictly temporal and they are always limited by their budgets. It's books that can do anything. It's words as they are put together purposefully that can produce movies in people's heads."

Since *Ragtime,* Doctorow has published a fifth novel, *Loon Lake,* and a play, *Drinks Before Dinner.* This month, Random House is bringing out his first collection of short fiction, *Lives of the Poets.* The novella from which the book takes its title is told from the point of view of a successful fifty-year-old novelist who lives in New York, whose friends are poets, painters, journalists—the creative elite of the nation—all of whom, like the narrator, seem to be experiencing crises of confidence in their personal and professional lives. "We are each aloof in our private beings," the narrator of "Poets" observes, as he seeks to abdicate the claims of marriage, home life, and politics. Since Doctorow's novels are notable for their engagement with large social and historical issues, the new book seems a departure in its concern with solitary, brooding individuals.

Jay McInerney: *Why short stories, after five novels?*

E.L. Doctorow: Oddly enough, I don't think of this as a collection of stories. I think of it as a novel about a guy who has written six stories. I worked my way into this scheme. In the first story ["The Writer in the Family"], which is very realistic and accessible, Jonathan finds himself through the act of writing. He comes to some realization that allows him to separate from his father, which he hasn't been able to do. I think of it as a parable about what I'm talking about: how do writers write? He understood his father without realizing he understood his father. I think that's a truth about the writer's intelligence. It's intuitive.

JM: *Would it be accurate to say that isolation, the retreat into self, is one of the main themes of the book?*

ELD: It seems to me quite true of our current, national, psychic state that we are in retreat. Certainly, the predominant trends in recent American fiction are toward privacy and isolation. With the novel's view of its terrain as the interior of a house with the door closed and the shades pulled, what goes on in the bedroom and kitchen and living room becomes the whole world. That's why I think *Lives of the Poets* can make a fair claim not only to describing the state of this artist's mind, but also to making him a representative of the network of our particular moment in literary history. American history. So that's the metaphor of *Lives of the Poets*. It's not just literal poets—it's novelists, columnists, painters, actors.

JM: *You once said, "I want to break out of the little world of personal experience which has bound the novel, to escape that suffocating closeness to the characters." It seems that this book reverses that program.*

ELD: It becomes necessary to say, "Why are things this way?" I can say what I think the novel ought to be, but why is this other thing happening? There must be something to understand from that. I think *Lives of the Poets,* in very specific terms, dwells in that kind of interior life, that isolation. Every one of these characters is alone. You've picked up on the insulated nature of all these narrative intelligences. But there are political implications to that. Into that vacuum the world advances.

JM: *The narrator finally commits himself to involvement in the world at large by becoming involved almost by accident with an underground railroad for Salvadoran refugees.*

ELD: It's not so much that he is *doing* something, but that, quite helplessly, he is open to the world. He is, after all, a writer.

JM: *He* is *a writer, and he has friends named Norman and Kurt. The reaction to this book may be that for the first time you have written autobiographically. Have you considered that just as we can't help connecting the Isaacsons in* The Book of Daniel *with the Rosenbergs, you are going to be the shadow that people see behind this narrator?*

ELD: I have. But of course as a writer everything you do is autobiographical.

JM: *But your previous works seems to resist that autobiographical focus.*

ELD: It becomes more or less coded from work to work. All I can say about this is that it is no more autobiographical than anything I've written. It's a fiction. It's invented. I use myself as I've always used myself, as all writers use themselves. That guy is not me.

JM: *But it seems to me that given the narrator's relative moral drift and his lack of political commitment, readers may take this as a statement about a change in heart from the man who wrote the book. You are, after all, known as a public figure, a man of the left.*

ELD: I think the so-called center has moved so far to the right that there are very few of us who aren't on the left. I don't think my principles have changed. It's true, there is a departure for me, both formally and in the ongoing argument we have with ourselves. But I wouldn't try to encapsulate it as my going autobiographical because I don't think that's sufficient. The metaphorical reference to the way we are now suggests itself as a fragmentation of the large traditional esthetic vision, the novel that will *do* society, that will say—*This is the way we are now.* I'm hoping that this book will accurately represent the way we are now. In breaking it down into the elements of this writer's mind, I am hoping that something whole has emerged. If you want to represent the whole now, you have to represent it as something shattered. I see this book as being the closest I've come to making a true representation of my life and times.

JM: *Your narrator says that something has changed in the last five years. What is that?*

ELD: Aside from the obvious political meanings, I think I am speaking of the loss of the romantic vision in even the most serious and the best people. There seems to be a kind of emotional exhaustion among all these people, and I think, as a metaphor for American art, that may be accurate.

JM: *What can a writer, an artist, do in terms of participating in the life of his times? To put it in terms of the metaphors of* Loon Lake, *should a writer be a passive observer, like the lake, or should he be active, like the loon that shatters the surface in search of prey?*

ELD: I think the writer's obligation is just to tell the truth, and that's the one commitment he can't betray without destroying himself. For the writer, the creative person, the practice of what he or she does is the connection between the inner and outer life, between political circumstances, economic and social circumstances, and his own internal being.

The Myth Maker: The Creative Mind of Novelist E. L. Doctorow

Bruce Weber / 1985

From *The New York Times Magazine* 20 October 1985, 24+. Copyright 1985 by The New York Times. Reprinted by permission.

Twenty-five years after the publication of his first novel, *Welcome to Hard Times,* E. L. Doctorow is reminiscing about a letter from one of its readers. Set in the Dakota Territory in the latter half of the 19th century, the novel takes the form of journals written by the mayor of a tiny frontier town called Hard Times. It's a dark fable, a literary western by a serious young writer, that employs the town's tribulations—and the mayor's attempts to record them—to explore grand themes: the nature of American culture, the mortality of men and their civilization, the eternalness of art.

"The letter was from Texas," Doctorow says, "and obviously from an elderly woman, written in a shaky hand. She wrote, 'Young man, when you said that Jenks enjoyed for his dinner the roasted haunch of a prairie dog, I knew you'd never been west of the Hudson. Because the haunch of a prairie dog wouldn't fill a teaspoon.' "

Doctorow pauses and grins, the professional storyteller timing a punch line: "She had me. I'd never seen a prairie dog. So I did the only thing I could do. I wrote back and I said, 'That's true of prairie dogs today, Madam, but in the 1870's. . . .' "

A small story, but it illustrates nicely the audacity Doctorow presumes as a novelist, his unconcerned subordination of fact to invention, his belief that the novelist's imagination is autonomous.

Edgar Lawrence Doctorow is 54, and on almost anyone's list he is counted among the leading dozen serious American novelists today. Although he is not simply a writer of entertainments, his books sell widely, and three—*Ragtime, The Book of Daniel* and *Welcome to Hard Times*—have been made into movies. Readers, some critics excepted, have come to relish the blending of fact and fiction that marks his odd scrutiny of the American past. His seventh book, *World's Fair,* will be published next month, and in it, he turns his historically inventive method on himself, drawing heavily on material gleaned from his 1930's boyhood. "Growing up in the Bronx, without the egg cream" is the author's flip description, but he has also called it "a portrait of the artist as a very young boy," and that is perhaps closer to what he has attempted. Although outwardly his quietest novel, *World's Fair* uses the Bronx, much as Joyce did Dublin, as a window through which to witness the tremors of a whole society.

Doctorow is a hearty-looking man with a surprisingly soft, speculative voice, an elfin face that crinkles when he smiles. He has the habit of squinting with one eye at a time, the expression of an amused skeptic. City-born and bred, he's become a suburban sort, and for some weeks he's been relaxing at his home in Sag Harbor on Long Island. He does keep a small apartment in Greenwich Village near New York University, where he teaches in the graduate writing program. For the most part, though, he and his wife, the novelist Helen Henslee, split their time between here and the house in New Rochelle they bought in the early 1960's and that served as the setting for part of *Ragtime.*

Doctorow's diverse and unpredictable fiction is known for its juxtaposition of familiar cultural, political and historical markers with prominent fabrications. But it is marked by a narrative style that is forthright, declarative and presumptuous of verisimilitude. In *Ragtime,* his chronicle of America hurtling toward World War I, Doctorow embellished his narrative with depictions of unlikely occurrences in the lives of famous people: secret meetings between Henry Ford and J. Pierpont Morgan; Freud and Jung visiting Coney Island and boating together through the Tunnel of Love; Harry Houdini's encounter with the Archduke Francis Ferdinand.

The magic of *Ragtime*'s invention was persuasive enough to win for Doctorow the National Book Critics Circle Award for fiction. And the novel garnered enough notoriety to sell more than 200,000 copies in hard-cover its first year; paperback reprint rights were purchased by Bantam Books for $1,850,000, then a record figure. The book's success launched Doctorow into the top echelon of American novelists, permanently enhancing his readership and the critical appreciation for the entirety of his work.

Doctorow's subject, to speak broadly, has been the evolution of the American perspective. He's interested in how our past is responsible for us as we are now. His novels shed their most provocative light on the contemporary world, and thus none of them could aptly be described as historical fiction in the conventional sense. "I have this concept of history as imagery," he says, "and therefore as a resource for writing. This is a very volatile society, con-

stantly changing, enormous. Every few years, there's a great infusion of immigrants, immigrant cultures. And so it's extremely difficult to find whatever
community there needs to be for a writer and readers to exist together. Somehow, I must have perceived that what we have in common is this country's
history."

This is a good time for Doctorow to reflect on his craft. He's just completed *World's Fair,* for which Random House has scheduled an initial print-
ing of 100,000, the largest for any Doctorow novel. Today, dressed in old
khaki shorts and open shirt, he looks easeful, a man who has given himself
over to a vacation.

The main narrative of *World's Fair* takes the form of a memoir, beginning
with the narrator's earliest recollections of his infancy and concluding before
his 10th birthday with two forward-looking visits to the futuristic World's
Fair of 1939. Doctorow's sixth novel, it follows a year after *Lives of the
Poets,* a collection of six stories and the title novella, the latter ostensibly an
examination of the mind of the man who has written the stories. In his new
book, he has named the protagonist after himself, the members of the boy's
family after those of his own. He sees the novel and the novella as connected,
portrayals of the writer's life from the two chronological ends of it he knows,
but he says quickly that though the lives of his most recent protagonists
superficially resemble his own, they are, at bottom, invented.

"Every book I've ever written, people ask me how autobiographical it is,"
Doctorow says "There's always that rich current of innocent readers who
think that what they ask is a compliment: 'What you've written is so believ-
able and so true that I have to ask you this question.' I, however, have always
been a writer who invents, and I think books are something you make. I make
books for people to live in, as architects make houses. I lived in it by writing
it. Now it's the reader's turn. When an architect does a house, do you say to
him, 'Is this house autobiographical?' "

Henry James has a parable about what writing is," Doctorow says. "He
posits a situation where a young woman who has led a sheltered life walks
past an army barracks, and she hears a fragment of soldiers' conversation
coming through a window. And she can, if she's a novelist, then go home
and write a true novel about life in the army. You see the idea? The immense,
penetrative power of the imagination and the intuition."

Doctorow's novels have, it would seem, been largely intuited. Until recently, his life has been sparsely evident in his fiction. The book before *Lives
of the Poets* was *Loon Lake* (1980), the story of an enterprising drifter during

the Depression, notable, among other reasons, for a boldly fitful narrative method that employs shifting, tough-to-track points of view. Before *Ragtime* came *The Book of Daniel* (1971), which had at its center the Rosenberg conspiracy trial of 1951.

Big as Life (1966) is a queer fantasy about people thrown together by an emergency in New York City that has been effected by the sudden, unexplained appearance in the lower Hudson River of two seemingly immobile human giants. Doctorow calls it "a rather weak book," and he won't allow it to be reprinted; hence, it remains his only work that is currently out of print.

By any standard, it is a strong output: experimental fiction that resists categorizing. *Daniel,* with its exploration of American radicalism, *Loon Lake,* with much of its focus on 1930's labor issues, and *Ragtime,* with its indictment of a complacent upper class and its portrayal of scabrous capitalists, have caused Doctorow to be seen as ideologically allied with the political left and identified by some critics as a political novelist. He has, in fact, given time to several liberal causes, speaking recently in New York against apartheid and at a rally opposing further nuclear-arms proliferation in Chicago. But as a writer, he says, his motivation is ethical rather than political:

"If I'm a leftist, it's because, as I think of them, the Ten Commandments is a very left dogma. What is just? What is unjust? That's where it all begins for me. But I tend not to accept any modification of the word novelist," Doctorow says. "So if you ask am I a historical novelist, I say no. Am I a political novelist? No. Am I an ethnic novelist? No. I'm a novelist." Asked if there is a signal authorial mark that links his books, he points out that in every one except *Big As Life* there is a storyteller within the story, the invention of an authority other than his own. "There are always characters in the books who do the writing," he says. "I like to create the artist and let the artist do the work."

In contrast to the variety in his imaginative life, there is a fundamental stodginess to his actual one. "My life is very quiet, dull, bourgeois," Doctorow says. "A wife and three terrific children. We have a close family life. Sometimes I teach. I tend not to get in fights in bars. I don't go hunting for big game in Africa. I don't box. I love tennis."

Doctorow was born in 1931, the second child of second-generation Americans; both his mother's and father's families were Russian Jews. Doctorow's was a Depression upbringing and amid the immediate practical concerns and the household's intellectual and political ideals, he conceived an affection for literature. His parents were readers. "Books were important to them," he says, "books and music." He was named after Edgar Allan Poe. And he remembers his older brother returning from the Army in 1945, enrolling in a creative writing course, and writing a novel sitting at the kitchen table. It was never published, but "I was very impressed," Doctorow says, "a sanctioned adult, doing that."

Doctorow was educated at Bronx High School of Science and Kenyon College in Gambler, Ohio, where he was a student of the critic John Crowe Ransom and a classmate of the late poet James Wright. He spent a year in the graduate program in drama at Columbia, where he met his wife, before serving in the military from 1953 to 1955. Jenny, the first of their two daughters, was born in an Army hospital in Frankfurt. He had hoped, on returning to civilian life, to support his family on his mustering-out pay, while he, like his brother, wrote a novel. The plan proved unrealistic and he had to seek steady work, first as a reservations clerk at La Guardia Airport, and then as a reader for CBS Television and Columbia Pictures.

"I was reading a book a day and writing a synopsis," he says. "It's actually not a bad apprenticeship for a writer. You can't help but develop an editorial capability, doing that kind of work on a daily basis. It's also good for young writers to see how much bad stuff is published. It's very encouraging."

He wrote *Welcome to Hard Times* in response, he says, to all the dreadful genre novels he was exposed to on the job, and shortly after completing it, he went from movies into publishing as an editor, first at New American Library, subsequently as a precocious 33-year-old editor-in-chief at Dial Press, and eventually, the publisher there as well. "There was a wonderful sense of indeterminacy floating through that place," Doctorow says. "It was a 60-hour-a-week job, easy. And I found myself dealing with formidable literary personages—Jimmy Baldwin, Mailer, Vance Bourjaily, Tom Berger—but it was a very small, unbusinesslike place." He tells the story of lunchtime chess games with Richard Baron, the publisher who preceded him. "Of course, the game would start getting interesting and last long after lunch should be over. People would be waiting outside the door. There were decisions to be made, and we'd be in there, playing the game."

By the time he had decided to leave Dial in 1968, he was at work on the manuscript that would become his third novel, *The Book of Daniel*. It was a decision he made with initial misgivings. *Big as Life* had been received coolly, and he was struggling with the new book. He withdrew from Dial by increments, requesting a three-month leave of absence, which he was granted with pay, and then requesting a second three-month leave, which he subsidized himself. Fortuitously, by that time, he had been offered his first teaching post, at the University of California at Irvine, and he took it.

Since then, Doctorow has taught at Princeton, the University of Utah, Sarah Lawrence and now New York University. But his devotion has been otherwise solely directed to his craft. "It wasn't just the time I needed to write," he says of his decision to leave publishing. "I had reached a point where I had to make a commitment. The book I was working on was an ambitious book, and I wasn't going to be able to pull it off unless I gave myself to it entirely."

Giving himself entirely to the craft of writing is the key notion for Doctorow. He believes that writers' lives are altogether too public, and that such publicity has a tendency to deflect attention from what is more crucial—the novels themselves. "The minute you ask a question about a writer's life, you're not dealing with the book," he says. "In one sense, we deny authors by wanting to know about them. In another, we learn to ignore them the same way. I'll tell you right now that more people in this country who think of themselves as cultured know that Faulkner was a heavy drinker than have read *Light in August.*"

He writes, he says, "because one likes to think one matters," and mattering, in his view, is something that American literature is not currently doing. In a recent address at the University of Michigan subsequently adapted in *The New York Times Book Review,* he noted, "Today, fiction suffers from a reduced authority. . . . It seems valid to say there is a timidity to serious fiction now . . . an exhaustion of hope that writing can change anything."

According to Doctorow, too many novelists have succumbed to self-absorption. Our fiction is no longer a risk-taking one, a condition that shows itself, he says, both in the work of young writers—"a lot of which is very well written but single-voiced"—and in the literary lives of established writers, "who have become careerist-minded. They're independent entrepreneurs, what Lionel Trilling called 'writer figures.' "

Doctorow's concern with the purpose of fiction is addressed in his novella, *Lives of the Poets.* Its narrator, Jonathan, is a writer in his early 50's, Doctorow's age when he wrote it. He's separated from his wife and living in an apartment in Greenwich Village that has the same view of Houston Street visible from Doctorow's apartment there. A poet friend of his whom he's known since college has recently died of cancer under circumstances that parallel the demise of Doctorow's old classmate, James Wright. He worries that his body is crumbling. He's having a crisis of confidence about his work.

In short, Jonathan's life seems frail to him, meaningless, a sense that leads him, in the end, to accede to an act of political engagement, housing in his apartment a family of illegal aliens from El Salvador. But even this is a half-hearted move, and the reader is left with Jonathan's desperation.

What is fiction and what is not?

"For me," Doctorow says, "the novella is meaningful only in terms of Jonathan's typicality. He's a representative creative person. It's told in a way that's confessional, but he's not me. It's not my marriage. The apartment was never a sanctuary for anyone. The novella is an allegory for what I take to be the state of American writing today. What the hell are we doing? We've lost touch."

He pauses, considering. "Maybe I'll give something away here. I hate to put it so baldly on the table, but here it is. There's a character in the novella who is represented as Jonathan's girlfriend, his mistress, who is traveling around the world. She was with him once, but now she keeps going further and further away, and there's some question about whether she'll return. When the book was published, that created a lot of curiosity in people. They wanted to know who she was.

"Well," he says, and the emphasis is final, "she's the muse."

For Doctorow, a book begins with surprise. "I've discovered that you cannot start a book with an intention, a calculation," he says. "You start writing before you know what you want to write or what it is you're doing."

The catalyst, the spur itself, "could be anything." The germ of *Loon Lake,* he explains, was a road sign in the Adirondacks reading "Loon Lake." "It can be a phrase, an image, a sense of rhythm, the most intangible thing. Something just moves you, evokes feelings you don't even understand." He talks of a book's "yielding," giving itself up to be written, and to illustrate tells how *Ragtime* was born.

The novel begins this way: "In 1902 Father built a house on the crest of the Broadview Avenue hill in New Rochelle, New York." After having worked for several months on a novel based on the life of Dr. James Pike, the controversial Episcopalian bishop who disappeared in the Israeli desert in 1969. Doctorow found himself stuck and brooding, staring at the blank wall of his study in his winter home. "It was in the back of my mind to be starting with Pike's childhood," he says, "which would have put it at the turn of the century. Suddenly I made the connection: 'Hey! This house!' And all these images came to me. I was off on my book and it had nothing to do with

James Pike. This is what I mean by material yielding. *Ragtime* is the book that yielded. You just punch around until something gives way. Then, if it keeps going, it's a book."

During the going, Doctorow is methodical and diligent, "getting up for work in the morning like anybody else," writing for about six hours until midafternoon, shooting for a production of between 500 and 1,000 words. He obeys rules: Hemingway's dictum about always stopping when you know what's coming next; until a draft is completed, never rewriting more than two pages earlier than his furthest progress; never rereading a working draft when he's tired. His drafts are typewritten, single-spaced, he says, "because then more of the landscape is visible at one time." And he has resisted purchasing a word processor, "because I like the physical aspect of writing. I like to tear up a piece of paper and throw it down and put a new piece of paper in the typewriter. When I've decided to change something, I like to retype the whole page."

Asked about research, Doctorow freely admits that his is spotty. He studies painting and photographs in order to familiarize himself with the tenor of the times he's writing here." Today Doctorow is reading galleys, but because it is a superb Sunday, he quits and suggests moving outdoors.

World's Fair reconstructs the early life of Edgar Altschuler, now a middle-aged man attempting to put straight for himself the seminal events of his past. Edgar's chronologically ordered remembrance is the novel's central body, and it is concerned with fundamental things: first and foremost, a child's home and family; second, his initial venturings away from them, off his block, into the world. This is augmented by the commentary from Edgar's family members. We hear from several of them, the prominent exception being Edgar's father who at the time of the memoir has been dead for years. The father's voice is conspicuous by its absence; hence, he himself stands out as a character, the only character drawn entirely from the outside, by others.

The narrator's voice shares qualities with the author's spoken one. They have the same quietude, the same insistent, exploratory hue. Then, too, his memoir has technique, which is to mimic in its quality of observation and deduction the maturation of a child's mind. As the young Edgar's engagement with the world at large grows, his personal revelations are informed by it with increasing frequency. Thus, his parents' squabbling over practical matters is seen in clearer light as the boy begins to perceive the cruel economics of the Depression. The encroaching war in Europe touches him when a schoolmate of his brother's announces himself a Nazi. The explosion of the zeppelin Hindenburg teaches him tragedy; he'd seen it wafting over the Bronx the day before. By the time the novel ends, he's aware of life's enormous dimensions. Earnest, baffled and healthy, he's about to be spilled into his future.

"I wrote the book on the presumption—which I realized after I started—that a child's life is morally complex," Doctorow says, "and that a child is a perception machine. A child's job is to perceive, that's his business. So the novel is the sentimental education of a kid, a *Bildungsroman,* if you will, that simply stops at the age of 10. And I had material at hand. I grew up in the Bronx. It is true that I have an older brother Donald, a mother named Rose. We actual Doctorows, including my late father, lived on Eastburn Avenue." His voice has taken on a mild edge. "These are all true. But the book is an invention. It's the illusion of a memoir."

As Doctorow speaks, it seems that what he's done in the novel is still becoming clear to him. Only just now is he realizing what his intentions have been all along, and he's sizing up his achievement against them as they come into focus. The sections of family commentary, for example, are written as if they have been elicited by questions and spoken aloud, and they stand as a kind of transcribed oral history in contrast to Edgar's crafted one. "I like the idea of composing oral history," Doctorow says, "Writing the way people speak. Behind it is the larger idea of trying to break down the wall between the real and the written.

"So what I wanted to do was write something with narrative advance that did not depend on plot, that is to say, that seemed to be life, not a story. To break down the distinction between formal fiction and the actual, palpable sense of life as it is lived, the way time passes, the way things are chronically dramatic without ever coming to crisis. And that is the strongest impulse in 20th-century literature, to assault fiction, assault the forms, destroy it so it can rise again. You let go of the tropes one by one. You get rid of the lights, you get rid of the music, you forego the drum roll, and finally you do the high-wire act without the wire."

This last metaphor is coyly chosen, for it comes directly from a scene midway through *World's Fair.* In it, Edgar recalls being taken by his mother to the circus, where he was fascinated most of all by "one wistful clown who climbed the high wire after the experts were done, and scared himself and us with his uproariously funny and incredibly maladroit moves up there." When the clown doffed his costume and revealed himself to be, after all, the star of the high-wire act, young Edgar was significantly affected: "I took profound instruction from this hoary circus routine. . . . There was art in the thing, the power of illusion, the mightier power of the reality behind it. What was first true was then false, a man was born from himself."

Thus is the artist in Edgar born, and the scene supplies an answer to the overriding concern of the narrator in the novel: How did I become what I've become? How did I get here from there?

Sitting in the sun in Sag Harbor, Edgar Doctorow answers those questions about himself. "The presumption of writing," he says, "is that you can speak for other people, that you can live lives through your work that you have not lived, and that you can do that adequately and justly. Writing is an exploration. You start from nothing and learn as you go. If you do it right, you're coming up out of yourself in a way that's not entirely governable by your intellect. That's why the most important lesson I've learned is that planning to write is not writing. Outlining a book is not writing. Researching is not writing. Talking to people about what you're doing none of that is writing. Writing is writing."

A Conversation with E. L. Doctorow: Writing Is Often a Desperate Act

Alvin P. Sanoff / 1985

From *U.S. News & World Report* 99 (16 December 1985), 73–74.

When I write, the first part of the work is uncalculated. I write to see what I'm writing. Then I find a voice or an image or some idea or feeling—and the true work begins. Something is evocative enough to pull me after it.

In *World's Fair,* I realized I was writing about a child's life. But I didn't know how it was going to end. Then one morning the words *world's fair* popped into my mind. Why? Maybe because I realized that this child was born in 1931, that his life would intersect with the New York World's Fair of 1939. Then, somehow, I had what I needed to create the boyhood of someone who had gone on to become an artist of some kind.

The act of composition is a series of discoveries. You find things just as you turn the corner. Eventually, you reach the stage at which it becomes an editorial, cerebral act as much as an intuitive thing. The further along you go, the more inevitable the course of the book.

The presumption of *World's Fair* is that childhood is a time of great moral complexity. Children perceive to a degree that we don't realize or cannot bear to think about. Their perception is their means of survival and their way of catching up to the world in which they find themselves. There is a tension between a child's total dependence on his family and his developing faculty of perception, judgment and moral understanding that is his independence. That tension is the state of love, and becomes the prescription for adult lives thereafter.

Many readers have told me that they recognize themselves and their families in the book. It's a kind of catharsis for them. I think that's because the real dynamic from childhood to adulthood is one of forgetfulness—and then to be reminded of what we all know about ourselves, the scandalous truths about our childhood, is a release. We had not wanted to remember our losses, our humiliations, our fears—the shame of what we were. We didn't realize how extraordinary we were as children.

Growing up, becoming an adult, is in a sense overcoming a period of time that we'd rather not remember. The interesting thing about middle age is that all those defenses we erect against our own perception and capacity to perceive in childhood begin to crumble. That's when we get into trouble.

World's Fair is constructed as if it were a memoir. I call it the illusion of a memoir. The most interesting technical discovery I made in the writing is that the adult narrator, who is re-creating his childhood, is taken over by this recreation. The memories possess him, so that as the book goes on his language gets younger and younger. By the end of the book, he's not only the adult recollecting his childhood, he's the child. This is nothing I anticipated until I realized that I was doing it. It may violate a major principle of craft, namely that the voice be consistent from the beginning to the end of the book. Well, it is and it isn't. The voice gets younger. It's as if the narrator, in describing himself growing up, is growing down. I rather like that.

People ask me if *World's Fair* is autobiographical. Every book I've done is autobiographical even when I've written about other times, other places than my own. Every invention encodes your life one way or another. Each book is a different code. I grew up in the 1930s in a house in the Bronx much like the one I describe in *World's Fair,* but the characters are compositions. It's very hard to explain to people that everything you write is both autobiographical and invented at the same time. This book reads like a memory book. In fact, I have a terrible memory.

Everyone around me remembers more than I do. And now that *World's Fair* is published, people have been telling me about my old neighborhood in the 1930s. Really fabulous detail, just achingly good stuff. Perhaps I should have talked to them before I wrote the book. On the other hand, if I had, I'd probably have forgotten most of what I was told. Memory is a principle of composition. Bad memory is a more disciplined composition.

Writing is very often a desperate act. After I finished *The Book of Daniel,* I was profoundly, emotionally exhausted. But I didn't know it. I sat around for a year trying to write. I wrote endless pages that didn't take me anywhere. I got so desperate that I started to write about the wall that I face when I write. As it happened, that was the wall in my study in New Rochelle, N.Y. That house was built in 1906. So I started to think about that house and that street and what it must have looked like in 1906. Out of that emerged *Ragtime.* You never know how it's going to start. But I do know that if I don't write, I feel as if I'm turning inanimate. I don't think of writing as a career,

I don't think of it as an occupation, I think of it as the way I'm alive. I don't know how to exist otherwise.

The process of composition is so vast. Writers make up things, and then the people who read us take what they need from our books for their own compositions. They take from us, take from what they see, take from everything said and done. It's a great march of consciousness, in order to advance the race an inch or two every 100 years.

Any novel, any poem, any piece of art substitutes one world for another. I take a kind of phenomenological view of things and believe that we are all in an act of composition constantly. The values and judgments we bring to events determine what those events are. A book is an illusion, obviously, in not being a stone or a wall or a table. It's a construct of language. Language itself is, in one sense, totally artificial. It's a set of sounds and symbols, so whatever depends on those sounds and symbols is illusory.

Having said that, I will also say that I am committed to the proposition that the imagination produces and finds truth. My discipline, that of fiction, excludes none of the data that, for instance, scientists might exclude. I believe in intuitive knowledge, a certain comprehensive moment of revelation that an empiricist might scoff at.

In my novels, I have dealt with historical figures and events. My research on these matters is idiosyncratic. I find what my intuition tells me I have to have. I'm not a grubby scholar who has to read 17 books to find out what happened. I realize that some people think, given the bias of our time, that I'm irresponsible to facts. But *Ragtime* is scrupulously accurate in its historical intent. Furthermore, if anyone took the trouble to investigate the assertions in that book, he or she would find that a very high percentage of it is historically accurate.

For example, I decided to take two of the characters on the streetcar out of New York to Lowell, Mass. I knew that there were interurban streetcar lines, but thought I'd better do some research to see that such a trip was possible. I dug up a wonderful book in the New York Public Library, a corporate history of streetcar companies, and learned, yes, you could in fact go from New York to Massachusetts by streetcar. That's an example of the way I work.

It is true that I reject information on the basis of my own judgment and have invented some things that have no historical verification. Nevertheless, I deal in truth. I will claim, for instance, that my portrait of J. P. Morgan in *Ragtime* is truer to that man's soul and the substance of his life than his authorized biography. If I didn't think I was telling the truth, I wouldn't write. So, idiosyncratic yes; irresponsible, no.

When I was a boy and a young man, every writer I read was my favorite. Now I think about the writers who really moved and staggered me. They include Hawthorne, Melville, Mark Twain, Dreiser and Scott Fitzgerald of the Americans. From England, Dickens and Conrad. Then the French, Flaubert, Stendhal and, to a lesser extent, Victor Hugo. Then the Russian masters, Dostoevski and Tolstoy. And finally, there's Chekhov.

Ah, Chekhov. He is the sanest, wisest writer in the world, the most natural voice. You read Chekhov and realize how much else is *machismo* posturing, forced ego—distortion. If we think of literature as a kind of distortion of what really is, I'd say there's the least distortion in Chekhov. That ideal of having literature indistinguishable from life always exists for me. I'm always going to look for the way to make words into life. Chekhov is a supreme genius, a sort of literary saint.

I have said that American writers have lowered their sights. Novels are made smaller today—craftier, but tending not to grapple with the big political and social issues of our time. Though there are wonderful writers today in America, there just doesn't seem to be any context for the political novel. Those who do it are exceptions. When someone does a book that is socially ambitious, it's seen as a sort of aberration. But enough things are starting to happen to make me think there's going to be an immense flourishing of the social novel again.

As for why it's been relatively quiet, why the novel has been domesticated, there are a few possible reasons. First, the techniques of fiction have been stolen by all the other disciplines, including journalism and the social sciences. Everything on television is dramatized—commercials, the news and weather. And, in a certain sense, the codifications of modern psychology are like the industrialization of storytelling. All these descriptive psychological concepts that we have now—Oedipus complex, borderline personality, object relation—we can compose ourselves out of these interchangeable parts of psychological codification.

The novelist has always tried to find a territory that's his own, but in trying to do this he's retreated, he's allowed himself to be disenfranchised, or, to put it another way, he's come into the house, closed the door and shut the curtains. Outside there are wars, riots, sirens, screams. But he records life as a whisper.

The bomb may be another reason for the quiet. There's a kind of post-'60s coercion of cold-war thinking in this country. Writers, along with everyone else, have pulled inward and miniaturized the significance of their lives. On the other hand, it may also be necessary in order to psychically survive.

None of these answers is entirely sufficient. It just may be that what has happened is a matter of cultural rhythm, a compression of our cultural psyche before we explode in some brand-new age of literary creativity.

A Talk with E. L. Doctorow

Liesl Schillinger / 1987

From *The Yale Vernacular* 1 (March/April, 1987), 10–13. Used by permission.

LS: *You once said that much of modern fiction "takes an act of will to read." Do you think there is a crisis in modern fiction?*

E.L.D.: I think I was talking about the condition of reading now, which is self-conscious, as compared to putting a tape on the VCR, or listening to a record. So I was not speaking of the quality of modern fiction but of the contemporary consciousness. There is after all a history we all have now—eighty or a hundred years of optical technology to deal with, and that has, I think, changed the way people read, and has changed our capacity for patience. And altered our interest in discourse.

L.S.: *It must be hard to write in order to sustain the attention of the impatient reader.*

E.L.D.: Novelists have always had to persuade their readers that what they were reading was not fiction, but a kind of urgent truth. And, at least temporarily, to break down the distinction between fiction and non-fiction in the reader's mind. DeFoe pretended to be the editor of *Robinson Crusoe,* rather than the author. Cervantes claimed at one point to have found this manuscript *(Don Quixote)* in an Arabian bazaar where he bought it for six reals and had it translated. Authors have always had to accomodate the skepticism or resistance of the reader. So do we today, except that the overall conditions are different. In our time fiction doesn't come only in the form of novels and stories; we have films, television, songs, news magazines, and the social sciences, which do a kind of fiction. They employ fictional techniques. Modern psychology which codifies mental attitudes is a kind of industrialized fiction. So the serious writer of fiction tends to feel not as central to society as, perhaps writers did in the last century.

L.S.: *You often address American society as a whole in your books—in* Ragtime, *for example, you portray a lot of disparate political and social figures, and expose many 20th century injustices. Is there a "central" message to be found there?*

E.L.D.: There was an old time movie-producer named Sam Goldwyn, and he came out with a film, and someone asked him what its message was. He said, "If you want a message, go to Western Union." The word "message" to me is a dirty word. A message is something that can be delivered briefly and concisely in a few words, and if I thought anything in my book could be reduced to that, then I wouldn't have written the book.

As a writer, you avoid bringing any calculated, thematic political or social intention to the book, because, if you do, you're in grave danger of becoming didactic. I think that the act of writing confers a degree of perception on the writer that he or she doesn't ordinarily have. The presumption of any art is that ordinary messages are insufficient.

L.S.: *You mentioned that there are many different media, as well as genres, available in the 20th century. Have you ever written for film or for television?*

E.L.D.: I've never written for television. I've written the film version of *Book of Daniel.* I've written screenplays for *Loon Lake* and for *Ragtime,* but those screenplays did not get produced.

L.S.: *There was a movie* Ragtime; *that was not based on your screenplay?*

E.L.D.: No. That was based on a screenplay by the director and another writer. I suggested some changes, but it was largely their work.

L.S.: *I know that you weren't pleased with the film version of* Welcome to Hard Times, *you said it was the "second worst film ever made." Were you pleased with the film versions of* Ragtime *and* Book of Daniel . . .

E.L.D.: *Ragtime* is a highly-polished film, and there are some wonderful scenes in it. I just don't think it has much to do with my book. *Daniel,* of the three films, is the most faithful. *Daniel* is a novel-film; it has a certain novelistic structure to it. And since I wrote the screenplay to it, I think it's reasonably faithful to the book, probably the most faithful of the three films. While we made some critical mistakes, I like that film very much.

L.S.: *About the idea that it takes an act of will to read in this very fast-paced society: Do you think that literature has been impoverished to any extent because the writer can't count on a very great attention span, or patience in the reader?*

E.L.D.: Not impoverished, no. The writers have changed along with the readers. So, for example, we don't do exposition as we used to. We explain less. We like to cut—just in the way of film. We chop up time, and space.

Discontinuity is now a reasonable aesthetic principle. We're less innocent, all of us, than we used to be. We know reality is construed. It's something we all fight to create. None of that necessarily makes for impoverished.

L.S.: *Your novella in* Lives of the Poets *seems to reflect the malaise of the times, in a way your earlier works haven't. Do you think that "Lives of the Poets" is noticeably different in structure and in general effect than your other writing?*

E.L.D.: I rely on readers and critics to make determinations like that. I just want to do them.

L.S.: *One critic said that the personal malaise you describe in "Lives of the Poets" stands for a general malaise that you feel is gripping the country. Is that true?*

E.L.D.: If you're doing a piece about your character's life and no one else's, then it's of no value. It doesn't come off the page. There has to be truth in it so that people recognize it for their own lives. It is true that the hero of "Lives of the Poets" is falling apart. It is also true that falling apart is a national predilection.

L.S.: *One of the interesting things about* Ragtime *is that there's almost no dialogue—it's almost as if you were recounting a history. Did you mean for that to be understood as a history?*

E.L.D.: *Ragtime* uses the mode of the chronicle. Historical chronicle is a kind of fiction that is not history, but it's not personal intimate writing either. It's somewhere in the middle between history and the modern psychological address; between history and the intimacy of the average contemporary novel. But it's still fiction. My use of historical chronicle was very much inspired by Kleist, the great German writer of the early 19th century. The character Coalhouse Walker, for example, derives from a figure of German literary legend that Kleist used, a man named Michael Kohlhass, who was a horse dealer stopped on the road one day and forced to pay a toll. One thing led to another, and all hell broke loose.

L.S.: *Some of your other books are chronicles as well. With a large canvas you've chronicled in different ways early-century western life, mid-century urban life, and on through the 80s. In any way do you see yourself as a historian or chronicler of this century in America?*

E.L.D.: No. Someone showed me that it is possible to put together four of my novels and get a unitary vision of the last hundred years of American life.

That you can start with *Welcome to Hard Times,* then read *Ragtime,* and then *Loon Lake* and then the *Book of Daniel,* and then you have it. But if that's true it didn't come of any plan or scheme on my part.

L.S.: *Which of the authors we see on the shelves today are your especial friends?*

E.L.D.: Many of the authors who live on the east coast in the New York area are friends or acquaintances. It just happens we run into each other. In our time, there are two schools of literature in the United States: the school that summers on eastern Long Island, and the school that summers in the Vineyard.

L.S.: *When I was reading* Lives of the Poets, *the novella specifically, it seemed to me that there was a more direct feminism than I had seen before in your books. Still, you've always had strong female characters. In* Welcome to Hard Times, *for example, there's so little shame attached to prostitution, and you don't romanticize or trivialize women. Do you have explicit feminist views, and are they changing?*

E.L.D.: To me, regardless of the particular events of political feminism, and the debate that goes on internally among feminists, feminism seems to me an indisputably important advance in human apprehension of what life is. It seems such a simple thing, that women are human beings. That's basically what's being said. On the one hand, it's discouraging that there's a struggle to push this simple idea into the institutions of society. On the other hand, it's happening, and that's good. It should have happened a thousand years ago. As for my work, I don't think I've every consciously written from an explicitly feminist point of view.

L.S.: *This is sort of a nuts and bolts question, but how long did it take you to write* Ragtime; *and how much time does it generally take you to write a book?*

E.L.D.: *Ragtime* needed about two and a half years. *Loon Lake* about three. *World's Fair* was very fast, in under a year. *Lives of the Poets* a year.

L.S.: *What about* World's Fair, *how autobiographical is it? Is it really ten years of your life? You do use your name.*

E.L.D.: Every book encodes your life, but the code changes from one book to another. In any case, you have to remember that something *cryptic* is going on. Either all the books are autobiographical, or no one more than another. They're acts of composition. It's not what your material comes from but how you use it that matters.

L.S.: *I've noticed that you always write about families; there has to be a family. One rises out of the dirt and somehow forces itself to exist in* Welcome to Hard Times. *In "The Writer in the Family," family dynamics is the theme, and of course, the family unit is crucial in* Ragtime *and* World's Fair.

E.L.D.: Well life usually constructs itself familially. But you're right *Book of Daniel* is about the destruction of the family, and in *Welcome to Hard Times,* Blue constructs a family out of disparate pieces of broken lives. I suppose there is a preoccupation with family life. Certainly children figure prominently in just about every book. Someone said to me once that there are a lot of children in my books. And there are. But it's better for me to do these things and then move on, than to think too analytically about them when they're done.

L.S.: *Do you plan to do more with short stories in the future?*

E.L.D.: I don't know. I'd like to, but I find them difficult. If you look at the stories in *Lives of the Poets,* they're not traditionally built, most of them. We may be leaving the era of the classic, modern short story. Anyway, if I'm to write more of them, I have to find out how they stand in my mind. How they're to be made. I'm not sure I know right now.

L.S.: *Are you working on something now?*
E.L.D.: Yes.

L.S.: *What is it?*
E.L.D.: I don't want to talk about work I'm doing. Makes me nervous.

A Multiplicity of Witnesses: E. L. Doctorow at Heidelberg

Herwig Friedl and Dieter Schulz / 1988

From *E. L. Doctorow: A Democracy of Perception,* Herwig Friedl and Dieter Schulz, editors, (Essen: Verlag Blaue Eule, 1988), 183–98. Used by permission.

Question: The feeling I have with your books is that although social engagement is necessary, it takes place in a context of society and history which is viewed as essentially absurd. Would you say that your vision of social engagement can be located within a philosophy of existentialist pessimism?

Doctorow: Existentialism was a momentous philosophical response to fascism and the rise of the totalitarian state in Europe. I wonder if we can appreciate what happened to the European intellectual mind when there sprang from the heart of Western civilization a monstrous society of death, a hellish barbarism. It was zealotry that powered the fascist movement and so the only possible response was the opposite of zealotry—which was distance, philosophical alienation. The existentialists went back to the beginning, to a world without dogma, to the brave recognition of an amoral universe. There were only things in themselves, what Sartre called the *en-soi,* and human consciousness, the *pour-soi,* portrayed as an emptiness longing to be something other than empty. I grew up on Sartre and Camus and others like their predecessor Husserl. I trust the existentialist vision. Like much metaphysics it is really a form of poetry, but I trust it insofar as it forgoes dogma and accepts the creativity of man as a kind of glorious noise in the midst of silence. I think that is what an existentialist means by absurdity. So then ethics is only a human invention. On the other hand, our sense of right and wrong is no less strong for that. We do have values and a working sense of meaning that can be violated, and the violation may cause us to feel outrage which is the most productive emotion in terms of activism, or engagement. So this is my gloss on existentialism. Is it pessimistic? I don't think so. It assumes the obligation to engage to construct a just world—at least as I read it—on the chance that meaning and God can be found that way. There's always that chance. The sense of absurdity is very pragmatic, skeptical of absolutes, of easy answers and political messiahs. It is actually quite hopeful, given the history of human society in the twentieth century.

Question: I have the impression from your novels that you enjoy taking pieces of history and manipulating them to create a subjective fictional overview. This leads me to think that you might see history as no more than a huge illusion. Is this so, and if so, do you hold any hope of progress for mankind?

Doctorow: I think history is made; it's composed. There is an objective event, but until it is construed, until it is evaluated, it does not exist as history. As Nietzsche said, you need meaning before you know what the fact is. For instance, if you're walking along in the street and you see a woman hitting a child—that is an event, that is factually verifiable. But until you make a judgment about what is going on, it has no meaning. Is the woman abusing the child? That's one meaning. Is the woman disciplining the child for the child's own sake (if the child threatened to run out in front of a car, for example)? That's another meaning. Until you make such an evaluation, and come to some judgment, unless you have a context of meaning, the event does not intelligently exist. Events in the past, too, don't totally exist until we construe them, and quite clearly, since they can only be recorded in words or in pictures, the judgment that is made has far more leeway. But history is not so much a discipline as it is a source of our own sense of ourselves, and therefore it is too important to be left to the historians and to the politicians, who are the two classes of people who use it all the time always construing it to reflect the values that they want to maintain or that they themselves represent. So I suppose my view of history is a phenomenological one, and you might call it cynical or pessimistic, you might say it verges on the existential, but there is a saving grace: since history *can* be composed, you see, then you want to have as many people active in the composition as possible. A kind of democracy of perception. Thousands of eyes, not just one. And since we're not only talking about history, but reality as well, then it seems to me a noble aspiration of a human community to endow itself with a multiplicity of witnesses, all from this ideal of seeing through the phenomena to the truth. So the absurdity, the futility may still plague us, but not painfully. And we may hope some day to transcend it.

Question: Do you think the only possible view is the subjective one: that there is really no possibility of reaching an objective viewpoint?

Doctorow: I think you may hope to reach the objective view with a multi-

plicity of witness; the important thing is to have as many sources of information, as many testimonies as possible—because if you don't, history turns
into mythology. If you don't constantly recompose and re-interpret history,
then it begins to tighten its grip on your throat as myth and you find yourself
in some kind of totalitarian society, either secular or religious. So the test of
any society is its resistance to the subjective. That is the way to truth and
freedom.

Question: Two years ago, in London, I bought a book called *Blacking Up,*
about minstrels in America. In a sense, the book is also about history and
how history is created by time. It's a book that would probably not be published in the United States. Several years ago, also in London, I bought Sid-
ney Poitier's autobiography. It was twice as long as the American edition.
Now, before you can achieve some kind of objective analysis of who you are
and your place in society, you have to have, as you said, as many witnesses
as possible, right? But as the publishing industry decides what will or will
not be available, we are often faced with, and are in danger of creating, a
kind of false history. So when a student goes in search of Jewish-American
or Black American history, where are his sources? Who are the witnesses?
What sort of perspective can that student acquire about the subject he's writing on?

Doctorow: Well, you do have a point, and a good one. But it goes beyond
an individual publisher's flaws or failures. For years in the United States we
laughed at the Russians because of the way they played with history, claiming
this or that scientist had discovered something that clearly was discovered
somewhere else, or inserting this or that politician in one edition of an ency-
clopedia and dropping him, denying him existence in the next edition. But in
fact, in the United States we've done the same thing; it wasn't until the 1960s
and the rise of the civil rights and counter-cultural movements that Black
Studies was created as a subject, as a discipline in the universities. Before
that it was as if in the United States there had been no black people or no
contribution of black people to the building of the United States. And what
scholars discovered in the 60s was that there was an enormous literature of
black testimony buried in the libraries: black biography, black autobiography,
black scholarship, that had been totally neglected. To this day, there is no
concerted or large effort to understand historically the tremendous contribution of the Chinese people to the developing of the United States. The role of
women in our history has only recently begun to be defined in Women's

Studies Programs in the colleges and the universities. All over the world
people are struggling with these things. The struggle to make history usually
comes to a point in textbooks for children in grade school. A couple of years
ago it became apparent that Japanese educators were busy rewriting their
textbooks to hide from children in grade school the atrocities committed by
Japan in the 1930s in Manchuria and in China. It's not just the Russian government that edits and composes history for its own purposes, but every
government in the world. So I would enlarge your critique not only to include
publishers, but writers and historians as political acts, and, of course, there's
a good deal of self-censorship. I mean, they didn't write the strike in because
it would have been very expensive to shoot, with masses of extras and so on;
but there are other scenes in that picture that were expensive and it's possible
this was a self-censoring act. On the other hand, what Forman did concentrate
on, and what interested him more than anything, was the violent rebellion of
Coalhouse Walker—which is pretty rough stuff, if you think about it. When
you are working, or when these people are working, some of them have a
good deal of independence and Forman had $32 million of independence.
But his idea of film making is that a film should be about one person, you
see. He has an idea for films that makes them equivalent to a short story: one
person, and one person's revelation, and one person's fate—that's all. That
was the real censorship of that film, that my friend Forman didn't see the
larger canvas. I think censorship in film comes more from exhibitors and
distributors than from film makers. A film that I think possibly might have
been censored in the distribution was the film based on *The Book of Daniel,*
a far more difficult story for the American public to accept or think of as
anything but esoterica. There the censorship was sort of ingrained in the
national climate and was reflected in the resistance of exhibitors and movie
theater owners to show the film.

   Question: We haven't seen it here. It was never shown over here.
   Doctorow: Even when it was shown nobody came. Even where the reviews were good. It is a grim movie, undeniably. And so one of the great
commercial disasters of our time.

   Question: You just said you were very fond of Emma Goldman, but aren't
you also fascinated a little by the other side of life, namely the established-
power side of life, Bennett in *Loon Lake?* Because sometimes I get the feeling when reading your novels that although your heroes start off being outsiders of the American mainstream, and in the end they are incorporated into it

and they thrive on it; becoming like Joe Paterson, just as he becomes the son of Bennett. I just wonder what is your relationship to these characters, I mean, isn't there a contradiction? I start off reading your books and I think, Oh, this is a criticism of the American way of life—and then your characters seem to be exactly an affirmation of the incorporative myth of America.

Doctorow: Well, criticism is very difficult. And sustained rebellion is very difficult. And I think it's a truth that many people in my country are gradually accommodated by the very thing they criticize. America's capacity and governments. It's because of that tragic or tragically absurd fact that reality is amenable to any construction placed on it, that makes it so important that we all generate as much witness as we possibly can.

Question: My question concerns self-censorship; that is to say, when the artist does the job himself rather than leave it to others. In your novel, *Ragtime,* I see Emma Goldman as a very central figure. In the film adaptation, which we've just seen, she is eliminated completely, along with the strikes and the massacre of the innocents, and the novel's motivation for Tateh to change his life. This seems to me to be censorship of a highly political kind. Did these cuts take place with or without your approval?

Doctorow: Let me talk first about Emma Goldman, of whom I'm very fond as you may suspect. The director of the film, Milos Forman, did film a sequence in which Emma Goldman was featured, and it lasted eight minutes—which is a very long time in film. He showed me the rough cut of the film and he and the producer, De Laurentis, were having an argument. De Laurentis wanted the film to be shorter, and Forman appealed to me as a fellow artist to mediate between him and his producer. The object of their contention was this eight-minute sequence in which Emma Goldman met Evelyn Nesbit and, in the movie, castigated Tateh for treating his wife badly and so started a street riot and then ran away from the riot with Evelyn Nesbit. And I, as a fellow artist, I walked into the screening prepared to defend Forman's film from his producer, De Laurentis. But when the film was over I agreed with De Laurentis that the Emma Goldman sequence should be cut. It was badly written, it was badly directed, and it was an offense in that it misrepresented the kind of woman Emma Goldman was and the kind of thing she did. Emma Goldman never started riots, which she was represented in the sequence as doing, but only tried to prevent riots. Whenever she spoke they were usually started by provocateurs, by the police. I advised Milos Forman to cut the sequence, because it was not up to the level of the rest of the film. So I myself may be responsible for the disappearance of Emma Goldman, and I think I did the right thing in that instance. Now as for the rest of it, Tateh's motivations, or the fact that the strikes weren't portrayed, or that Freud and Morgan and Houdini were not visible: I don't think that was censorship so much as, if I may say so, the inadequacy of concept on the part of the director and the screenwriter. They did not realize that everything that I had in there was necessary to make the whole thing work. And at the end of the shooting, but before the picture was released, Forman said to me, You were right, we should have had this, we should have had that.—It's easy to see these things to absorb criticism is immense, it even sometimes rewards the critics, a form of national self-defense. I do have the feeling, though, that it's possible that there are ironies intended in these books when this or that character starts out in some kind of state of rebellion and ends up manifesting just those characteristics that he had criticized.

Question: But the very fact he does so, doesn't this show also your belief that it is still possible in America to be accommodated?

Doctorow: It seems to me Joe Paterson writes a lament, basically, a song of remorse. The book is about loss. Novelists are not politicians.

Question: Yes, but what about Tateh in *Ragtime?*

Doctorow: Well, there, Tateh in *Ragtime* describes, it seems to me, one of the truths of radical life in America, that people convert from their radicalism and use that same energy and genius to make themselves personally successful—without losing the conviction that they continue to be radicals. There are several ex-Communists I know in America who live in very fashionable apartments on 5th Avenue now, and they think of themselves as highly radical people. The thing about Tateh was that he broke and could no longer sustain his ideals under personal torments he'd gone through, and simply took that energy and that wit or brilliance of his and directed it along the lines of flow of American energy, as I think I wrote. He becomes a success, but always maintaining that he continues to be a member of the Socialist Alliance from the Lower East Side.

Question: I have the feeling that you're also an idealist trying to confront the American public with its own ideology, trying perhaps even to shock people into an awareness of how government operates, of how the situation really is. But how could someone, an ordinary U.S. citizen, who also feels the same way but is not a writer, go about changing things? Isaacson was executed, Warren Penfield fell into despair, and Tateh gave up. What does a plain old nowadays radical, or former radical do?

Doctorow: Well—you know, in America there is no left to speak of in the sense of a political party, or a national movement. A lot of people talking and meeting and having conferences and putting together demonstrations of one sort or another and benefits—and there is resistance to Reagan's foreign policy, ecological policy, and so forth—but it is all minority opposition and marginal insofar as the loyalty or the conviction of the majority of the people in the United States are concerned. There is a growing opposition to the generally right-wing inclination that we have in America right now, but it's not yet terribly visible. If you're a Hegelian, you may take great comfort from this, because you will see in the extreme uniformity of thought in America right now the makings of its own antithesis, and that something will happen, as for instance an invasion in Nicaragua, that will set fire, illuminate or somehow reveal or articulate a mass opposition that will then begin to make itself felt in American politics as it did in the sixties. But I have to tell you I don't think in slogans. I can't tell you, or anyone, what to do. You'll have to figure that out for yourself.

Question: I have a question about the relationship between the writer and politics. People think that a writer needs to spend a lot of time alone. Do you think this is a drawback to your occupation as a writer or do you find that you like solitude as much as you do writing?

Doctorow: It's true that people who do this kind of work must spend a lot of time alone, that's absolutely true. I have no problem with that, although, generally speaking, on a daily basis, it's hard to create a life for yourself in which you're alone when you want to be alone and with other people when you want to be with other people. But if you're talking about the conflict between a kind of solitude and separation that is required for the writer and political engagement, that is a very big problem, virtually insoluble. There I would have to say that I seem to have made a decision: that if I have anything to offer, if I have a contribution to make, it's in the act of writing books, and so that's what I do with most of my time. I do participate in this or that political action or protest, but I'm not programmatic, and I'm jealous of my own diction and my own time. It's a very unsatisfactory, irresolute state I live in most of the time, but at least I get my work done.

Question: I would like to go back to the question of history and hear your ideas on the dangers a relativizing, subjectivizing view of history might cause. For instance, recently here in Germany, there's been a controversy about some people who have come forward with publications that simply denied the fact that many Jews were killed during the Nazi period, claiming that it just didn't happen, that it was only a fiction of history. My question is, isn't it dangerous if individuals or politicians can simply revise history? What happens to moral responsibility and the responsibility towards history, if it's possible to simply relativize or subjectivize unpleasant facts away?

Doctorow: Well, that's exactly the point I'm making. It seems to me that the artist who displays the elusiveness of historical truth in his work is performing a legitimate function. He is a Distant Early Warning System in the defense of reality. Not only these people you refer to who are doing this kind of desecration are on my mind, but the kind of history of the genocide, the murder of six million Jews, the world would have, if, for instance, Hitler had won the Second World War. How would that be represented in contemporary history, as not having happened? Or perhaps as the incidental destruction of a minority group of no consequence to life or anything important? That's exactly the point I'm making. That's why you need as many witnesses, you see, as you possibly can muster. That's why a free society is so important, because then there will be a multiplicity of witness, and the elusiveness of history, its inherently delicate nature, its susceptibility to construction through official ideology, is modified by the number of voices and the number of perceptions that rise from us all, so there can be some kind of built up consensus of what the objective truth was, or is. I remind you, there are never any failed revolutions in history, only lawless conspiracies.

Question: Reading your last work, *Lives of the Poets,* led to the assumption that this was your most self-revealing book. In how far would you create a distance between you and the narrator Jonathan, or Jonathan writing about Jonathan I in the first six stories in this book? Or is there no difference between you and this Jonathan at all?

Doctorow: If you decide this work is autobiographical, then all my works are autobiographical. No one is more revealing than the others. I think that what happens is that essentially the same mind is mapped and charted over and over again by any writer, but what the map is describing changes: it could be a weather map, it could be topographical, or a map of rivers, or of roads and highways. It's always the same territory, but the writer is giving you different aspects of it. Among the other interpretations I've heard of my work—and I tend to embrace any reasonable interpretation, as long as it doesn't claim to be exclusive—is that somehow all my books are about writers of one sort or another, all of them are *Künstlerromane*. That's not a bad idea—although I don't think it's the whole idea. But to the extent it's valid, then Jonathan is just a brother of Blue and Daniel and Joe. The confusion comes, because in *Lives of the Poets* I use the confessional mode. You know, confessional writing is very popular in America and has been for several years both among the poets and the fiction writers who like to report on their own private lives and torments of their own private relationships, and so on. So I thought that it might be possible to construct a fiction in the confessional mode. The only difficulty is, then, people think I'm being autobiographical. The truth is, I'm not Jonathan. For one thing, I think I'm a better writer than he is.

Question: What drives you to write about artists or *Künstler?* Do they incorporate everything you're interested in, or can't you write about anything else?
Doctorow: Yes to both questions.

Question: You said you are very fond of Emma Goldman and you also seem to express very radical and extreme ideas in your books. And I am quite surprised, actually, to find such a normal person here, a family man, and middle-class, and I wonder now whether you draw any personal consequences from your ideas, or do you have a clear-cut line between your personal life and your writing?
Doctorow: You think because I'm wearing a coat and tie, that I'm normal and middle-class?—Actually, I am an actor employed by Doctorow to represent him.

Question: Why did you choose Daniel as narrator in *The Book of Daniel?* In the Old Testament, Daniel is led into captivity, he faces execution, and he can save his life only by interpreting the king's dreams and telling the truth. Why didn't you choose a narrator from middle America, for example? Is it necessary for the narrator to be more gifted than other people, to have more intuitions and deeper insights than ordinary people, and are you writing for life or death?
Doctorow: Writing for what?

Question: Life or death?
Doctorow: Good God.—I didn't choose to make Daniel the narrator. You know, one of the things about this sort of work—well, I'll tell you about the

composition of that book: I wrote 150 pages of it in a very straightforward way, simple past tense, totally chronological. And *I* was the narrator, not Daniel. And it was very—bad work, and I threw those 150 pages away in great despair and I decided to give up writing, because I didn't understand how I could take a subject of that magnitude and make it so dull. I decided I couldn't go on. So at the moment I gave up totally, the moment at which I was as close to total despair as I've ever been in my life, I started to type something, almost in mockery of my own pretensions as a writer, and what I typed was the first page of *The Book of Daniel.* And the discovery I made through that torment and agony was that *I* shouldn't write the book, but that Daniel should. So much for choosing him. Now the fact that because he was named Daniel he had a relationship to the biblical Daniel I didn't realize until I found him, my Daniel, going into the Bible to look up the original. In effect, I think there is a possible analogy there, because he does interpret the prevailing dreams of his society—a society that has had the power to destroy his parents. And in the act of interpretation, his book, he manages to survive, whereas his sister does not.—As to the last part of your question: I write for life. No question about that. Both mine and my posterity's.

Question: Something that struck me in reading all your books was your way of presenting sexuality. Most of all in *Loon Lake,* probably, I found a kind of preoccupation, and reading other Jewish-American writers, contemporary writers, I found the same preoccupation in their books as well. So I'd like to know a bit about your attitude towards sexuality and whether you think there's a connection to other Jewish-American writers. I'm thinking of Philip Roth mainly, and Joseph Heller, and I think their ways of approaching sexuality are similar to yours in a way.

Doctorow: I would differ from you. I don't think the sexual preoccupations or the manner of treating sexual life in my books is particularly Jewish. I see such preoccupations in the work of writers all over the world, of many different religious backgrounds. I think more likely it is a preoccupation having to do with sex as power, either perhaps using sex as a metaphor for political relations, or helplessly annotating what passes for sex in a society that suffers paternalistic distortions. I have to think of Wilhelm Reich in this context who among other things decided that there could be no new society without a transformation of the sexual preoccupations of Europe in the 1920s, which he saw as generally sado-masochistic. Certainly Germany in the 20s and 30s was kinky. And he tried to set up sex clinics for people, so as to free them of their political uses of sex, their power uses, their repressions, their self-destructions—through these sex therapy clinics. This was an idea that offended the two groups he was closely involved with, the Freudian analysts and the Communist party. Each in turn kicked him out—the analysts because they were terrified of being thought of as political and the Communists because they were terrified of sex. But I accept his judgment, his description of sexuality in industrial societies, as being largely sado-masochistic and helplessly so. And therefore I think it is so in the modern writer's descriptions of sexual events which often mean or represent anything but sex and love in the engagements of people. I would take strong exception to your attribution of this as Jewish. You here have a particular responsibility to distinguish literary criticism from demonology.

Question: I concede that point; but, nevertheless, I do find parallels in other Jewish-American writers who are your contemporaries, and it may well be that this stems from, I don't know, the surroundings in New York, maybe. I just found the way of presenting it similar, so that's why I'm asking, is there any connection? I don't know.

Doctorow: Is Günter Grass Jewish, do you suppose?

Question: You said *The Book of Daniel* was the book the writing of which brought you closest to despair. Was there a book that you thoroughly enjoyed writing or perhaps loathed from the beginning?

Doctorow: Actually, I've enjoyed writing all of them, and despaired of finishing any of them. It is not easy for me, as a writer, to distinguish between happiness and despair.

Question: I heard you've been in Europe before in a number of different capacities including a spell in the military, I believe. I wonder whether your European experience has in any definable way fed back into your feeling or sensing what it's like to be an American.

Doctorow: This is a very good question, and it has come up one way or another on this trip. I think about my own experience as a child in New York in the 1930s. At that time there began an immigration into New York City of refugees from various Western and Eastern European countries. In the thirties and forties when I was a boy, I grew up with Viennese children, French children, German children whose families had fled fascism. I would meet them in my classrooms. There was a coloration to my life as an American child, very much to my advantage, and to all of us who lived in New York in those days, because of Hitler and World War II, so that I did absorb an awful lot of European culture, European music. The composers came over, the scientists, the scholars. Bartok lived in Manhattan. My own background as child of a Jewish family in New York almost necessitated the presence of European culture in my house, art and music, and the reading of European authors. As I grew older and went to museums, I favored the Museum of Modern Art in Manhattan. There I found Van Gogh, and Oskar Kokoschka, and Picasso, the Cubists, the Surrealists, all European. A common mistake of Europeans thinking of America is to believe that the influences have all gone the other way, that American culture has flowed across the ocean to Europe with our movies, and our jazz and rock, our Coca Cola, and all this sort of thing, but the fact of the matter is that there's a lot of flow the other way as well, certainly to my generation. I had to think about this when the question came up in Vienna. In *Ragtime,* the description of European influence, art, architecture, and so on, of European figures from Freud to the Archduke Franz Ferdinand affecting America, is quite deliberate. And that was generations ago. I wonder at this point how different we are. I think there's a difference everywhere between urban and provincial, which I can see in every country. I might feel closer to a community like this, for instance, in Heidelberg, than I would to a small town in the deep South of the United States. But to speak in political terms, to speak of nations, there can be no question that we of the United States learned imperial ambition from Europe. The United States confiscates the wealth of smaller countries on the European model. We came into being as a nation in an act of deEuropeanization, but certainly since World War II we have been reEuropeanized. The CIA, for instance, is essentially our version of a European idea—the secret worldwide intelligence apparatus of a government. And if you worry about it, let me assure you that we do too.

Question: You wrote a foreword to an American edition of Kleist's plays. Could you tell me what it is that interests you in Kleist?

Doctorow: Kleist is a great master. I was first attracted to his prose, his stories, and the location of his narrative somewhere between history and fiction. He was neither as far from his subject as the historian nor as close as the modern novelist who is inside the head and the genitals of his characters. He wrote a kind of chronicle fiction which to this day dazzles me as no other. The other astonishing thing about Kleist is connected to this—the rate of narrative advance, both in his plays and in his prose. The relentless almost predatory movement from one sentence to another. Nothing is still, in Kleist.

Nothing is commentary. Characterization is never indulged for its own sake—it is rather a circumstance of plot. The action is headlong—and generative. The fact that many of his characters are totally insane is of great appeal to me, too. All those fainting fits, and trances! I don't know how one accounts for one's susceptibility to one great writer rather than another, but when I first read Kleist I recognized a brother.

Question: Was that the reason why you built in similarities between Michael Kohlhaas and Coalhouse Walker?

Doctorow: Oh, absolutely. *Ragtime* is a quite deliberate *hommage.* You know, writers lift things from other writers all the time. I always knew I wanted to use Michael Kohlhass in some way, but I didn't know until my black musician was driving up the Broadview Avenue hill in his Model T Ford that the time had come to do that.

Question: On the subject of writers you have felt close to, I am particularly interested in whatever influence the romance tradition, maybe as exemplified by Hawthorne, might have had on you.

Doctorow: Hawthorne had an immense impact on me when I was a student, and I read him very closely. He did not give you ordinary life but a precipitate of it. And it seemed to me his vision of fiction, the identity he proposed for himself as a writer of romances rather than novels, suited me particularly well. Somehow I applied this idea to my first novel, *Welcome to Hard Times,* which takes place in the West in the 19th century. I had been trying without success to write a realistic novel until I conceived of this one. I realized I was, like Hawthorne, not an exemplar of realism but a writer of romances. I was interested in imagery as a kind of moral data. And I was at home in the past. I'd never been to the West when I wrote that book; I had never been west of Ohio. As a matter of fact, I thought Ohio was the West. Yet I seemed to think my own experience or lack of it was quite irrelevant— that in fact it was my justification. What got me going was just the image of a place that had no trees. I wrote the whole book out of that, to me, very evocative geographical fact. A land with no trees. That was a purely Hawthornian impulse, I think. To this day realism, its patient accumulation of data, does not excite me as work does which cures life—like Hawthorne, like Kleist.

Question: I wonder if you could tell us why you gave Joe of Paterson Joseph Conrad's name.

Doctorow: Perhaps to confound the Ph.D.s.

Question: I wonder what sort of audience you have in mind when you write. You have said you write intuitively—which sounds to me like a claim for genius. Paul Levine has said that you don't have to bother about who your readers are, as you understand them very easily. Then you said that art has to be taken to the people. Or are you, perhaps, even writing for an academic elite who have to read your books because it's their profession?

Doctorow: Basically the question is, "Who the hell do I think I am?" I'm afraid you'll have to make your own determination. You might do well to follow D.H. Lawrence's advice. He said, "Trust the book, not the author." I have no audience in mind when I write. My mind is the language of the book, I am a function of the book, attached to its words like their spirit. When I am writing I am only the book, so I cannot have any audience in mind, or anything in mind because my mind is wholly the meaning of the words of the book, and the sounds of the words and the rhythm of the words. In this way I may hope to speak for other people, by never having them in mind as I write.

Question: It seems to me that when we look at film adaptations of literature, we should remember that we are not viewing an attempt at reproduction, but rather a particular interpretation by the director. A reader's perspective then, not a writer's. Would you agree? Also, why did you become involved in the filming of your novels?

Doctorow: Yes, the director is a reader, which is why I have tried in these instances to inform his reading. I haven't been too successful. I might be mistaken to allow films of these books in the first place. Films are very specific; even a good film does not exist in the mind as the text of a book exists in the mind. When you read a book, the text is like a circuit through which your own life flows, but when you see a film, that's a particular actor playing Daniel, or a particular actor playing Coalhouse Walker, and your options, your imaginative responses are severely limited. You ask, then why I've had anything to do with films and I say it's because I'm weak and they gave me money. I admit I'm jealous of the enormous impact they have. People I respect, scholars like Professor Levine, think film is extremely important and they attend to it very closely, and in a sense they're right, but I'm beginning really to be angry at films because they are essentially nonverbal communication. Ninety percent of the meaning of a scene in a film derives from the set design and the lighting and the position of the camera, the background music, the actors' faces and postures, even their costumes and the way their hair is dressed—hair is very important in film and gives you indications of someone's social class and income and education. So, there's not much left for a simple writer once film gets through with us. So I've decided to wage a one-man campaign against film and all its progeny such as television. I think what I will claim is that the medium of film is culturally regressive, non-verbal, simplistic, and a cause of rising illiteracy around the world.

Question: I wonder if you could define a little more closely the term 'witness of history' that has been used here so frequently. How can a writer call himself a witness to a history of which he was never a part?

Doctorow: I think the writer's faculty is not that of a journalist or the witness in a trial. It's more like religious witness, and someone who stands up to witness Christ, say, does not have to have been there 1985 years ago.

Question: How come you gave us a computer as narrator in *Loon Lake?* Do you have strong feelings about computer technology?

Doctorow: It's Joe who does all the writing in that book, I think, and the computer language as I see it, is his computer mimicry which he practises ironically and perhaps even with a kind of self-disgust. You will remember that he has spent some time with the CIA. As for computers generally, I think they are of no particular value to most of us. It is being reported in America these days that more people have them in their homes now than know what to do with them. They may be quite unnecessary. Computers are very useful in business, of course, and in government, and they are particularly dangerous in government, because they can be used to destroy the idea of private life, and as they can establish connections among police departments all over the world and credit bureaus and so forth, they can produce dossiers rather quickly and effortlessly—and disseminate information that can really undermine the very idea of personal freedom. So in a political sense, computers are—well, like all technology, they're quite neutral, but they are a potential tool for tyranny, and for every writer who enjoys his word processor there are ten intelligence officers rubbing their hands with glee, I think.

Question: Children figure prominently in your novels and stories—both as protagonists and as narrators. My impression is that you employ children to convey a particular perception of the world to us; perhaps a more truthful interpretation of the history they live in. Is this the case in your new novel, too?

Doctorow: It's true in my work I've always been very attentive to children; I've even granted them certain kinds of supernatural gifts in *Ragtime,* in which the two children are agents of coincidence and have capacities of perception that adults don't realize they have. I think I was trying metaphorically to represent the state of being a child, in that book. In the new novel, *World's Fair,* I'm more descriptive of the immense, complicated moral life that children lead, and in one sense their struggle to be moral beings is what that book is about. An aspect of their moral nature is the incredible degree of very intense high-level perception that they're capable of; they must perceive, they must be almost engines, machines of perception and judgment, in order to catch up to everyone else. Childhood is very often a humiliating state for the individual who has these sophisticated powers of perception and understanding without having any power to effect change or control what happens or even gain recognition as a sentient being in the adult world. The child's basic study, of course, is the adult family, and that is the story of *World's Fair.* As to why I'm given to this—I've no idea. Perhaps I feel that innocence is a tremendous moral and intellectual endowment. Perhaps I haven't grown up yet.

Question: Do you distinguish as a writer between the general reader and people like us who subject your work to academic criticsm, analysis, and interpretation?

Doctorow: I was talking with one of your professors at dinner who didn't, in her analysis, in our conversation, make the distinction between a critic and a reader, and I liked that very much. People like you, as you describe yourself—what are you except more closely attentive readers perhaps than people who are not in a university? You know, people read books for very selfish reasons; you read not for the sake of an author, you read for yourself. You take what you need from books, and whether you're a scholar or a critic or a person who just happens to walk by a paperback book rack in an airport, the need and this wonderful selfishness of reading is the same thing. So I won't make any distinctions among my readers. I'm grateful for all of them.

Question: When you start writing a book, how much of it do you already have written in your mind? Do you start with a plot? Do you know how it's going to end?

Doctorow: Sometimes you have an idea of a subject, as I did in *The Book of Daniel.* Sometimes you have no more than an image or a sound of a voice and that's the way you begin. And you pursue the thoughts and emotions evoked by that image or that sound and perhaps you find yourself writing a book; and then when you have enough of it, and you see what you have, you get very editorial and very cerebral and you begin to create strategies, you arrange to make good on the premises of the book that you've discovered simply by writing. If you think of writing not as a calculation but as an action, you'll have the idea. I write to find out what I'm writing, and everything, even the ending, comes out of that.

Question: I perceive a rather close affinity between Günter Grass's narrative techniques and your own; between his concerns and yours. Do you admire his work?

Doctorow: Well, I like the *Tin Drum* very much. I don't feel a particular affinity between us as writers. Perhaps as kindred spirits politically, yes. And I like him and admire him as a person. But when I read your paper on this subject I'll be better able to judge our affinities as writers. And since that is the last question Professor Levine will permit, I want to say that this has been a very bracing experience for me and I offer you my compliments for the quality of your questions and your attentiveness. I am happy to be here and to have had this chat with you. Thank you.

An Interview with E. L. Doctorow

Winifred Farrant Bevilacqua / 1988

This previously unpublished interview was conducted on 23 September 1988 in Budapest, Hungary, in connection with the conference "Revisioning Fiction and History: The Example of E. L. Doctorow," organized by Professor Paul Levine at Eötvös Lorand University. Used by permission.

Winifred Farrant Bevilacqua: *You majored in philosophy at Kenyon College. To what extent has your training in philosophy helped shape you as a writer?*

E. L. Doctorow: Well, it's difficult for me to know. I took to philosophy very readily as it came in college. Beginning at the age of seventeen I was very excited by the philosophical mode of thought. It seemed to me there were some basic, very simple, but incredibly valuable categories of understanding, for instance, epistemology, monism, dualism—the basic elementary curriculum of Western philosophic ideas. It was as if my mind had been waiting for something and found it. I was fascinated by the never-ending argument between the empiricist and the idealist, the platonic view of the ideas that inhere in things, that a chair was not only itself, but an example of the idea of the chair which preceded it and without which any individual chair couldn't exist. There was the wonderful excitement of Plato's Myth of the Caves and the Force Light, the True Light, and the idea of a Philosopher King which I loved before I understood the dangerous political meaning of it. All of this was very important to the extent which these ideas influenced me. When I went to college, the existentialists were very current and important in philosophical halls. I studied Sartre and Heidegger and Camus and Husserl and there it wasn't just excitement about ideas but some kind of emotional recognition. As a young man, I responded to that sense of freedom and desolation together, and I've never quite shaken that response. So I'd say that existentialism is extremely important to me and has probably been important all through my work.

Have you ever wished you had been an English major in college?

No. I did take many English courses but was seduced by philosophy. Which was all right because then I was able to take only the English courses

I wanted to take. Whereas if I had been an English major, I would have had to take everything. Of course, the most important professor in my training was John Crowe Ransom, the poet and critic who was at Kenyon at the time. He was very kind to me. I wrote some really bad poems.

In graduate school at Columbia University, you studied drama. How has this affected you as a writer? Is there a connection between it and the fact that your books create vivid visual images?

My attraction to drama and to theater preceded the writing of any novels. Drama probably taught me to look for some sort of symbolic or metaphorical, or even allegorical, resonance in the confrontations of people and the troubles they have. However, I think I have also been influenced by Hawthorne whose idea of romance is very important to me. So, that disposition for drama and for the Hawthorne vision of romance is all of a piece. I don't know how to separate these things. It must have been some sort of disposition in me in the first place, some vulnerability for this sort of thing. People always talk about how visual my writing is, and even cinematic, but the people who think it's cinematic do not include the filmmakers themselves who tell me how difficult my work is to transfer to the screen.

Perhaps that's because there is a lot of moral life in your books that is difficult to express in the usual cinematic way.

That may be true.

Besides drama, do you feel influenced by any other art forms, such as music? To me, ragtime music seems to act as a "sound track" for Ragtime *and I wonder if a link between narrative and music operates, more subtly, in other works.*

It's looser than a deliberate link. Some music is useful for me. I was quite taken by ragtime music at the time I was writing *Ragtime*. For *The Book of Daniel,* I was listening to a lot of 60s rock music and folk acoustic music and popular songs of the great rockers. I found myself constructing the novella *Lives of the Poets* according to the principle of phase music which doesn't have a linear way of advancing. You hear the same piece endlessly with slight modifications. It's sort of oriental. Philip Glass uses this kind of formal approach. The narrative in my novella does not advance directly but spirals around and around. It uses six or eight motifs and each time it comes around to a new motif it changes cycle.

In "False Documents" you write "there's no fiction or nonfiction now, there's only narrative." Is that a philosophical or a political statement?

I wrote that essay after *Ragtime* was published and it was an attempt to deal with critics who felt that somehow I had abused history by mixing up fact and fiction. In Don DeLillo's novel, *Libra,* Lee Harvey Oswald and other historical figures from the Kennedy tragedy appear as characters with their own names. No one said this was an impiety, that the fiction writer should stay in his own territory and not intrude in this way, mixing up fact and fiction, using real names. But in 1975 I was called to task and in response I wrote "False Documents." I wrote it in a somewhat ironic spirit and with some astonishment that people had to be told that reality was amenable to any construct placed upon it. It's essentially a political idea rather than a literary-critical idea or an epistemological idea—trying to see the tremendous advantage of certain elements of society who can control the society's myths and therefore control the people who believe those myths. Perhaps "False Documents" is a piece of fiction without any characters except certain historians who are mentioned by name. I remember composing it with joy and relish.

Aren't there potentially dangerous political implications in a view of reality that excessively blurs the distinction between fact and fiction?

I had thought that in mentioning the Nazi extermination of the Jews in "False Documents," I had pretty much indicated where I stood on this matter. The Holocaust, a monstrous historical event, comes to us today with immense documentation, with an enormous literature of personal witness. There are films that are official documents from the Nazis themselves. There's no question that six million people died from this kind of racial ideology. Yet despite this fact, the overwhelming nature of the event, the repercussions of which are felt throughout the world today, to this very moment there are some professional historians who are attempting to disprove that there was a Holocaust and that it was engendered by German National Party policy approved by Hitler and carried out by members of the German government with the approval and complicity of various elements of European society both in Germany and outside. Nevertheless, these people are going ahead trying to revise this truth. Now suppose Hitler had won World War II. Suppose the Nazis had prevailed and all of Western Europe was under Nazi control and perhaps the United States as well. What would the Holocaust mean under such circumstances? It would be perhaps a footnote in a historian's account of that period of time, saying that this strange weird little people had to be disposed of because they were unpleasant. There would be no moral dimension, no monumental dimension, to those six million deaths. The point of "False Documents" was perhaps to reveal, through the irreverent, irresponsible work of a mere fiction writer, that the world is a lot more elusive than people normally think it to be and that moral life requires an effort for its definition and that this definition doesn't exist objectively out in the air but has to be imagined and re-imagined and re-created by the most responsible members of society for the benefit of everybody else. That was the meaning behind the essay "False Documents."

What is your sense of your own relationship to the literary tradition?

I don't think you ever achieve independence from the great writers of the past, the ones you revere. I doubt if they ever achieved independence. This is because every book is an answer to another book. Sometimes a very direct and conscious answer, like when Tolstoy wrote *Anna Karenina* he was in effect responding to a book called *Fathers and Sons* by Turgenev. He was saying: "that's not the way Russia is, *this* is the way it is." Indeed, there are some critics who claim that all literature can be considered a dialogue among books and that this is an eternal self-contained system in which all books function. I think that's partly true so that, in effect, when you use a convention you're answering somebody else. If you achieve independence, you may make a contribution someone else will recognize. Yet I don't think you ever really get away from the writers you revere—but then, who wants to?

Which contemporary writers do you admire and do you feel that any of them has influenced you?

I don't think we are influenced by our contemporaries. I think we are influenced by the masters we choose when we are younger and whom we continue to read. There are a lot of fine writers I admire. The writers I admire are those everyone admires. Italo Calvino, Primo Levi, the early Doris Lessing, the early Günter Grass, Gabriel García Márquez, Carlos Fuentes. There are many fine American writers, like Don DeLillo. Black women writers like Toni Morrison, Alice Walker and Gloria Naylor have created an interesting body of work in the last fifteen years. I think Robert Stone is a serious novelist, and of course, the late Raymond Carver. And many others. I probably read ten times more slowly than you do. When you write, you don't read—it's another kind of signal coming in that you don't want. I only read when I am in between books and sometimes I just read to see what the author is up to.

A few years ago, you expressed concern about what you described as "the reduced authority of fiction" in the minds of some young writers who "seem to want to take on less and less of the world" in their work. For you, what is the best balance between personal life and broad social concerns in fiction?

I made that statement in a lecture to young writers at the University of Michigan. I was trying to suggest that somehow the ambitions of novelists had declined in the past thirty years in America, that American writers had become miniaturists, had become technically very competent. The young first novelist in America today is far more technically accomplished than the first novelist was forty years ago. I said that there was a loss of ambition, that the horizon had come down, that the novelist had decided that the only reasonable subject he or she had was private life. As a result, the novel of large social dimension had not entirely disappeared but it wasn't common any more. Novelists came into the house and closed the door and lowered the shades. They thought about what went on inside the kitchen and the bedroom and so on as if there was no street outside, no town, no highway, no country. That's what I was talking about and I suggested that this attitude leads to a kind of narcissistic small fiction. There's nothing wrong with private life in fiction. Jane Austen ignored all that was going on around her to tell the story of the three Bennett sisters and what their relationships were. However, there's not that broad meaning for all of society in many miniaturist novels today that you nevertheless find in Jane Austen. Personally, I've always preferred to invent and to disguise myself and the events of my life in my books. The books are codes of my life, maps of different kinds of events and in that sense they are autobiographical. But they are encoded and their value or their thrust is not the real me, it's pointless to say something else. In one book, *Lives of the Poets,* I went so far as to use the confessional mode, to pretend to be writing about myself. Of course, I wasn't doing that any more than I had in my other books. And I got into a lot of trouble because people thought I was telling all the scandals and stuff about myself. I had to get out of town for a while.

Do you have any reader in mind when you are working on a novel?

I become my own reader at the moment the sentence is written and so I am writing the book and reading it at the same time. I'm the reader that I have to satisfy. The sense the writer has of himself is an objective sense. You treat yourself objectively. You treat your own writing objectively. The moment of writing is instantly transferred on to the objective mode of thought.

One of the problems about young writers is that they don't keep those two
things in balance and they no sooner write a line than they judge it critically
and this paralyzes them. This happens to the character in *The Plague* by
Camus. He spends the entire book writing the first sentence of his novel and
he can never get past the first sentence because the critical factor is so strong
for him that he is not released to take a chance, to the freedom to go on to
the next line, and so he keeps changing the clauses in the sentence. He's
trying this one sentence over and over in different ways because that objective
quality is overdeveloped in him. It's a joke that all writers recognize. He is
never going to get out of that first sentence. What you have to do to become
a writer is to teach yourself to keep in proportion the freedom and the recklessness to write the line and the good judgment to judge it and see whether
it should survive. When these two things are working in harmony then the
book will be produced and presumably your good judgment will continue to
work.

Would you agree that your work can be associated with postmodernism?
    I don't know exactly what you mean by postmodernism but when I began
The Book of Daniel, I was attracted to formal experiments of the time in
which writers sort of broke down the compact between reader and writer and
intruded in ways to suggest to the reader that the material was totally unreliable and not to be trusted. Whenever you want to suspend your disbelief and
believe what you are reading, the writer will intrude and say: "Ah ha! I
caught you that time. Don't believe this. There's no such thing as human
character and all stories are sham and I am telling you this and now we'll go
back to the story." That appealed to me, if that's one of the signs of postmodernism. Of course, the great presiding postmodern presence, I think, is Lau-
rence Sterne. I definitely was taken with his kind of play and used it in *The
Book of Daniel,* where Daniel is constantly intruding and transgressing and
violating the most basic conventions of narrative. He changes the tense, he
changes the person, he assumes other guises, he's sardonic, so that at any
given time you don't know what to expect. That all provided the book with
the kind of energy I wanted, the energy of discontinuity, of confounding the
reader and of keeping the reader on his toes. That was all very valuable to
me. In that sense, I used certain postmodern devices. However, I did that, I
think, for very traditional novelistic purposes. Frank Kermode once said when
I was talking to him: "you seem to be experimental but for very traditional
reasons and intentions." I think that describes it very well. My final intention,

or faith, is in the traditional novel, or the traditional function of the novelist. In other words, whatever denials I practice are in the service of keeping the novel alive. This happens all through the twentieth century. I think the novel has been kept alive by virtue of the practitioners who have assaulted it, like Virginia Woolf who said she wanted to write a novel without a subject because she detested plots and because the quality of relentlessness in narrative oppressed her. All the advances we have made with the form have come out of this kind of impatience or sense of exhaustion. I think I have shared that. But it's not a denial of the great social importance of fiction—it's an affirmation of it.

Can you tell me something about your writing habits? Is your writing schedule always the same or do you alternate between periods of greater and lesser intensity?

I write every day on the theory that the writing generates the writing, that if you have that discipline, that habit, then you trust the writing. At the beginnings of a book you don't know what you're doing and you're just writing to find out what it is you are writing and that's a wonderful state of mind to be in, to find out what you are writing and then gradually the material begins to direct you, to present itself to you in certain ways. You see, it's not an entirely rational activity. It's the response of a whole being, you accept all data, all the information you receive through every sense. If an idea is strong for you, if there's meaning for you, you pursue it wherever it leads and somehow, if you are doing your job correctly, it produces knowledge of a sort.

What is it about writing that gives you the most pleasure and the most anguish?

The anguish is in simply not achieving what I want to achieve in a work or even in a given day's work, finding that there is some disparity between my hopes for the lines and what they really are. Although once I accept the fact that, on any given day, I have failed, it's a very liberating feeling. As a matter of fact, all through my career I've had moments of great crisis when enormous chunks of work have suddenly shown themselves to be disatrous. And so far, after that terrible anguish and despair, I usually have found the freedom to get on to what I really need to get to. That seems to be one part of the cycle, to almost give up before finding the voice that I need to find. Then I experience the pleasure. I think pleasure, though, is a demeaning word for the state of transport you are in when you are released from yourself and you have no identity other than the lines through which your own mind is flowing. That's more than pleasure. I don't know what the word is for it, but it's a kind of justice. A kind of harmony. A feeling that somehow the brain is humming and singing. And then it's really a kind of peace, that's what it is. And when you are out of it and you recognize that you have done all right that day, you have a sense of, I don't know what—of exoneration.

Why do you think there is such an interest in writing programs on the part of the young?

Some of the young people who come to writing programs do so because they want to write for the sake of writing or because they are helpless to do anything else. Those are the best. Then there are the people who see writing as an instrument for some sort of escape from whatever it is they are escaping from. Some see it as a kind of therapy. Some see it as a way to make money. They are the most foolish of all. But there has been a bad spirit in the country. I don't necessarily think that this is connected to writing programs, but some young people see art as a way to become quickly famous and rich, an attitude encouraged by the New York art scene and the New York literary scene where the demand for the new, the fresh, the brazen, has brought some young writers to public attention who ideally should be left to themselves for a few more years while they practice their craft.

Why are you fascinated by teaching creative writing?

Well, I enjoy it. Around people who are just starting out, you are reminded what a long way you have come, what a long, difficult vocation this is. And you remember your own arrogance and fear and that keeps you honest. On the other hand, there's also a social commitment, I suppose. It's a way of communicating with other people, of expressing the instinct we all have to be a mentor eventually, when our own egos have been satisfied, when our own ambitions are slaked. Then I think everyone in every field takes pleasure in saying: "I know a few things and let me tell you what they are."

Throughout your career you have worked with various genres of the novel and have certainly revitalized them in many ways. When you are planning a book is this apparent desire to experiment with genre a determining factor in any way?

It was probably a determining factor in my first novel, *Welcome to Hard Times,* where I made a quite conscious decision to see what could be done with something as disreputable as the Western. It may have sneaked into the second novel, *Big as Life,* which was an attempt to use, for the most exalted literary purposes, the Science-Fiction/Fantasy genre. Since then I have learned a little about writing which is to have no aesthetic that governs all books, to write so as to find the book, to find the book that works, and if it doesn't work, to recast it until it does work. To find the voice for it, not to plan to use a genre or not use it, not to be difficult or to be accessible, not to plan any of these things but just to accept the book that comes out of the act of writing.

Welcome to Hard Times *is, among other things, a "New Western," indeed, one of the first Westerns to be written in an ironic and questioning manner. Why do you think so many serious novelists and film directors in the 1960s turned their attention to a reexamination of the Western?*

I don't know. Perhaps it was the appeal of some sort of fundamental myth that is easy to work with because it has some very simple elements like good vs. bad. There are times when this sort of simplicity is very appealing in a society. I can't make any analysis of that. My own reason for getting involved was simply that I was a reader for a film company and I was reading all these terrible books about the West. They were really awful and I decided, as I've said before, that I could lie about the West better than the people I was reading. So I tried my hand at a Western.

Could you comment on the fact that in The Book of Daniel *some of the dilemmas Daniel faces as he searches for knowledge about the past resemble the problems historians now say they face in doing historical investigation?*

Well, I imagine historians have always faced these problems. They may not have admitted it but historians today are the last people to claim that science is on their side and that their discipline is objective. They know better than anyone else how creative they are, and furthermore, how susceptible the material is to their own instrumentation. It's like the Heisenberg theory of indeterminacy in physics which specifies that the act of investigating physical phenomenon changes its nature. Events in the past don't totally exist until we construe them and quite clearly, since they can only be recorded in words and pictures, the judgment that is made can be viewed, and used, in various ways. You don't have any naive security about history once you find out what the score really is.

And yet, The Book of Daniel *engages historical and political material in substantial ways.*

I wrote *The Book of Daniel* toward the end of the 1960s after certain things happened that were very disturbing. There were four students killed at Kent State University by National Guard troops and President Nixon and Secretary Kissinger bombed Cambodia. The anti-war movement was at its height, the New Left was in constant battle with the police, all over the United States campuses were in turmoil. I began to think about radicalism in America and how it functioned, what happened to radicals, and then I began in my own mind to think about the radicals in the 1930s and how they were different from those of the 1960s. They were more intellectual, more problematic. They were Marxist and they read and argued. The 1960s radicals were kind of anti-intellectual and non-problematic and anarchic. And somehow in between these two I found the case of the Rosenbergs executed for espionage in the United States and that seemed to me to be the fulcrum of these two ages and so one thing led to another. I'll tell you what happened. I worked for six months and produced 150 pages of the worst, dullest material before I gave up in despair. One day I threw it all away and sat down to make fun of myself as a writer and I found myself typing the first page of the novel. That's how the book came to be written. The history in the other books I usually pick up as I go along. I never research books. If you are working well, things come to you out of the sky. You are like a great magnet, you create this force field around you. Things come to you just as you need them. I am talking about walking through the library and a title catches your eye and you open the book and there is a picture of something or you hear somebody saying something on a street corner and suddenly you have a character.

Do you agree that Ragtime *is a historical novel?*

I call *Ragtime* a novel. I've always found myself resisting any modification of the word novelist: historical novelist, American novelist, ethnic novelist, regional novelist. I always resist whatever word is put in front of the word novel or novelist. I automatically disagree. I set my novels very often in the past but if you think about it all novels are set in the past even those that are written about the present. The very act of writing is a delayed reaction. So whether it's the immediate past or far past it's always past. The problem is that in English the historical novel has some kind of connotation of a consumer product. Gore Vidal writes historical novels, the kind in which the novelist is essentially dealing with research and showing you what a wonderful researcher he or she is. That's not what I do in *Ragtime*. I think it's very accurate but it's also a naughty book. It transgresses, it's a rebellious book, it has historical characters doing things nobody has any record for.

What attracted you to Heinrich Kleist's "Michael Kohlhass?"

I think I had read Kleist first in English and then some, strugglingly in German, many years ago, many years before I wrote this book, and he became very important to me and I learned a lot studying his texts. I was intrigued by the idea of the smallness of the provocation and the enormity of the result and that once it began, it seemed inevitable, there was no way to stop it. Anyway, somewhere along the line as I was writing *Ragtime* I realized I was writing chronicle-fiction with a certain mocking or ironic tone but nevertheless with the same distance from the characters that you find in chronicle-fiction, that is to say, a distance not as great as a historian, not as close as the post-Flaubertian novelist, but somewhere in the middle and maybe that's why I remembered then that I'd always wanted to use "Michael Kohlhass" in some way, it was a story for me. But it wasn't until I envisioned Coalhouse Walker driving up the hill in the Model-T Ford and realized that the car would be his string of horses and that somehow it would get him into terrible trouble, as it turned out to have done when he went back down the hill and past the volunteer firehouse, that the whole thing clicked and I realized at last that I'd been waiting for years to steal Kleist's story and now I was able to do it. More particularly, it's the idea of writing a relentless narrative that I learned from Kleist. The rate of narrative advance in his work is incredible. When you read a play or story of his, you realize nobody else can do what he did, and so, in one sense, it was a technical exercise to see if I could write a narrative as relentless as a Kleistian narrative with Kleistian factors such as the chronicle mode. That's a beautiful story. All Kleist's stories are beautiful. As I've already mentioned, I really do think we answer books in our books and this is inevitable so it's all a meld. It's our lives but also books that are parts of our lives to which we respond and certainly there's an attempt to identify with a writer I revere in *Ragtime,* there's no question about it.

How did Billy Bathgate *begin for you—with an idea, a character, an image, a metaphor . . . ?*

This novel began with the image of men in dinner clothes on a tugboat. I don't know where the image came from but that was the beginning. It was like the center of a painting and I started to paint in the details around the edges. Actually that scene, which is the first chapter, was the very first writing I did on the book and I just went on from there. Of course, every book presents an opportunity for another book, and after *World's Fair,* which is about a good boy, it occurred to me that I could write about a bad boy. Also, the idea of doing a book in which crime was the milieu appealed to me. The portrayal of life in the extreme appealed to me. Billy insinuates himself into the heart of a major criminal enterprise, a post-prohibition gang run by a historically verifiable figure named Dutch Schultz. His attraction for the disreputable, which is true of me as well, figures greatly in the dynamics of the story.

While listening to the chapter from Billy Bathgate *that you read to us yesterday, I was struck by the lyrical quality of the prose. Was this style something that was born with the book or did it emerge gradually?*

I never start with a plan, stylistically. I am restricted or controlled by the voice I find and that tells the story. In this case, it goes back to that scene I just mentioned. It was such an odd thing, the juxtaposition of elegance and formality with grubby working materials. I couldn't imagine what those men were doing on the boat and then it occurred to me they had to be gangsters and then it occurred to me they had to be on that boat because they were taking one of their number out into the harbor to drown him. Then I wondered how I knew that and I decided I knew that because someone was watching them and that someone was Billy Bathgate. He jumped on board the boat just as it was leaving so he witnesses this awful ceremonial ritual murder. I didn't know what his name was but I was able to learn the first sentence of the book in his voice and that allowed me to continue. His voice was the voice of a fifteen-year-old boy who writes, in long sentences, very rhapsodic, what he sees. One thing led to another and I was off on this book. The imagery and the voice preceded any intention of writing a particular kind of work in a particular style.

Why are your works so often presented through the perspective of a boy or a young man?

I think probably it has happened in several instances because the *Bildungsroman* is a very suitable container. It's a very useful way to go about things. Nobody expects a fellow of my age to wonder at simple ordinary things but if I have a fifteen-year-old or a ten-year-old boy who wonders about ordinary, obvious things then I can get away with it and I can indulge my own capacity for wonder and find language for it that pleases me. Second, to begin with some sort of presumption of innocence allows you to impute to the narrator certain observations and feelings that set up the entire dynamic for the book. If you have to begin somewhere, you may as well begin with innocence and then go on to the corruption of it. You see, there's a certain built-in kind of dramatic advantage to that sort of thing. But I'm not so sure that's the whole reason. It may just be because I'm very slow and I'm only now in middle age. Middle age beginning to be able to deal with youth. If I had another fifty years maybe I could deal with middle age.

Loon Lake, World's Fair and Billy Bathgate are all set in the 1930s. Why does your imagination return so frequently to that decade?

Since I grew up in the 1930s, that period made an enormous impact on me. In some ways, it was an estimable time. In America, it was the time before the era of the superstate and the militarization of society. It was the time when it was still possible to see good and bad rather clearly. Certainly, it was a time when writers had more connection to what was going on and were part of the national argument very clearly. Every writer, good or bad, knew what was happening and was trying to deal with it. Which is not true today, I think, when people are in some sort of somnambulant state.

However, we no longer read some of the writers who tried so hard to deal with what was going on in the 1930s.

I know. It broke a lot of writers, of course. I'm not saying this created great literature. But when it's all toted up, it may turn out that we've written as badly in our time as they did in theirs. Certainly, ideology, politics, is a great danger to a writer. We all know that. Auden said "A writer's politics are more dangerous to him than his cupidity." I guess I subscribe to that idea.

Does politics affect the writer in America today?

This touches on a problem that is a constant irritation to writers. One abandons the disguise of fiction in order to make a statement or to use one's celebrity or reputation in the country to come out for this or that politician or idea. We all have our own ways of dealing with this. My feeling in the past few years is that real politics in America is not electoral politics. It's not what you read about in *Time* magazine or in the *International Herald Tribune*. The real politics in the United States is a grim kind of politics being fought out in school boards, in various communities and at the local government level in terms of citizen resistance against the nuclear power industry, in terms of organizations trying to organize homeless people on a political basis, in the anti-nuclear movement generally and in the ecological movement generally. All these kinds of politics to which I and many of my colleagues lend our support to one degree or another, to one subject or cause or another, are not electoral politics. However, every four years, we all become weak-minded and weak-kneed and we start to believe that electoral politics is very important. Every four years the general anxiety level in America goes up as this contest, usually between the center and the right, occurs. This is the kind of contest we have now, the contest between a mildly liberal decent man and a political opportunist of a conservative stripe. My own feeling, once again, is that it is an extremely important election because one candidate, the conservative, is using the diction that American politics has used for the past forty years. It's nothing new, it's opportunistic, it's depressing and it's the kind of thing representing values that have driven us down. But the other fellow, the Democrat, whom I am for, has not been able to conceptualize a new diction, a new politics, a new vision of where America should be going, what we should be doing, where our ideals should be and what our identity is. He has these instincts to re-create the American political and national idea but he doesn't have the equipment yet to formulate this in ways that masses of people can understand. But to the degree that I'm engaged, and I'm terribly engaged, we all come to believe in the importance of electoral politics every four years.

Since we are in Budapest, it seems appropriate for me to ask you to comment on the situation of the writer in the West and in other parts of the world.

Of course, as an American writer, I am extremely privileged. In "False Documents" there is an ironic statement to the effect that writers whose governments stare over their shoulders are to be envied, that writers who are put in prison are paid the ultimate compliment of their importance to their society. Naturally, that's an exaggeration. To be a writer in a Republic where, when censorship occurs, it tends to be local rather than national and where people are not put in jail for what they write, not exiled, not tortured, obviously, to say that this is a less desirable condition for writers has to be an ironic statement. However, there are certain things about the condition of the American writer that contradict such a statement. One of them is that America is generally an anti-intellectual country and the literary life occupies the attention of a very small number of people. A serious book that happens to get a lot of attention and even a lot of sales generally goes unrecognized and unknown in the majority of American communities, which is not true in other countries in the world. One of the reasons for this may be that we are very big, although there are other big countries in which this is not the case. Another reason for this may be that we are so overcommunicated, overwired in the United States, with chain newspapers and radio, that most people take their knowledge and information from the media and what the media leaves is quickly appropriated and used up by the social sciences, which I also said in that essay. The social sciences have intruded on the realm of fiction in the United States and I think some of the best fiction today is written by sociologists. This is the general framework of that point of view. Whenever one of the major network anchor correspondents says something that could be remotely construed as critical of the administration, a phone call comes from the White House to the network news immediately, and it doesn't matter if it's a Republican President or a Democratic President, it just happens, over and over again. Whereas in books you can say anything you want to and you'll never hear a word—because television has great distribution and books have very small distribution. That's why the freest expression today in the United States is done on the stage or in the format of a book. The more distribution an opinion has through newspapers, radio or television, the more likely it is to feel the inhibitions of the society, to feel the rules and regulations of propriety or a conservative kind of timidity. So we who do books have relative freedom, except we just discovered in the past year or so that the FBI has kept dossiers on every major American writer since the FBI was formed. Everyone from Dreiser to Hemingway to Katherine Anne Porter up to Truman Capote and, I am pleased to say, myself, it has been revealed . . . We have been watched, listened to, and files have been kept on us in spite of the fact that no one writer in the twentieth century has ever been brought to trial, convicted, or even accused of a crime. The FBI now claims they do not keep track of us any more, that they stopped, but of course nobody knows if it's true or not. Nevertheless, in comparison perhaps to other countries in the world, it's very, very benign. And I tell you how weird it is, even as the FBI was keeping track of me I received an invitation to the White House to come to dinner. So that may be the most destructive thing that could happen to writers in America. On the one hand, you feel good because they are keeping a file on you. On the other hand, they invite you to the White House as if what you'd written and what you've said and what you've stood for mean absolutely nothing.

The Audacious Lure of Evil

Alvin P. Sanoff / 1989

From *U.S. News & World Report* 106 (6 March 1989), 56. Copyright © 1989 by *U.S. News & World Report.* Used by permission.

E. L. Doctorow *has gained a reputation for bringing 20th-century America and its myths alive in his novels. His new book,* Billy Bathgate, *tells of a 15-year-old boy's apprenticeship to the Bronx gangster Dutch Schultz.*

Like the rest of us, my character Billy Bathgate is attracted to the disreputable. The question is: Why? Perhaps what appeals to us and him is the realm of high audacity in which gangsters operate. Most of us are not contemptuous of law and morality. But we have a weakness for the idea of the person who makes his own rules and who lives free of ethical constraint. For the same reason, we conduct our ordinary lives in metaphors of violence and death. In business, we make a killing; in sports, we beat or clobber the opponent. We all have roots in the deep past, the primordial. So, a longing for criminal license may be basic to all our activities and relationships—the desire to be Dutch Schultz.

How did you pick Dutch Schultz as your gangster?
I probably liked the sound of his name. He had a mythic dimension in my imagination that the other gangsters of the period did not. It's hard to explain. When I did *Ragtime,* for instance, I could write about J.P. Morgan but not Andrew Carnegie, even though they were both tycoons. Similarly, I knew that I could write about Schultz. That his actual name was Arthur Flegenheimer also was appealing. Schultz was actually the name of an earlier gangster who had been killed. The name was bestowed on Flegenheimer as a kind of honorific by the members of his gang.

Schultz always portrayed himself as a victim, somehow, a guy just trying to get along who was frustrated by people stealing from him or putting things over on him. So, he felt justified in whatever he did. There's a kind of mirror system of morality in evil. People don't say, as they more or less do in Shakespeare, "I'm by nature bad." They say: "I had to do this; it was necessary. I didn't start it, but nobody's going to play me for a sucker." Schultz does that all through the book; he talks about himself. He's something of a dialectician. That's what comes out of the mythic Schultz.

You often interweave fact and fiction in your novels.

When people are public figures, when they have media lives, you can write fiction about them because they have already invented themselves and made themselves into fictions. So, I'm dealing with inventions people have made of themselves.

The way we respond to our experience creates the theme of our lives. That theme can be deviousness, innocence, failure, success or what have you. When I deal with characters who are historically verifiable, I am responding to the themes of their lives as they were worked out publicly. I can make judgments.

At the same time, the basic events that I describe and refer to are fairly accurate. Schultz did grow up in the Bronx and started out dealing beer during Prohibition. He did get into the numbers racket and was indicted on a federal rap. He actually was tried twice—one case involved a hung jury—but I could use only one trial in the book. And he was shot in the Palace Chop House and Tavern in Newark in more or less the way I describe.

This is your second novel with a youngster as hero. Why?

It's a wonderful strategy that enables a writer to deal from the point of view of someone who is a comparative innocent still capable of wonder and discovery. But coming up with a youthful hero is nothing I calculated. Billy Bathgate just emerged in the initial sentence. I heard him breathing. In that sentence I had everything—the rhythm of his speech, his diction, the circumstances. The same thing happened with Edgar in *World's Fair.* In a very rough sense, Edgar is my Tom Sawyer and Billy is my Huck Finn. Edgar lives a fairly ordered life, while Billy is a tougher kid with less of a purchase on middle-class verities.

There's a great literature of boys' books by authors such as Robert Louis Stevenson, Charles Dickens and Mark Twain. And there is an idea in contemporary literary criticism that all books answer previous books, whether consciously or not. So, when a writer works in a convention that others have worked in, in a sense he is saying: "Here's what I say in reply." And if I'm any good, maybe someone will think I'll be worth answering in the next generation.

It's very peculiar. The hero of my first book, *Welcome to Hard Times,* which I wrote in my 20s, is a 49-year-old man. Now that I'm past 49, I find myself writing from the point of view of a boy.

Is Schultz's story a metaphor for wealth and power?

If you're asking if this is an allegory, I have to say that I find it hard enough to write these books without interpreting them. That's for others to say. The writer's job is to stay within the universe of images that he has created.

All I knew at the outset was that a boy had propelled himself into a rather forbidding situation on a tugboat with Dutch Schultz. My next problem was showing how he got to that point. It's precisely at such moments, when I face a problem, that it becomes possible to continue. Everything that happens creates yet another question that has to be answered. In a sense, every book is not only itself but a record of the writer's mental events during its writing.

E. L. Doctorow, Novelist

Bill Moyers / 1990

Moyers: Do you still think, as you did a couple of years ago, that our literary life is quiet compared to earlier periods in our history?

Doctorow: That's my impression. I don't believe we're doing work equivalent to our nineteenth-century novelists or even to some of our early twentieth-century novelists. Beyond that, several things have happened that have constricted us as a group or "trade." One of them is the movement of the social sciences into the realm of fiction. Anthropology, psychology, and sociology are now using many of fiction's devices and forcing us to become more and more private and interior. We have given up the realm of public discourse and the political and social novel to an extent that we may not have realized. We tend to be miniaturists more than we used to be.

Moyers: Miniaturists writing in small strokes.

Doctorow: We look for the major statement that comes from the metaphor rather than trying to put together the sloppy, all-encompassing novel of a Dreiser, for example. We do less reportage than we used to do in terms of the great social issues. Fortunately, there are exceptions. Novelists are writing about Vietnam. Black women novelists have been writing very social and political material. But, as a generalization, I think it's true that we've constricted our field of vision. We have come into the house, closed the door, and pulled the shade. We're reporting on what's going on in the bedroom and in the kitchen, but forgetting the street outside and the town and the highway.

Moyers: The big story. You once said our writers are less and less inclined to take on the big story. What is the big story?

Doctorow: The big story is always the national soul—who are we, what are we trying to be, what is our fate, where will we stand in the moral universe when these things are reckoned? That's always the big story. But all this is not to say that we're doing bad work. As a matter of fact, writers today are technically more expert than fiction writers have ever been in this country. The average first novel is far more accomplished today than it was forty or fifty years ago.

Young writers today know a lot more, too. They have a degree of self-consciousness that perhaps comes of the fact that you can now study the craft of writing in college graduate writing programs all over the country. This is a great thing, but it has its drawbacks. The technical proficiency is an obvious advantage, but the fact is that too often the young writer goes through school, gets a degree in writing, and then stays in school to teach writing to other people who are going to get degrees in writing. There's a tendency to make the writing profession academic. It gets very guarded, and the sensibility becomes a little precious. You're with other writers all the time, and you're working out this little space for yourself and this little voice for yourself, and all the possibilities become smaller.

Moyers: What do you miss when you're focusing so narrowly?

Doctorow: There's something to be said for a writer being out somewhere. Now I don't subscribe to the idea that writers should go out and seek experience. We're all given more experience than we can handle. As a matter of fact, that's why we write. Most experience is probably bad anyway. But, nevertheless, I think of the novelists of the past who came out of journalism, who worked in newspapers. Dreiser was a newspaperman, and he wrote knowledgeably about every element in the society, from the bottom to the top. And Hemingway, of course, worked for the *Toronto Star.* He got to see an awful lot of what was going on.

Moyers: Of course, a lot was going on then. The novelists I read as a young man wrote in the early part of this century. Faulkner, Hemingway, Dreiser, Algren—they were engaged with the great issues of the times, when society was literally falling apart, and it seemed that America was no longer nourishing life.

Doctorow: That's the other thing—the passion they had. Things seemed to be falling apart—rising tyrannies in Europe, the collapse of the American economy, the immense poverty of the Depression. Writers connected with this and began to talk about it. They wanted to report on the misery around them, on what they saw. And they had this passionate involvement with their lives. The critic Malcolm Cowley has pointed this out: Whether they were on the right or the left, whether they were Marxist or Southern agrarians, whether they believed in the past or the future, they were all vitally connected to the crisis, which everyone recognized. I'm not so sure that our crisis today is something that we writers recognize or that we have any particular passion for.

Moyers: The political passion in fiction today is coming from abroad, from people like Nadine Gordimer in South Africa, Günter Grass in Europe, Gabriel Marquez in Latin America. Why is that?

Doctorow: As a practicing writer, I am, of course, happy to put some of the blame on the critics. There's no critical fraternity today that has that much regard for the political novel in America. But when political novelists come along from other countries, the value of their work is recognized. It's almost as if we're too good to need political novels in this country. It's like President Reagan's feeling about trade unions. He likes them as long as they're in Poland. We like our political novels as long as they don't come out of this country. We think if you write from a political awareness, you're bound to preach. We've always had a bias against preaching in our art. We like Tolstoy, but we don't like his moralizing, his essays on history. We like the individual witness. We have a feeling that to the extent politics or political passion or social or religious passion gets into a novel, that it's an impurity.

Moyers: Aesthetic malpractice.

Doctorow: Yes, that's our propriety as practitioners, that any of that stuff that gets in is ruining the work. I subscribe to the idea that you want your convictions to come up out of the work, not be impressed upon it. That you have to trust the act of writing to scan your brain and to represent whatever beliefs you have, but you cannot impose those beliefs on the work, you cannot twist it and bang it and torment it into shape, because if you do, you become a propagandist, a hack, an entertainer, or a shill. All that is true. It's a valid point of view, but as a piety, it restricts us.

Moyers: I think it has some validity. Are writers the best ones to deal with the great political themes? Shouldn't they stick with what you once so elegantly described as the moral immensity of the single soul?

Doctorow: Ah, well, you can do that any which way you want to. You can do that as Jane Austen did, who ignored what was going on around her politically and socially, just to report on the lives of this family of sisters in an English village. Or you can do it on a large social canvas, as Dickens did. That is what we always want to do. I get a little worried talking about this too much because I never want to be in the position of telling any writer what to write. There are no rules, there's no one way to write a novel. As a form it has room for everybody and for every vision. But I can wonder why our work has gone in the direction it has. The artist isn't immune to his life and times. To a certain extent he is conditioned by them and has to overcome them. Ireland was always in Joyce even though he left and wandered around. You see that when you read his work.

What I mean to say is that it's not just the writers today, although you would expect more of them if you were an artist: It's everybody. We seem to be living in a state of mind that's controlling us as a nation but that we haven't quite defined yet. We're living a national ideology that's invisible to us because we're inside it.

Moyers: Like a fish in the ocean cannot analyze the ocean. But what is this general climate that we don't quite seem to be aware of?

Doctorow: Well, I would rephrase that to say we've been living according to premises that we haven't examined for a long time, premises that seemed to be valid and workable for us right after World War II, but which now, forty or forty-five years later, continue to go unexamined, even though they direct our national life. Our unexamined premises cause even artists to reflect the conformity of our thinking. For example, many young artists want to get rich painting. They have no passion for painting, just for the painting game. We have young writers who take up the craft to become famous, so that the doing of it is not what they love, it's the being of someone doing it. Another example is the level of political discourse in this country as it's existed in the past eight or ten years—the pieties, the simplistic reliance on the worst impulses we have to make us fearful or easily patriotic, to make us stop thinking.

Moyers: In fact, one critic criticized your novel *The Book of Daniel* and Joseph Heller's *Catch-22* because he said they were flawed by an adversarial spirit toward the republic.

Doctorow: I found that appalling. The most active and vocal literary and intellectual personages today have been people we call "neoconservative." They've been very shrill advocates of very nonintellectual ideas—like the idea that if you speak out or take a critical position, you're somehow giving aid and comfort to the enemy. Well, who is the enemy? The enemy is clearly Russia, the enemy is communism, the enemy is totalitarianism, the enemy is the enemy. There is that enemy out there, and anything you do to shake things up, to rock the boat, gives aid and comfort to "the enemy."

Moyers: So if you criticize the United States policy toward Nicaragua, you're encouraging Moscow.

Doctorow: Exactly. Dissent is seen as a form of betrayal. Free speech is seen as being most appropriately exercised when it is not exercised at all. Democracy is maintained by not thinking democratically.

Moyers: And fiction is judged by an ideological standard, not by the measure of truth.

Doctorow: Yes, to a certain extent it sometimes is. But the whole idea of dissent has been discounted. The average American no longer sees the value of dissent. People who say things you don't want to hear, people who point out things you'd rather not have pointed out, people who nag and say, "This isn't good enough, that's not good enough—try this, try that"—this kind of discourse is not valued today.

Moyers: You're not talking about the writer as a critic of this or that program, you're talking about the writer whose works challenge the underlying belief system of the rulers or the prevailing mythology of society.

Doctorow: Yes, the key thing is mythology. When ideas go unexamined and unchallenged for a long enough time, they become mythological and very, very powerful. They create conformity. They intimidate. They coerce. The person who says, "Wait just a minute," is going to find himself in a very uncomfortable position. I can't remember who said it—probably a French writer—but there's a line that goes: "My job is to comfort the afflicted and afflict the comfortable."

Moyers: This is an important point. The novelist of the thirties wrote about the failure of America to nourish life. But today that's considered in many quarters an unpatriotic theme.

Doctorow: Or more likely, too tiresome to be borne. There is a definite disinclination to accept writers who take on these big social, political ideas. It's the "Who do they think they are?" sort of criticism. We seem to prefer the perfection of the miniaturist. That may be a reflection of the orthodoxy we live in today.

Moyers: Orthodoxy?

Doctorow: Yes, a cultural orthodoxy has ruled us for some time. There's no more avant-garde, for example. It just doesn't exist. If you were to consider the proposition that culture is something generated to express society's values, then it is the culture that compliments the society that is encouraged and developed by the various commercial establishments of art and criticism.

Moyers: So the writers are being created by culture instead of creating culture.

Doctorow: Exactly. We're not making it as much as we're in it. We're reflecting it. And that's wrong.

Moyers: Alfred Kazin has a notion that the thirties, instead of being a revolutionary period, was a counterrevolutionary period and that instead of extolling the autonomy of the individual and the freedom of the soul, there grew up in the thirties a relish for the power of the state. He says the thirties produced an orthodoxy, not a revolutionary ideology.

Doctorow: I think he's probably right. All I'm speaking of is the great activity, the ferment in culture as it attempted to figure out what was going on in those days. All I'm really saying is that the social impulse, that connection with the larger world, doesn't seem to be characteristic of many of our writers, or more generally, our intellectuals.

Moyers: How do you explain that so many intellectuals today are in service to orthodoxy?

Doctorow: It depends on the generation. Of those notable members of the intellectual class who are on the extreme right today, one generation of them is simply terribly bitter—they're leftists who felt abandoned and betrayed by Stalin and who turned in exactly the opposite direction. But there's a younger generation who simply were absolutely traumatized by the war in Vietnam and the cultural agitation in this country of the 1960s, especially by the anti-war movement, and it's anti-intellectual manifestations—students, for example, would stand up in class and shout at their professors and call them tools of the imperialists and that kind of thing. That coarseness, that abuse of the intellectual dignity of the teacher, was unforgivable. The young people were seen as thankless and angry and anarchistic and nihilistic. Very many of them were in school and didn't appreciate that they were in school rather than out fighting. So lines hardened, and polarization set in. That was another component of the growth of the right-wing intellectual community.

The third element is very interesting, and I think it's been under-reported—and that is the immense influence of the emigré, Eastern European intellectuals who've come over here in the past fifteen or twenty years. Many of them are quite brilliant writers and professors of different disciplines. They have tended to see American life in terms of their own background and suffering, which has been considerable, as people in exile from regimes who have done terrible things to them and their families. They come of the terrible European legacy of monarchism and the reaction to it. So every attempt we make to legislate some advance in our American society, some social enlightenment, they see as a dangerous left-wing weakness leading toward totalitarianism. They've had enormous influence in the American intellectual community. They tend to see things as either/or and feel that you must be rigidly against any idea of improvement because the idea of perfection is what kills society and creates totalitarianism. The utopian ideal leads to revolution. They seem to forget we had our revolution two hundred years ago. Our history is not theirs.

We've always gone out into the barn of the Constitution and tinkered. That's our very pragmatic history. I don't think these people understand that. So any time we tune something up and fix something and make it more just, make it work a little better, they become alarmed.

Moyers: Or anytime the writer champions change or the belief that while we may not be perfectible creatures, society can be a little better than it is.

Doctorow: Exactly. All these things contribute to the state of mind of the union in this particular decade. At this point in our history, anticommunism is a degenerative force in American life. It is doing terrible things to us. It encourages the creation of secret government, it fosters scorn among our public officials for public accountability, it contributes to our loss of sensitivity to civil rights and civil liberties and the loss of honor, and it encourages the self-righteousness in lying, and doing things against the law even though you're in office to uphold the law because you see yourself above the law. All these things come of the state of mind where national security is the shibboleth, and everything else must conform to it.

Moyers: The justification for this behavior comes from the notion that if we live in a lawless world, we cannot ourselves always act lawfully. Defeating the Communists justifies any effort to beat them at their own game. The Cold War has been the canopy for the last forty years, under which writers have had to write.

Doctorow: I'm a Cold War writer. I published my first book in 1960. My whole life as an adult writer has occurred during the conditions and terms of Cold War. It's been a very peculiar experience for all of us. Part of it, of course, is the bomb and the rise of a militaristic culture that must be fed with

money, money, money to keep it going. This has eroded our national identity
terribly. It's certainly one of the things I've tried to talk about as a writer one
way or another, metaphorically or explicitly.

Moyers: You must be somewhat encouraged by the recent scenes of Ronald Reagan embracing Gorbachev.

Doctorow: If Mr. Gorbachev continues and succeeds, and is what he
seems to be, he could be seen eventually as one of the major statesmen of the
twentieth century. The murderous Soviet state paranoia itself seems to be
relaxing a bit. It would be nice to see our own national self-righteousness
relax to the extent where we could begin to admit our mistakes and our errors.

Moyers: Do you think that is happening?

Doctorow: You and I are now talking during an election campaign. It's a
shame that the political discourse so far is at a very, very low level—who
recites the Pledge of Allegiance and who doesn't. This simplistic kind of
name-calling, clutching the flag, not dealing with problems or issues, but
waving symbols about, is disheartening.

Moyers: In the sixties and the seventies the intellectuals, to a considerable
degree, were opposed to the policies of the state. Now many of the intellectuals support the policies of the state and the ideology of the Reagan years. Is
it the duty of the intellectual always to be only against or does the intellectual
also have the privilege of serving the people in power?

Doctorow: I think the ultimate responsibility of the writer, for instance, is
to the idea of witness: This is what I see, this is what I feel, this is the way I
think things are. Writers have the responsibility not to corrupt that point of
view and not to be fearful of it, not to self-censor it. There's a certain dogged
and sometimes foolish connection to the ideal of just telling the truth—seeing
into the delusions, the self-deceptions, the lies, the pipe dreams, including
his own. Now, if you do that, you're going to get in trouble both ways. You're
going to get in trouble both by being against something and by being for
something. Finally, when all of the dust settles, the writer who emerges will
be recognized as the one whose work is closest to the reality of the truth.
Reality is our ultimate concern. The writer can stake out a very remote place
for himself where he doesn't see anybody or do anything, but just sits in the
woods and is a recluse. And that can be seen as aesthetically pure. But it can
be a very self-satisfying and essentially corrupting position to assume, as
dangerous as its opposite—being too attached to power, loving it and admir-

ing it and looking to be patted on the head by it. Any position the writer assumes may be dangerous to him or her. It's a very difficult profession, it really is.

Moyers: You say it's not the role of the writer to save society.

Doctorow: No, you can't have that kind of self-aggrandizing view of yourself. You like to feel that somehow, you might inch things along a little bit in a good way toward civility, toward enlightenment, and toward diminishing the suffering. But you don't want to get too pompous about that. Really what you do is distribute the suffering so it can be borne. That's what artists do.

Moyers: How does a writer do that?

Doctorow: If you or I read a book, and we learn about someone else's life and torment, to the extent that that book is effective and good, we will be participating in that character's suffering. Presumably, when we close the book, it will give us an enlarged understanding of people we don't usually think of looking at. We are at the level, the depth, of the universal. In others we see ourself. So fiction really enlarges our humanity. Poetry, too, shares its perception of what life is, and raises to illumination our awareness of its profundity. That's why political diction and aesthetic diction are always antithetical. Because to get elected or to do what he wants to do, the politician has to appeal to prejudices, symbols, biases, fears—all the ways we have of not thinking. But the artist is always saying, "Wait, this is too simple, this is a lie, this is an untruth, this is a fraud." His diction is more like the texture of real life. Politics scants reality. It diminishes it and makes it small. That's the problem with political discourse.

Moyers: I watched both conventions, and listened to both candidates, and I haven't heard any description of the reality I know as a journalist in the world. It seems to me the rhetoric has been distancing us from the reality of life.

The grammar of politics today is a visual grammar. Videos introduce the candidates, the political commercial says, "This little seven-year-old girl has known nothing but peace and prosperity for seven years." But if they put a different child in there—a poor white child in West Virginia or an inner-city kid—they couldn't make that claim. The video grammar of politics today manipulates our emotions.

Doctorow: Yes, and look at the structures from which they give their speeches—those huge, high podia over a great assembly of cheering people.

That's begun to look a little ominous to me lately. When you get everyone feeling the same emotions at the same time, and thinking the same way at the same time, you're in trouble. This is when the myths go unexamined, and the coercion sets in. The rise of religious terminology on television is unfortunate.

The prominence of religious terminology today in the media, the televangelists, and the coercion of fundamentalist religious thinking as it effects its will in various kinds of censorship and as it expresses itself in political terms, seems alarming. Regardless of this or that particular scandal of this or that preacher, I think as a discourse, it violates my sense of what religious thinking should be.

Religion is a private matter. Religious thought, to have any kind of integrity at all, must be the most private, tremblingly sacred kind of awareness we have. When religious terminology is bandied about, it loses its religious character and becomes entirely political and coercive.

This has happened during the growth of civilization over and over again, to the detriment of countries and nations. In fact, it accounts, at least partly, for the founding of this country. Our forefathers ran from this sort of thing. The terrible destructiveness of religious orthodoxy as it infects and comes into the political realm is an indisputable historical lesson that we're perhaps forgetting.

Moyers: Religious dogma is at odds with democracy because democracy invites and tolerates the clash of opinions. It can't choose one dogma over another. You once said that the mind of the writer has to be a democratic mind. What did you mean by that?

Doctorow: Partly this: When I was younger and would see some production of a play by George Bernard Shaw, or I'd read Shaw, I was always very impressed by how he gave the best lines to the people he disagreed with. That touches on the idea. To do justice to all your characters and all their points of view, to give them all honor—that requires a rather democratic mind.

Moyers: Every truth has an answering truth?

Doctorow: Exactly. You have to allow the ambiguity. You have to allow for something to be itself and its opposite at the same time—which political discourse cannot.

Moyers: The religious mind, seized by the conviction that this is God's truth, cannot tolerate an answering truth.

Doctorow: That's right. Faith is closure. It's very hard to discuss faith with militantly faithful people.

But the democratic mind of the writer is also a sign of great chaos. The openness of it will only find order in the work that's created. Out of the chaos of that mind somehow will come an orderly vision. If the writer knows what he feels before he writes and knows indubitably what's right and what's wrong and who's good and who's bad, and that this politics is the only politics, and this religion is the only religion, he's going to write worthless prose.

Moyers: So that's what you meant when you said that at its worst, the writer's mind can be the tyranny of one argument.

Doctorow: The minute you find yourself too convinced of an all-encompassing "Idea" as a writer, then you're in trouble.

Moyers: The writer is so often at odds with the political order because the tendency of the political order and the need of society is for orthodoxy, for a center that holds, stability. The writer's mind challenges or questions orthodoxy, right?

Doctorow: The writer relies on his own witness. And truth can be very, very uncomfortable and inconvenient—it's sometimes perceived as dangerous. I think it was Gorky, the writer-hero of the Russian Revolution, who was dispatched in the 1920s by Stalin's secret police because he couldn't be relied upon to say what they wanted him to say. He'd say, "Isn't our great, grand revolution wonderful? Then why are our glorious Red Army troops on such-and-such street looting that shop?" He got into greater and greater trouble doing that sort of thing. Of course, in this country, we don't erase our writers that way, which is a good thing.

Moyers: No, but the mind closes very quickly in response to a parochial loyalty. Whatever the record, immediately after Senator Quayle was selected, Republicans said, "He's our man," no questions asked. The National Guard said, "He's one of us, so don't bother to raise those difficult questions." Parochial loyalty brings the mind to heel behind it. The writer has to assault parochial loyalty.

Doctorow: Yes, we tend to be wary of orderly rows of marching people, all going along at the same beat, to the same drum.

Moyers: A couple of years ago, you said that in their nonpolitical, pragmatic vision, artists may be expressing the general crisis of the age. What do you take that crisis to be?

Doctorow: The loss of our identity as a democratic nation with constitutional ideals. I seem to be sensitive to that as a crisis—not as a sudden thun-
derclap kind of loss, but as a slow, almost invisible transformation of
ourselves under the pressures of our history and our time and our ideologies.
I'm reminded of de Tocqueville's remarks that when tyranny comes to the
United States, it will be very, very quiet. It will be the somnolence that comes
over quiet and pacific industrial animals. He compared us to sheep. I think
that's true. We'll just forget who we are and what a raucous bunch we used
to be, so outspoken, so aware of the dangers to our freedom. I don't know if
we're that aware of them these days.

Moyers: Do you think we are becoming a passive society?

Doctorow: It seems to be so easy to intimidate and coerce people. For
instance, look at the vulnerability of people to television. We see in polls that
favor or disfavor expressed toward politicians is directly connected to the
amount of exposure the politicians have on the air. That's frightening. It
means something is happening to our thinking, and something is happening
to the debate we should be conducting at the most serious levels.

Moyers: It's very easy to turn an opinion without presenting a reasoned
case. The right commercial will do it, the right sound bite will do it, the right
emotional manipulation will do it.

Doctorow: It's theatricalism. I wrote a play once, and while we were re-
hearsing it, the director—a man I respect—said he hated audiences. I thought
that was an odd thing to hear from a director. Then when we started performing the play in front of audiences, I understood immediately what he meant.
They were so easy to sucker, so easy to turn, so easy to manipulate and twist.
To the extent that that kind of theatrical cynicism enters the political dialogue,
as it has been doing lately, we're in danger. Anything that substitutes for
thought—that seems to be thought but is not thought—is dangerous. I may
be a bit of an alarmist about this sort of thing. I remember someone sent me
an old copy of *Time* magazine for the week I was born, and in it some Swed-
ish Air Force general was rightly predicting the coming World War in Europe.
This was in 1931. *Time* magazine's reaction was to call him a Cassandra, an
alarmist.

Moyers: A bringer of bad tidings.

Doctorow: So it may be that is the sign I was born under. But I do worry
about this kind of thing—Wilhelm Reich said that the average man's mind is

structured for fascism—for authoritarianism, for dominance, for power. The mind attaches itself to power, it respects power, it defers to power greater than its own, it uses power on individuals' minds that are weaker than its own. If that's true, then it's very much easier for the right to win an election in this country than it is for the left, because it has such a little way to go to tap into the worst instincts of all of us. The true democrat who wants to enjoin us as a society to be better than we are has to go a long way to find some sort of connection with the voter.

Moyers: The instinct to order in a chaotic world is not to be denied. The need for stability at a time when, as Gabriel said in *Green Pastures,* everything that's tied down is coming loose, is real. This has been a violent century, a genocidal century, a century of enormous evils. Don't you have some feeling for those people who have an impulse toward orthodoxy and conformity?

Doctorow: The violence and evil came out of order. Fascism was order. Communism was order. The Holocaust was performed in a monstrously orderly way. There's a difference between the social order that creates civility and certain shared values of decency and understanding and the order that convicts people who think a little differently or wear their hair a little differently or worship God a little differently. The order that wants everything to be the same everywhere and all people to think the same way and look the same way and speak the same way and come from the same background— that is the kind of order that we have to resist.

Moyers: Do you see a tendency toward that kind of order in America?

Doctorow: Perhaps in the stimulus of this conversation I'm overemphasizing this—but I'm certainly aware that the power of government has increased in a malign way in this country in the past forty years. The greatest problem any nation ever has is to deal with its enemies without becoming its enemies. I'm not so sure that we're managing to do that.

Moyers: In the competition of the Cold War, we take the techniques of the Communists to defeat the Communists, and that changes us?

Doctorow: We begin to scant on our own strengths, to cut into our democratic sense of ourselves, to condone secrecy and deception and assassination and all sorts of un-American things. We condone defending democracy by preventing people from having their own. There's a contradiction there. You can't maintain yourself as a power for any length of time without corrupting yourself. After all, the bomb first was our weapon. Then it became our diplomacy. Then it became our economy. Now, if some of the things we've been saying about American culture have any validity, it's become our culture, too. We're becoming the people of the bomb, even though we have evidence everywhere that we're going to go down this way. The Japanese are now the prime economic power in the world, and the European nations are economically powerful and threatening to us. While we've been wielding this bomb, life has been going on all around us in ways that we haven't been perceptive to. Presumably that kind of understanding will help change us a bit and relax our ideological self-satisfaction.

Moyers: Something also happened to the intellectual under that canopy of the Cold War. He began to be a servant of the very state he once warned us was getting out of hand. I found it an interesting sign recently when Irving Kristol, the so-called "godfather" of the neoconservative movement, moved from New York to Washington, putting him nearer the scepter of power, for which he has become a very able spokesman—the intellectual at the service of the state.

Doctorow: That change is reflected in the behavior of two writers, both of whom I've regarded highly. In the sixties, Robert Lowell refused an invitation from the White House because he was opposed to the war in Vietnam. Yet, at the PEN Congress a couple of years ago, the president of the American PEN Center, Norman Mailer, invited George Shultz to come speak, presumably because it would lend a certain dignity or panache to the proceedings. Those two events reflect on some of the things we've been talking about and on the writer's changing view of himself.

Moyers: The poet Joseph Brodsky said that you can tell a great deal more about a candidate for the presidency from the last book he read than the last speech he gave. Do you think there's any truth to that?

Doctorow: I'm sure it's partial truth. If he does his own reading and doesn't write his own speeches, certainly that's true. But I should imagine a President would be under such enormous pressure on a day-to-day basis that his reading would reflect his need to get out of the Oval Office, and even out of himself. But maybe not. Apparently, Mr. Reagan likes the work of Louis L'Amour, a mythologist of the West who uses a classic good guy/bad guy formula—which does reflect Reagan's own approach to political discourse.

Moyers: John F. Kennedy liked spy novels.

Doctorow: John F. Kennedy liked Ian Fleming's spy novels—and did give the okay for the Bay of Pigs Invasion. So I imagine there's some quick and insubstantial truth to that idea. Maybe it's a half-truth. Mr. Kennedy also liked the poetry of Robert Frost.

Moyers: Are you ever tempted to follow the example of Tolstoy? At the age of fifty, Tolstoy abandoned the writing of novels. He said he was tired of pandering only to people who had time to read novels, and he became a prophet for justice. He began to preach Christian nonviolence, and he began to teach the peasants how to write. He decided to do something about the condition of the world instead of simply describe it. Were you ever tempted to follow that example?

Doctorow: I have talked almost jokingly with my friends about finding the opportunity, sometime in the future, to just see what would happen if I announced my candidacy for the House of Representatives of some district. That's hardly the degree or the magnitude of Tolstoy in torment. But I can't imagine not writing. I'm too weak to abandon it. I love language. I love to be in it. I love to have my mind flowing its way through sentences and making discoveries that I hadn't anticipated. I need that. If my mind has any distinction at all, it comes of that process, or the commitment to trust the act of writing and see what it will deliver me into.

Moyers: But you also have a passion to change the wrongs you see. You have a streak of the prophet in you.

Doctorow: I'll accept that if you define a prophet as a not necessarily perfect person, who tells people not what's going to happen but what's happening. Very often, everyone knows it anyway, which is what makes prophets so tiresome. No, I don't want that job.

I don't know anything that anybody else doesn't know. But the act of writing conveys some degree of heightened awareness. It's not a function of the ego, it's the opposite. When you write, you're less the person than you usually are.

Moyers: Why?

Doctorow: Because of that democracy we were talking about, that opening of yourself to all the discomforts of contrary perceptions and feelings and guilts and improprieties of thought, and working through them somehow with a story and language to find some sort of truth. I can't imagine giving that up. I may have to. It may be that, like ballplayers, our legs go eventually. But until that happens, I wouldn't imagine myself voluntarily stopping.

Moyers: I've always envied the writer because you can make happen what you imagine. Journalism can't do that.

Doctorow: We all do that to a certain extent. I've written about historical subjects and have caused some people to wonder if I've been quite fair to my subjects. I think I have. I think I've been honest. But I haven't only stuck to the facts. The facts are not the sole source of truth.

Moyers: But we journalists are supposed to stick to facts. You can create a Moyers, but I cannot contrive a Doctorow.

Doctorow: No, I don't think I could create a Moyers. Journalists are very creative. Journalists cover "stories," a word from fiction. What they decide is a story is important. That's very creative. Assertion is a strong part of creativity. There's great creative power in journalism.

Moyers: I like what I do, it's just that writers make a world. They don't just report on it.

Doctorow: We do try to make people feel whatever the experience is that we're describing. Flaubert had an interesting observation. He said something exists in fiction if it's worked upon by something else. The window exists because the sun comes through it, and the street exists because the wheels of the cart go over it. That's the way you make fiction. You make things in relation to other things. His fiction is so unsurpassingly great because he invokes all the senses all the time. He'll tell you how things smell and not just how they look. And he'll give you ideas of temperatures, and of the air that someone is walking through. He is constantly invoking the sensate responses of his reader.

Moyers: Do you remember the first time a word on the page became a sensuous creature to you, when you really discovered there was life and power and joy there?

Doctorow: I don't remember the first time, but I remember as a blur my addiction to reading as a child. I loved reading and was indiscriminately absorbed in whatever I read, whether it was trash or great. I would go down the shelves of the public library and pick up stuff that looked interesting, not knowing what it was. I read *Don Quixote* just because I found it. I didn't know who he was or what that book was. I read detective stories and Westerns and everything I could get my hands on. Somewhere along the line I began to identify with the people who were doing this sort of work. I read, not just to find out what was going to happen next, but with a degree of consciousness that someone had composed this material that I was reading. I looked at how it had been done. So I made that identification with the author as some sort of older colleague. And when I concluded the book, I felt that somehow the author and I had written it together. I don't remember the moment when I realized that was for me. It may not have been a moment, it may have been a gradually creeping addiction. When I tried it myself, fortunately, there were always some teachers around, and people in the family, to say, "This isn't bad, keep at it, you're good at this." I was very, very lucky as a kid to have that kind of help. And then, of course, I thought of myself as a writer for years before I ever wrote anything.

Moyers: Why?

Doctorow: It was just some sort of declaration to myself. That's not a bad way to begin as a writer.

Moyers: To think you're a writer.

Doctorow: Yes, to think you're a writer, and not to feel any necessity to write anything to prove it.

Moyers: Thinking about it is a joy, doing it is something else.

Doctorow: The fantasy is like someone who wants to be a ballplayer. The kid who goes out in the schoolyard and puts a Mets cap on and plays with a ball and a bat all by himself, and announces the game, and plays all positions, including the umpire—that's the same kind of thing. I just happened to fix on writing.

Moyers: Do you think writing changes anything? Has literature changed that observable world out there?

Doctorow: Well, it's very inefficient. The poet W.H. Auden said that none of the anti-fascist poems of the 1930s stopped Hitler. That's undeniable—but maybe the poems weren't good enough. Sometimes works are written that serve no apparent social utility, but which are predictive and become recognized later on. There are all sorts of weird ways consciousness is changed by literature. Certainly, I can't imagine my mind, or the mind of any of us, without Chekhov, or Joyce, or Mark Twain. All the writers I've ever read or admired constitute my brain, in part, or deliver me to some point in civilization that I wouldn't have reached otherwise. I have to assume that this is true of most people.

Moyers: This is unprovable, but there was a time when those images resonated throughout society, even among people who had not read the literature.

Memories of Shakespeare, fragments of Shakespeare, and others, had come down to us from the general culture. We had a sense of a common heritage even though we might not, ourselves, have read the literature. I wonder if that's as true today, given the dispersing power of television in sending so many disparate images. Is the loss of a common body of literature a danger to us?

Doctorow: That's undeniable. One of the reasons writers are let alone to the extent we are is that we're not perceived to have the same distribution for our ideas that people in television have. It's become quite standard for presidents to be very sensitive to the evening news reports. The basic network newscasts are very orderly, moderate, and basically uncritical. They are barely curious, let alone adversarial. But presidents are always saying, "Why did so-and-so say that?"—and they get on the phone. They don't feel that way about book writers, whose depth of discourse is naturally heretical, because we're not seen to have much distribution for our work.

Moyers: It's intriguing to me that Lyndon Johnson wasn't embarrassed by anything Robert Lowell wrote, but he was embarrassed when Lowell refused to come to that White House reception, because television would cover it.

Trying to change things is a slow process. If you're never really sure you do change anything, why write?

Doctorow: I've never had a rational or thoughtful answer to that question. It's a kind of faith. Basically, you want to make something that stands. It's really very selfish. You want to make something that's good and true and something that didn't exist before. You hope it will last. That's all. That's all, but it's everything. It's a monumentally arrogant wish and desire, but it's also very simple. Just out of your own inadequate mind, to make something that stands and holds and becomes something that someone else will use to walk us another bit further toward whatever it is our destiny might be. Enlightenment, one hopes. Salvation. Redemption. All those things.

Fiction Is a System of Belief

Christopher Morris / 1991

From *Michigan Quarterly Review* 30 (1991), 439-56. Used by permission.

Morris: As an undergraduate at Kenyon you studied with the godfather of the New Criticism, John Crowe Ransom. What philosophers interested you at that time? And do you still read philosophy today?

Doctorow: At that time there were those we had to read because we were assigned them and there were those whom we were interested in. I tried to read all the major philosophers. Epistemology occupied a good deal of my attention. Which meant Hume and Kant, finally. And metaphysics, which I read with a much warmer disposition to Plato than to Aristotle. In a small department, just two men, Phil Rice and Virgil Aldridge, both given to a naturalist, philosophical bias, we read Clarence Lewis, in value theory, who I gather is not read that much any more. C. I. Lewis. But we were made very aware of G. E. Moore and Wittgenstein, of the school of analytic philosophy. I was bad in logic, very bad in anything requiring attention to mathematical symbols on a page. But finally, emotionally I came under the spell of the Existentialists who were not really taught at Kenyon except, one semester, by a Belgian visiting professor named Wilfred Desin. But that bleak sense of freedom of the Existentialists, the absurdist vision, seemed to fit what I knew. I came away with a phenomenological view of what reality was, and how much of it was composed, how much of it was invented. But by the time I graduated, my revered professor, Phil Rice, who was to die in an automobile accident a few years later, turned out to be a much stronger influence than Ransom. It was Rice's courses that had so excited me into giving up my English major for one in philosophy. Rice told me on my graduation, "Doctorow, you're probably one of the four best students I've ever taught, and of the four you're the least informed."

Morris: You were making it up as you went along.

Doctorow: Exactly. I did a lot of good creative work in philosophy that always got me the A's but I didn't do all the reading that I should have done.

Morris: You were composing.

Doctorow: I was very temperamental as a reader, and I could tear through some of the texts and just couldn't abide others, and with that kind of undisciplined approach, everything showed. Rice could see it quite well. I managed to graduate with honors, but I should have done more. They all knew I was interested in writing. As a matter of fact Ransom got me into the Yale Drama School on graduation day by talking to Robert Penn Warren, then at Yale, who was in town to receive an honorary degree. I ended up at Columbia, but it meant a great deal that Ransom spoke up for me.

Morris: In your short story "The Songs of Billy Bathgate" and other works you create narrators who either *are* orphans or are like orphans. Would you comment on the function of orphans in your work?

Doctorow: I grew up in a normal home with a mother and father. I was twenty-four when my father died, at which time one thinks of one's self as an adult. And my mother is still alive. Nonetheless, there's a very strong sense of loss in several of the books, certainly in *The Book of Daniel* and *Billy Bathgate* where the missing father is crucial to the composition of this boy. I don't know where that comes from, but it's undeniably there. Some kind of inconsolability that, if I had never written anything, I wouldn't think to claim for myself, but I can't deny it. I can't deny it.

Morris: So there *is* a connection between writing and the inconsolable situation of a orphan?

Doctorow: Well, there is in writing a certain need to redress grievance, I imagine. That may be a nicer way of acknowledging the basis of neurosis in art generally. I've never found it necessary to deny Edmund Wilson's proposition in *The Wound and the Bow*. It seems to be self-evident and, in fact, so self-evident as to be almost useless as any kind of critical tool. But redressing grievance could include a metaphysical disturbance of some sort or longing apart from one's own personal psychic construction, and certainly to be orphaned or the state of orphanage is just a useful metaphor for all sorts of injustice.

Morris: *The Book of Daniel* seems death-haunted, as do all of your novels, so this seems a useful place to ask you about the way your work returns to death in scenes of obsession and certitude unrivalled in any of your predecessors except maybe Hemingway. What's the fascination of death for your narrators?

Doctorow: I don't know how to answer that question. I don't think of myself as particularly fascinated by death. But it's a condition of narrative, just as it is of life. Isn't it Walter Benjamin who talks about the way death confers a dignity on the most wretched person, as his life might not have? That the fact of death elevates our humanity? I think I would have to burrow back into my interest in telling stories in order to begin to feel my way to a proper answer.

Morris: So there is a connection between narrative, story telling and preoccupation with death?

Doctorow: Maybe it's simply that death is the most obvious and easily evoked kind of closure for your story. Or maybe it's more. Now this is either to run a gloss on Benjamin or disagree with him, I'm not sure which, but it seems to me there would be no moral ascription to any death without an understanding of the cause of the death, the means of the dying, or the circumstances of it. Indeed, the necessity for it. Or the manner in which it occurs. So we're not talking about death anymore, we're talking about injustice. The moral value of the death of a man who's lived a long and righteous and honored life and dies in his nineties is quite different from that of a boy who's cut down in war at the age of twenty. Or from a death by starvation. Or from a death that is self-inflicted. Or from a death applied as in the case of the Isaacsons, in *The Book of Daniel,* by society. Each of these deaths means something else, and the preoccupation is not with death itself but with the meaning of it, the judgement we make of it. Every death of course has a degree of injustice. Death is ineffably a terrible fact. But this one is pathetic, that one is brave, another is monumentally tragic. These boys in my books, Billy and Daniel, they're seeking some sort of patrimony, some kind of justice in the world for themselves, just as Dickens's boys do. I couldn't think about just the deathliness of these books without thinking of the life that qualifies the death.

Morris: Let me take you back to a reply you made in the Heidelberg interview, when you were asked about the naming of Joe Korzienowski, Joseph Conrad, at the end of *Loon Lake.* To the question, "Why did you do it?" you replied, "Perhaps to confound the Ph.D.s." As a follow-up question on *Billy Bathgate,* the novel, and "The Songs of Billy Bathgate," is the intertextual connection there to confound the reader?

Doctorow: No, there is no attempt to confound there. I wrote the story in 1968. It was written in the form of record liner notes. In those days on record albums the artists would say something about each song. The idea of the record liner note, of the singer offering an explication right there on the

package, intrigued me. I thought I could do something with that. Ted Solotar-
off published the piece in *New American Review*. It's an attempt to deal with
the '60's using two characters roughly equivalent to Bob Dylan and Joan
Baez. The writer-singer whose album notes you're reading is Billy Bathgate.
A few years later I reread the story, and thought it badly needed editing. I
liked the chance I took and the loopiness, but I thought there was some false
poeticism in it and some things that just didn't come off. I had gone back to
it because someone wanted to produce it as a radio broadcast and to write
music to go with the lyrics. They wanted me to flesh out the lyrics I had
written for the songs. I liked the lyrics, or I did then, probably better than the
text. In any event, one of the things that happens to authors is that they're
given to certain images, settings, even characters that they use over and over
again. As if they carried their own repertory company with them. One of
mine being the old grandma, whom I used in *Daniel*, whom I used in *World's
Fair* . . . the crazy maternal figure who's transformed in *Billy Bathgate* to his
mother. Another image that pops up, as you know, is the genial neighborhood
macrocephalic. Something about the nature of those images: you don't exor-
cize them by using them once. They come back. One of my settings is Bathgate Avenue, which appears in the story, and again in *Daniel*, and it may be
mentioned in *World's Fair*, I'm not sure. When I came to write *Billy Bathgate* I used that street again. And whoever Billy was he would not now celebrate Bathgate Avenue in a song, but he would choose that name, under the
pressure to find an alias, since it came out of his dream world, of the world
of plenty, the street of the riches and fruits of the earth. But I put together
the two names, Billy and Bathgate, as far apart as they occur in the book. I
used Billy the minute his mother called him Billy, very early, but he isn't
Billy Bathgate until they get up to the country, Onandaga, halfway through
the book. The minister asks him his name, and that's when he comes up with
this alias, Billy Bathgate. Then I realized it was the name of the songwriter
in the earlier story, and I thought, "Can I do this?" And I said, "It's a very
obscure story, it's never been reprinted—why not?" So I went ahead, and
that's how it happened.

Morris: You set me to wondering whether Billy Bathgate the folkrock
singer was going to be the child of Billy Bathgate the criminal, because the
dates almost match.

Doctorow: That never occurred to me. But maybe you could make the
case.

Morris: You mentioned Billy's mother as being an avatar of the various crazed maternal figures. She seems an important character in the novel, one who stands outside the rapacious world of the rackets that everyone else is contaminated by. Do you see Billy's mother as in any way a counter, a foil, some alternative to the world of Billy and Dutch Schultz—to the world of reading and writing and the rackets?

Doctorow: Definitely a counter to them in a way I didn't quite understand. I knew she was eccentric. She is very important to this boy. He could have done none of this unless she was the way she was. In a certain sense, he was doing it *for* her. He was fulfilling some sort of prophecy that was inherent in her madness. I've never thought further than that in my mind. But, in effect, it all plays out so that she can become sane, and her madness, in retrospect, I see as a kind of demand that some sort of justice be done in order to make the world right again. In that sense, she is a prophet of the action, and everything that happens in the book is Billy's fulfillment of her expectation.

Morris: I see a link here with some classic American fiction. You've often mentioned that Hawthorne was important to you.

Doctorow: He was very important to me when I was a student, and of all the reading I did in American literature, the sense of recognition I felt for Hawthorne was the strongest at that time. I had read Mark Twain at a much earlier age and was wildly crazy about him, but the thing with Hawthorne was a kind of recognition, unbidden. Subsequently I felt it with Melville as well. Those two, and, in the twentieth century, Scott Fitzgerald. But today, what I realize is that Hawthorne's idea of the romance has been very crucial to my sense of fiction. And a case could be made that I don't write novels at all, but I write romances as he defines them. They seem to fit his prescriptions. The idea of curing up life into meaning. The gamier taste, somehow, than you get in a realistic novel of accumulated data. And working in the past, working in the lag, as it were, which in fact I do, for the most part. So I would say that while I can read Hawthorne today and find a lot of him tedious—his rhythms very slow and some degree of self-consciousness—nevertheless, if you start talking about stories, the stories more than novels, I think, stories like "The Minister's Black Veil," "The Birthmark," or "Wakefield," which I salute in my story "The Leather Man," with the character who spies on his own household, an engineer named Morris Wakefield—well, these pieces stay with me, like stars, guidance systems.

Morris: We were talking about death before, and you said it's a good way to close a novel, I think facetiously, but I don't know. But on the question of

the endings of your works. Many of your works seem to subvert the traditional expectations of endings or closures. I'm thinking especially of *The
Book of Daniel,* with its three plus endings, or *Lives of the Poets* which ends
in mid-sentence, or *Loon Lake* with its computer dossier, although I think
one could make a case that the denial of the traditional, closed ending is
implicit in all of your works to a certain degree. Do you see your works as
challenging that expectation in terms of an ending?

Doctorow: I've always thought of endings in a very pragmatic working
writer way. To find the natural and satisfactory conclusion to the doings. I
like that ending for *Daniel.* I haven't read that book in a while, but it seemed
to me at the time that given Daniel and his character, three endings were
appropriate to him—he would do that. And they would all together be a
proper closing. I once found myself talking about that book to Frank Kermode, I think it was an interview he was doing for the BBC. His idea was
that I used the discoveries of what we now call postmodern works of the
Sixties for very traditional narrative purposes. And I thought that was true.
All that stunting around I do is in the service of a very traditional sense of
what the novel has to accomplish. Those three endings—that's Daniel talking. The commitment to his character is the naive, premodern belief in fiction.
Even though I bash away at lots of conventions in that book—tense, continuity, and person are all sabotaged one way or another—it's Daniel who's doing
it, because he *would* do it. I was criticized at the time of publication, less so
now, for the ending of *Billy Bathgate.* That it was a happy ending. But I think
the image of Billy pushing the child in that carriage down Bathgate Avenue
does not constitute a happy ending. I mean, what car is going to nose around
the corner and move alongside with its tommygun poking out the window?
Loon Lake was not written on a computer. But the idea of inanimate intelligence creating phrases and sentences seemed to me very much a part of that
book and my discovery of who its narrator was. And so at the end he would
run himself off as a printout. Some of the endings might be flawed and they
might be wrong, but in my mind they're appropriate and reasonable and
always in the service of the book rather than a result of some external mis-
chievousness.

Morris: Not there to confound the Ph.D.s.

Doctorow: Finally, no.

Morris: About *Ragtime.* One of the continuing puzzles to critics—perhaps
not to you—is the character Tateh. Critics seem to be roughly divided as to

whether we are to take Tateh ironically or, let's say, normatively. In the *Nieman Reports* colloquy, you remarked, "Tateh becomes an American success story, but at the expense of his socialist principles, I don't know if that is heroism." But I have a different question. Suppose you say, "All right, readers, you should take him ironically," or "All right, readers, you should take him normatively." Would that settle the case? To what degree can you answer the question as to how we should take Tateh?

Doctorow: The book poses the question. It doesn't answer it. It's a morally ambiguous state Tateh is in. That's the point. He's very charming and attractive, and I like him enormously, but he does have the faculty of insisting that he's the same person even as he drifts away from his principles from which he gets his self-identification.

Morris: He would not be the first film director to do so.

Doctorow: He would not be the first film director nor the first radical. There are people living today on Fifth Avenue, Park Avenue, who still think of themselves as radicals. That's funny. Moral ambiguity can be very funny. There was some thought on the part of conservative critics that I was sentimental about my leftists in that book and rather tough on the other characters. Actually I never divided them in my mind as left or right. I rather loved them all. But it was said that clearly my heart was with Coalhouse Walker and Tateh and Emma Goldman, whereas I was pretty rough on Morgan, Ford, and Father and so on, and I thought that was absolutely off the wall and wrong, and I tried to join in this critical understanding of my own work, something that I would rather not do. I pointed out that Tateh violates his own principles and drifts away from them, and, maintaining in his mind his socialist ideology or religion, simply goes with the flow of social energy; and I said that might be considered heroism, but it might also be hypocrisy. And as to Emma Goldman, she wreaks havoc wherever she goes. That's what truth tellers do. She can really destroy the people around her without even knowing it, because she has all this force of principle. There is texture in that idea, of a person who has these explosive truth charges at her fingertips—hardly the stuff of sentimentality.

Morris: Do you think it's misguided of critics to look for a character who represents the author, fully, completely, 100 percent?

Doctorow: Yes, in the case of this book, maybe all the books. The presumption in the novelist's mind is that fiction is better than anything else, I mean more capacious as to truth, reality, than any other discipline. That the novelist, with the equipment of his trade, has more of a chance to see. Because fiction is the discipline that includes all the others. Its language is indiscriminate, it accepts the diction of science, theology, journalism, poetry, myth, history, everything. That's why Lawrence said fiction is the whole hog. That's basically it. You embrace everything. Dreams, hallucinations, legends, facts, and the mutterings of crazy people in the street—it's all valid, and you use it all. Fiction is, finally, a system of knowledge—that's what I believe it to be. So the writer is not functioning properly if he limits his vision as a journalist might or an ideologue.

Morris: Will you discuss your disappointment with *Big as Life?*

Doctorow: Ah, well. That book. The unhappy memory I have of working on it. There was an earlier manuscript version about twice as long that was even worse. I think the problem is that I never found the nerve of the book. It was not excessive enough, perhaps it didn't go far enough in its . . . in its outrage, as an essentially outrageous idea. I have in my mind a few of the images, which I still like. The bass player, Red Bloom, wheeling his bass through the streets of New York or indeed the aliens themselves who move in another space-time continuum relative to their own size. That's a nice conceit. But overall I didn't come up to the conception. I've always had the idea I could fix it up, make it work, so I've not put it back into print. Although I have to admit right now this is not uppermost in my mind as something to do.

Morris: Let's go back to the work outrage. Outrage in the book against NYCRAD?

Doctorow: No, not in the ordinary attitude of the book, which is its satirical spirit, but in its imaginative rendering of all the possible aspects of this incredible event. Perhaps it's not dark enough, there's not enough evil in the book. There is an obligation with a conceit like this to really render it in all of its possibilities. Just as, for instance, Dos Passos, by calling a trilogy *USA,* presumes to give you every class of society and every region of the country. That kind of obligation toward some sort of totality of expression is perhaps where I missed. Perhaps *Big as Life* was too small-minded in the way I worked it out. But in any event, it's a very useful book now to chill me, every time I begin to get too self-satisfied. It is useful to be recalled to what an awful struggle writing is and what a risky way to live one's life.

Morris: I was drawn to a response you made about *Loon Lake* to Victor Navasky. "The reader has to figure out who and what the narrator is. The convention of the consistent, identifiable narrator is one of the last conventions that can be assaulted, and I think it has now been torpedoed. For the first time, I've made something work without the basic compact between narrator and reader, and technically I'm pleased at being able to maintain a conventional story despite giving up that security." Is part of the creative process, maybe part of its imperative, the need to give up security, of one sort or another, casting off assumptions, conventions, guarantees, while assaulting—in your phrase—the assumptions readers traditionally take for granted. Is that an imperative?

Doctorow: Yes, with this qualification: that when you're working, you don't think theoretically, you don't have an aesthetic idea that you're looking to fulfill.

Morris: It comes later?

Doctorow: It comes as critical discovery when you see what you've done. My remark to Navasky—that was an answer brimming with self-confidence that I rarely feel when I'm working. I didn't write that book in order to prove to myself that I could do a narrative without that particular trope to depend on. What I found as I went through the drafts is that the book could only work a certain way. That it wasn't there, it was not realized until this version of it in my mind . . .

Morris: Until you disconnected the compact between the reader and the identifiable narrator?

Doctorow: A lot of the work consisted of tearing it down, yes. Only then, oddly and paradoxically, did the book begin to find its tension. Sometimes, as a writer of fiction, you continue to write after the book is written. But what you're writing now are fictions about the book you've written. I was really strutting around in that answer, when in fact I found that book, as I do all of them, by a very grim and stumbling process of trial and error. The experience of writing is not a particularly intellectual experience. You don't know what you know. You don't know anything when you write. You work inductively from the text that you happen to produce, and when you see what you don't want or can't use, you begin to dimly see what you need. And you don't consciously learn all that much as you write, because each book is so specific and precise in its being that it basically gives you very little instruction that you can take away from it.

Morris: Coming to *Lives of the Poets*. In "The Writer in the Family" Jonathan learns about the truth of his father by writing letters in the name of his father, who is deceased. By making up fictions, he discloses something in the real world, or seems to. To what extent is that kind of demystification of the world through fiction really Jonathan's, and is it really authentic?

Doctorow: I'm not sure that demystification is the word I would use. As I understand that story, it's not the lies in the letters that teach him anything; what he learns at the end is what he knew through his writing, without knowing that he knew it. The writing led him to the truth, and I believe that to be true of writing. That generally speaking the act of expression is empowering. That's why fiction is a system of knowledge. The letter leads him to the truth before he knows that he's capable of it. So that's the paradox of the thing. By committing himself to the lie of these letters and then blowing up the lie, he finds out that he knows the truth.

Morris: Maybe put it another way. He learns belatedly, too, that it's too late to do any good for his father. Or his understanding of his father comes only after the fact, too.

Doctorow: Oh, well, of course. That's the way most knowledge comes. I mean you rarely learn anything in time. If Jonathan understood his father a little better when his father was alive I'm not sure it would have done his father that much good. But the events he describes—his understanding of the family dynamics and the conflict and competition for his father's attention, or the competition to define what the father was—are factors in his own life, in his child's life.

Morris: If Jonathan is the author of the entire collection, and I suppose arguably he is, then Jonathan is the narrator of that odd piece, "The Leather Man."

Doctorow: Yes. That story has puzzled a lot of readers. What is happening in the story is this: a bunch of government intelligence agency people are sitting around wondering if homelessness has the makings of some sort of radical conspiracy. Essentially a satirical idea. I *thought* that's what that was about, yet in the course of the writing, it becomes a rather brutal story of genuine, speechless suffering, so that people lying around the sidewalk or even stumbling around the moon are by that fact of their isolation suspect.

Morris: The category seems to expand over the course of the monologue.

Doctorow: Yes, the professional and police-intelligent mind considering dereliction finds its symbol in The Leather Man. Anyone who withdraws, anyone who is terribly private, anyone who seems not to exemplify the values of the society or the supposed values of the society, or seems not to live them contentedly, becomes an object of suspicion, and the whole point is that the category keeps expanding. Incidentally, there really was a Leather Man. He skulked about Westchester and Connecticut in the late nineteenth century. I read a piece about him and looked at a photograph of him. A huge, ungainly, bearish-looking man with this homemade leather armor hung on him and this great, enormous kind of dunce cap with ear flaps. And I found it very evocative, and that's how that story came to be written.

Morris: One of the extraordinary things about the collection as a whole seems to be the variety of styles, which seems to come out of nowhere in your career to that date. It just appears. And then it disappears, just as fast, in *World's Fair.* We could account for this, I suppose, by saying that this is not your medley of voices, this is Jonathan's medley of voices.

Doctorow: That could be my defense, yes. It's simply the idea that every work of fiction has its own voice. That it's not my voice you hear in the work. It's the voice of the individual book or story. Of course, that may be nothing more than a necessary illusion of mine. But these stories certainly, they're almost disturbingly unlike one another. I think of them now, each of them, as possible novels, and if I was somehow forced to, I could write a novel out of each of them. That's what happened with *Welcome to Hard Times.* It was a story, and then someone said, "Why don't you turn it into a novel?" So I just crossed off the title and wrote "Chapter 1." I don't know if I ever write anything without thinking it's going to be a novel. Any fragment, any odd thing, you always hope that this time you're on the nerve of something that will be a book. So I don't really know when I decided these *were* stories. I mean they may have existed for me originally as possible novels, rather than stories. In any event each of them has its own individual character, its own voice, and since I flatter myself enough to think that's true of my novels as well, the six stories attached to the novella became among other things an illustration of the idea.

Morris: Is there one Doctorow that is continuous from *Welcome to Hard Times,* up to *Billy Bathgate?* Could we infer a continuous identifiable entity with definite attributes as we could a Jonathan?

Doctorow: Yes, without question, and my claim is it would not contradict my idea that each book has its own voice. The books are different, but I see the underlying preoccupations. The formal connection of *Billy Bathgate* to *Welcome to Hard Times,* is very, very clear to me. Both books begin with a violent disturbing act, which propels the rest of the narrative. Both have young boys who become attached to figures of evil. And that leads to another characteristic—children populate these books, they figure in every one. So, in terms of each book having its own voice, yes that's clear. Diction, setting, the multiple universes of the books. But each one is written by the same person, although presumably he changes and grows older if not wiser.

Morris: Do we get any closer to you, the man sitting across the desk? Do we arrive at the author in the process of reading your works?

Doctorow: Well, I suppose, if that's what you want to do, eventually it can be done, like looking for a unified field theory. But why get closer to me? What would be the point? Is there greater critical enlightenment? The assumption of any one book is that it supplies everything you need to understand it.

Morris: About *World's Fair.* The art of ventriloquism, the construction of time-capsules, and the deception of high-wire acts are three activities from this novel that have been compared with novel writing. Yet each of those endeavors presupposes a kind of conscious determination of intention on the artist's part that doesn't seem to square with Edgar's exploratory and not fully-perspicacious narration. In what sense are these metaphors which have been compared to novel writing valid?

Doctorow: I didn't do the comparing.

Morris: I realize that; critics did.

Doctorow: Edgar doesn't identify that old clown routine with writing or art, he compares it to growing up and proving out to be stronger and tougher and smarter than he's given credit for. So it's a fantasy of fulfillment for him. He identifies himself as the super person he wants to be, disguised now in these ridiculous clown clothes of childhood; but underneath, he knows that he's got it, that he's the high wire act, the star.

Morris: So it would be misleading to apply that metaphor to Edgar as the author of his retrospective narration?

Doctorow: He doesn't know he's a writer, at this point in the story. The closest he comes to a metaphor for writing is in his desire to learn ventriloquism, his interest in throwing his voice, disembodying himself. When I found him wanting to do that, I was very pleased.

Morris: But my question really was this: In your remarks earlier this afternoon, you implied that writers discover as they write, and they don't begin with a foreordained plan, or map, or manifesto or something like that. The art of ventriloquism seems to be a very deliberate, conscious execution to create a voice and place it.

Doctorow: Right. Put a voice out there and animate something that is inanimate.

Morris: Would you accept such an analogy to your own work in the light of what you said about the not fully articulable endeavor of writing?

Doctorow: Yes, because you have written from an effective voice that's not yours.

Morris: But the voice that emerges is not necessarily the one that entered into the act of ventriloquism . . . The analogy breaks down somewhere.

Doctorow: Well, it does break down somewhere, unless you allow that the voice, the narrative identity, comes into full being discursively, as the book. Writing is exploratory and full of surprises, and it gives you gifts and things you didn't anticipate. The whole act of composition is, in effect, learning to accept what the book offers you. It's when you know everything in advance that you're in trouble. When everything is worked out too well beforehand. For the writer, what is written has to present itself with the same sense of discovery and surprise that it presumably has for a reader. When you're writing, you're in the position of a reader, reading right up to the blank part of the page. So, there's no question that it's a formative process and it occurs over time. But once it's done, it is appropriate to say that you have performed as a ventriloquist. Because without this thrown voice, you could not have written this particular book. The language you find precedes the intention of the book. I don't know if that satisfies you as an answer, but I don't see any particular contradiction.

Morris: In your novels women are sometimes—not always, and never primarily—associated with the phenomenon Robert Graves called the White Goddess, that is, a figure who sometimes lures her votaries into a form of catastrophe. I'm thinking of Lovegirl in "The Songs of Billy Bathgate," or Evelyn Nesbit in *Ragtime,* Clara in *Loon Lake,* or Drew in *Billy Bathgate.* How would you respond to the observation that these characters may be readable as perpetuating a representation of women that is part of a problem in American literature?

Doctorow: To my knowledge, I've not been criticized on those grounds. Now, you can take the characters out of context and make a case or leave them in context and perhaps not be able to. I suppose one could pull this thread out of the pattern and hold it up and make something of it. But Love-girl, in her story, doesn't destroy her lover. She destroys herself. Clara is not the only woman in *Loon Lake,* Mrs. Bennet, the aviatrix, is another. There is also the servant girl, Libby, up there at Loon Lake. And there is the young child bride, Sandy, recently widowed at the end, whom Joe goes west with for awhile.

Morris: Yes, but certainly Clara is the character who is pursued by the principal male characters.

Doctorow: Yes, she is. But I think she's presented as something or some-body with less control over things than the males have, and it's my under-standing of the White Goddess that it's a sort of a primary power not subject to any governance. Do I misinterpret that?

Morris: No, I think that's correct, although its primary power is ultimately analogous to that of the Muses, for Graves. So your female characters are not so much in control?

Doctorow: Evelyn Nesbit, in *Ragtime,* is attractive, seductive, yet like Clara ultimately subject to the male world's rules and standards. I hardly call Emma Goldman a White Goddess. There is a muse figure in *Lives of the Poets,* in the novella.

Morris: The one who keeps escaping from Jonathan?

Doctorow: Yes. And it's true that Drew has some of these qualities, in *Billy Bathgate.* But she is finally a nihilist, not a femme fatale. Billy is not destroyed by her. And I wouldn't know how to characterize the women in *The Book of Daniel,* except as vessels of suffering. So I would have to say on the whole, just thinking about this briefly, that I would disagree with the proposition.

Morris: Can interviews be classified as a kind of low-level fiction, or art form, born of journalism and perhaps influenced by television? Do writers adopt personae in interviews? You said earlier that first one writes the fiction and then defends the fiction with fiction. If that's so, of what use can an interview be to readers if it's another fiction superimposed on the original fiction?

Doctorow: The word "fiction" for me is not a pejorative term. And it's a kind of creative criticism you do, when you're questioned about your own work, as you're forced to think about it. Perhaps looking at several interviews

together would be a good idea, because one could see different aspects of the
same writing mind and find things that the subject-writer, of the interviews
as it were, never intended. So in that sense, one could consider a collection
of interviews as kind of a solipsistic novel and treat it on that basis. The
interview is ubiquitous in our society and there's really no way to avoid it,
but as a novelist I can't consider any literary form without wondering what I
can do with it. Whether it's liner notes on a record album or an inter-office
memo or a legal deposition or a newspaper story or whatever. Whatever the
form of discourse, one time or another I've probably considered it a possible
strategy for fiction, so . . .

Morris: The interview would fall in that category too?

Doctorow: Unquestionably. No interview I give, no substantive interview,
gets by without my editing, including this one. But all in all I think the reader
would do better to read books than interviews.

Morris: My last question refers in part to *The Paris Review* interview and
your comments there about Hemingway's *The Garden of Eden.* You said that
text, for you, marked no shift of voice for Hemingway, merely the same old
Hemingway repeating himself. But later on, in the review essay in the *Times*
called "Braver Than We Thought," you changed your mind.

Doctorow: I'm not sure that's correct. Because I think I gave the *Paris
Review* interview after I wrote the piece for the *Times,* although it may not
have yet been published. In both places I said that Hemingway created strategies for himself as a young writer that produced his great work. But that these
same strategies later defeated him when he tried to move onto new ground.
That book was heavily edited and cut and reduced to a small percentage of
its original manuscript length. The editor must have found that the stuff that
worked was the old Hemingway. What didn't was the new. I stand by what I
said in the piece: there are signs of a growing feminist sensibility, of a different treatment of women, and certainly if we were to believe accounts of the
parts of the manuscript that have not been published, he was struggling to
break out of what had become a sort of aesthetic prison for him, which was
the dramatic novel.

Morris: I asked out of interest in you and your work because in *The Paris
Review* interview, when you talked about the difficulty of finding a new
voice, you said that if a writer can't find something new, it's a kind of death.
And at the end of "Braver Than We Thought" you said it took great courage

on Hemingway's part to have attempted this change in his voice. More courage, you wrote, than looking down the barrel of his rifle. I was struck by those lines. This is a preparation for a question that has to deal with creativity and with the need authors may feel to create something new, without repeating something from the past, as might have been Hemingway's dilemma as you saw it at that time. When you're asked about how you come to write novels, you often reply with little anecdotes which I think are familiar to us now, like looking at the blank wall of the house in New Rochelle or seeing the sign in the Adirondacks. These answers seem to suggest that creativity comes about almost accidentally; it comes dropping down like manna from the air; there's no accounting for it. On the other hand, judging by what you've written about Hemingway, the desire to create something new is almost like the desire for life. It is so important that not to have it is a kind of death. I wanted to ask where it comes from—the ability to create something new without becoming trapped in a repetitive voice, that has been exhausted?

Doctorow: Well, there are always contingent circumstances, but I would say the constant under everything is desperation. I think that despair with what one has done, that dissatisfaction, that need to push on, is a very punishing thing, and it creates, if you're lucky, although from considerable stress and anguish, whatever it is you need to make the discovery that you're going to make. It's difficult to talk about. In the past, speaking of the sign at Loon Lake or staring at the wall, I mean metaphorically those things are true.

Morris: They seem incommensurate with the need to create. They seem somehow out of all proportion to the desire to create, these small accidents.

Doctorow: In fact the writing about the wall you're staring at is a measure of desperation, isn't it?

Morris: Like Bartleby.

Doctorow: Even after you have found the book or stumbled into it, you need the discipline to keep a blank wall in front of you so that the only way you can see out is through your sentences. And all of this suggests a degree of concentration and need that hardly goes along with the idea of a sort of effortless gift-taking through the air. The creative accident is just the beginning of the process, it comes in the moment when you have found the freedom to do anything you want to do, but it comes of desperation. The struggle to stay alive.

Morris: What kind of work is it that writers do? What work has been done by *Billy Bathgate?* Is work effected in the envisioning of something new, of something that hasn't been imagined before?

Doctorow: Well, this is a serious question. We're often filled with doubts as to the value of what we've done—but beyond that to the form itself, to the trade. How useful is it? What does it do? What does it accomplish? Is a good book as important to the world as a well-made house? That sort of thing you get plagued with if you allow yourself to think about it. Have I given my life to something inconsequential? Is the larger consciousness, if there is such a thing, advanced a quarter of a tenth of a thousandth of a millimeter? You know these are very uncomfortable questions, somehow devolving into the term "work," but if you think about what people generally call work—that is to say, something that is achieved as a result of an effort—then it gets interesting. Work, most work, is really very simple, and one doesn't have to go too far into the particular practice to accomplish it. In other words, I began to wonder if all work is in an accessible range, even the work of scientists. One masters a discrete number of facts or ideas or techniques and then can do "the work." One uses muscle, common sense, observation, basic logic, and reaches that most advanced results that way. Whether it's being a police-man or a president, whether it's farming or making movies or mixing chemi-cals, relatively little preparation is required, once one is committed to do this "work." Things are needlessly made mysterious. I mean, when I talk to a practitioner I respect in whatever field, it's astounding how simple things are. And what little distance that person has had to travel from his own being and personality in order to communicate what the work is . . . In physics, work is defined as moving a weight a certain distance. Why can't I call what I do work when everybody else calls what they do work? I guess I would have to rely on the belief or the faith in fiction as a system of knowledge. I move ideas, images, a certain distance. I try to make the invisible visible. I distrib-ute the suffering so that it can be borne. Fiction is an ancient way of knowing, the first science.

Works Cited

Doctorow, E. L. "Braver Than We Thought." *The New York Times Book Review,* 18 May 1986, 1 +.
———. "The Songs of Billy Bathgate." *New American Review* 2. New York: New American Library, 1968, 54–69.
Friedl, Herwig and Dieter Schulz, eds., *"A Multiplicity of Witness:* E. L. Doctorow at Heidelberg," in *E. L. Doctorow: A Democracy of Perception.* Essen: Blaue Eule, 1989.

Mills, Hillary. "Creators on Creativity: E. L. Doctorow." *Saturday Review,* 7 October 1980, 46–48.
Plimpton, George. "The Art of Fiction." *The Paris Review* 28 (1986), 23–47.
Navasky, Victor S. "E. L. Doctorow: I Saw a Sign." *The New York Times Book Review,* 28 September 1980, 44 +.
"Ragtime Revisited: A Seminar with E. L. Doctorow and Joseph Papaleo." *Nieman Reports* 31 (1977), 3–8 +.

E. L. Doctorow

Michael Silverblatt / 1994

This interview originally aired on station KCRW, on the program "Bookworm," a project of Santa Monica college. Used by permission.

Silverblatt: Hi, this is Michael Silverblatt and welcome to "Bookworm." Today my guest is E. L. Doctorow, the author, most recently of *The Waterworks,* and *Ragtime, Welcome to Hard Times, World's Fair, Lives of the Poets* and *Billy Bathgate.* I wanted to begin peculiarly. I suppose it's not fair to talk about a book that in some of its trappings is a gothic thriller, but many reviewers, who (out of an old-fashioned fear of telling the end of a penny dreadful) are not really considering the moral values of the tale being told, talk about it as allegorical without being willing to say allegorical of what. So, I thought I'd begin by asking you about Dr. Sartorius and how you came to invent him.

Doctorow: About ten years ago I wrote a small dream piece of about three pages called "The Waterworks," which I published in *Lives of the Poets.* In this story a man is standing on the embankment of a reservoir, and he's watching a model boat going through the waves, a child's toy boat, and it capsizes and sinks, and he rushes into the adjoining reservoir and sees the owner of the boat, a miniature, as it said in the story, like the boat. A boy who's been drowned and whose body is slamming against the sluice gates. The child's body is recovered from the water; he wraps it up somehow and rushes off with it, leaving a second man, who has observed this entire thing, to wonder what was going on and what exactly was happening, and as I wondered when the story was finished—when you finished something, you are usually rid of it. It's a form of exorcism that takes place if you do it properly and apparently, I hadn't quite finished with this piece. And I worried about it and wondered about it for several years. I wrote *World's Fair* and then came back to thinking about it, and then I wrote *Billy Bathgate* and it came back again, and finally, I guess, it was time to write the book. What I deduced was that this had to be a nineteenth century story because the transporting of water was the great accomplishment of that period—bringing it to the city, putting water under pressure. And then for some reason I've always associated the waterworks with the Croton aqueduct and the Croton dam, in upstate New York, and then I recalled that, indeed, in New York City there had been a reservoir at 42nd Street and Fifth Avenue, an Egyptian-revival monument, very odd, right in what is now the middle of the city where the New York Public Library stands. So I had my period, and I had my city. The man who wraps the child's body up and rushes off with it turned out to be Dr. Sartorius, and the other man, the observer, became my narrator, McIlvaine.

Silverblatt: It's funny because when I read "The Waterworks" story it seemed as if that figure was the police detective, Donne, at least as he originally appeared to narrate the story. He refers to the shrouded figure as "my man," and he seems to be very much an apprehending officer.

Doctorow: That's interesting. That's not the way it worked out in my mind. McIlvaine is the key to the book, I think. He is a reporter, an old newspaper man who is in effect telling us thirty years later about the story he never wrote. And he does enlist the help of police Captain Edmond Donne. Perhaps you're right: I split that fellow up into two, the apprehender and the observer, and turned him into two characters; that's quite possible. I'll have to read the original again to see.

Silverblatt: Those stories in *Lives of the Poets* seemed so mysterious as they appear there; you know, shards. I think they've lived in readers' memories as well, and it's not exactly a surprise to find "The Waterworks" fleshed out; in fact, I am surprised that others of those stories have not been.

Doctorow: In fact, I don't consider myself a story writer, I'm not a natural to the form, and to make a brief confession here, most of those stories I thought were going to be novels. So you see, if I was methodical and wanted to organize myself, I would take every one of those stories in that book and make a novel out of it. I don't think that's going to happen. The first piece in that book, "The Writer in the Family," did give me the sense that I could write a book about that milieu and that particular family, and that turned out to be *World's Fair.* So that's two of those pieces which have yielded longer work. But the point about "The Waterworks" is that it led me to thinking about New York City and the nineteenth century, and once I was on to this, you see, all I could see in New York was the nineteenth century. Every time I walked down the street there was a nineteenth century building, and it became apparent to me that in this city that's usually torn down every ten years or so and rebuilt, there is an enormous presence of that century, still there, right there: Central Park, the Jefferson Market Court House, Cooper

Union College, the armory on 67th and Park Avenue, the row houses in Harlem, the tenements in the Lower East Side, they are all there. But not only that, the very shape of the streets, the construction of the layout, the land-scape—that was all done in that period.

Silverblatt: The way you are speaking, it sounds the way Poe sounds when he is writing in "The Philosophy of Composition" how he came to write "The Raven." You know, that he needed a bird that could talk, and that if it said something it would have to say something eerie, and then the long vowel, the "nevermore," would be an eerie vowel and therefore, you know . . . Is that, in fact, the way this book was constructed?

Doctorow: D. H. Lawrence said, "Never trust the author, trust the book." It is true, since we are all writers, that when the book is done we keep writing. We even make up fictions about the book. This is the way I have fallen into talking about it; in fact, I have never quite believed Poe. It seems to me there was some determination there to react to what he thought was the dandyish kind of poetry that was around him and the affectation and the aestheticism of it, and he wanted to make poetry hard and practical and get rid of people like Longfellow. I think that was really what he was up to in that piece. But it is true that once you are on to something, you can get very practical about the construction of a book, the composition of a book. Once you know what your premises are, you have to deliver on them. And so your editorial mind is functioning simultaneously along with your creative mind, at least it always has with me. But the book here, as all of them, begins with an image of something very, very evocative that just won't let go of you. The entire book then turns out to be, in a sense, a deduction or an exegesis of the story, trying to render the feelings I had when I wrote that story.

Silverblatt: Now we are going through Sartorius—because the book, to me, seems constructed around him—to a question of morality and ethics and to ask the question, "What if, in fact, the mad doctor of Frankenstein, or Hawthorne's 'Rappuccini's Daughter' were in fact not completely a madman but a man more intelligent than those around him who has perhaps inched too far in his procedures?" As such, he seems to be, when he finally speaks, the most interesting man in the book. Yes, he has done things coldly, but he does know what he is doing. He is not a person who is escaping his own consequences.

Doctorow: No, hardly. He is a person who is simply doing what he has always done. During the Civil War he has effected procedures, surgical procedures, which have been of great benefit to the soldiers, wounded soldiers. He's developed post-operative therapies that have been adopted by the military medical establishment, and after the war, he's one of sanitary commissioned doctors who helped prevent a cholera outbreak in New York City.

Silverblatt: He reminds me a bit of that figure that Celine wrote his doctoral thesis on. Celine wrote about a doctor who insisted that doctors wash their hands before ministering to women giving birth and wash their hands afterwards. One delights in thinking of Celine insisting on this kind of cleanliness.

Doctorow: Yes, Sartorius projects himself through his intellect out beyond the realm of permissible behavior of the time. On the other hand, to speak in the other case, he is willing to accept the immense funding that he requires form old, wealthy men who simply want to maintain themselves at the expense of their heirs and families. He also seems to accept the protection of the Tweed ring without acknowledging that there are any moral issues at all to be thought about.

Silverblatt: Well, it's an interesting thing—because he appears in a novel, and his ideas are theoretical, I thought about something you had said about the artist, that the artist is a transgressor. Sartorius seems, for better or worse, to be the transgressor in this book. In other words, he seems more than any of the others to be the artist figure. And decidedly so, since the artist announces that he has turned his back on art, that he doesn't care, in fact, about art. So he seemed a much more problematic figure still than simply ethically problematic.

Doctorow: Oh well, I think that's true. Part of the fascination of the character for me was the fact that he seems to elude any easy ascription. In fact, one of the things I realized in writing the book which I give to McIlvaine is what he calls "villainy." All the villainy in the book is entirely elusive, and the villains in it—you can never quite get your hands on them, whether it's old Pemberton who is not seen, really, until he is dead, or, Pemberton's factotum, who is found on the beach, or indeed, Tweed himself, who is really not a major character in the book but more or less a presence like a configuration of the clouds, a kind of ethos that has settled on the sea like some sort of fog, a miasmic fog. Very elusive, as McIlvaine says. And you reach out to grab these people, and your hand hits the mirror. And the elusiveness of Dr. Sartorious, if he is indeed a villain, is his intellectual point of view which does not recognize any easy journalistic, moralistic ascriptions.

Silverblatt: Well, I thought that perhaps if he were an artist, he would be an artist that you might not entirely approve of. He would be an art-for-art's-sake kind of artist—uninterested in the milieu, the actuality of the world he lives in, interested like Valery, perhaps, in what the mind can reasonably project.

Doctorow: I accept that analogy. I think that's a good one.

Silverblatt: Well, I'm going to call in two big figures here—Valery, on the one hand, and Walter Benjamin, on the other. In different essays, you've admired Benjamin's essay on the taleteller and on the storyteller. On the one hand, Valery seems to be a worker in the ineffable. Benjamin says that the storyteller really is a craftsman, that the great virtue of the storyteller is that he seems to come from an artisan class and the trades. I guess the thing that gives me most pleasure in *The Waterworks* and *Ragtime* and in others is the kind of consequent chronicle narration that Benjamin sees as being very much the result of someone who cares about where he lives but has also traveled far and brought news back to the people he's telling stories to. I wanted to talk to you about craftsmanship.

Doctorow: Well, he's talking about oral storytelling—isn't he?—the days before stories were written down when craftsmen would move from village to village and sit with the local employer or fellow craftsmen as they worked together and bring the tale, and it would be told and retold and refined and polished and buffed just like whatever piece they were working on. But, if you ask me what my sense of the calling is, I take great pleasure in thinking about it as a kind of trade, in thinking of myself as getting up and going to work in the morning like everybody else. I certainly have never been a Valery-*esque* figure. In terms of my own personal life, I have lived a very ordinary, average kind of domesticated existence, which I think Flaubert also suggested is the way to get your work done.

Silverblatt: Live like a bourgeois.
Doctorow: That's right.

Silverblatt: Benjamin also talks about how in the course of this polishing of the tale through retelling, a mystery arises perhaps because things in retellings of stories have now been left out, cleaned up, dropped away, become irrelevant historically, and so you have almost an image from which psychology has been subtracted. In order to understand the story, you might want to add psychology, but you'd be doing it on your ownsome. And it struck me,

too, that in your work—obviously in what you've called the dream pieces in
Lives of the Poets—there is an interest in a sort of image-mystery which
psychology might help to explain, but the fiction seems to be rather uninterested in that kind of inner process.

Doctorow: Images are what always evoke the beginnings of books for me.
The sounds of words, images, even phrases of music, the slightest private
excitements are always the origins of books. Certainly the image of the toy
boat going down the reservoir generated something clearly for me in my
mind, and I like the idea of an image standing on its own and sort of shim-
mering for one and having some meaning which must be elucidated, which
must be sought out and worked on by the reader or the hearer. It's interesting
because in this century, the techniques of fiction have been adopted by the
social sciences to a great degree. There are even historians now who write
turning to fiction. In a sense, I think of psychology as the industrialization of
storytelling. They have all these interchangeable parts that can be applied to
any one of us. But, if you are suggesting that somehow I honor whatever the
ancient craft is, I am very pleased about that. Benjamin, of course, said that
the era of storytelling was over because we had now only the individual
writers who could offer us no counsel nor wisdom as the ancient storytellers
could. I don't happen to subscribe to that part of the essay.

Silverblatt: Well, it seems to me, in fact, that one of the things you've
adopted as the role of the writer is to offer counsel that—if anything—the
Benjamin advice that the writer has abjured his role as advisor to a culture is
one that you've sought to redress in some sense.

Doctorow: Well, but avoiding any pieties that that might imply or the
grandiosity of the role you might pick for yourself. There is nothing I have
ever consciously chosen to do: any ideas you have, any convictions, any
beliefs have to come up organically out of the work. You must honor the
process. You can't inflict on it and expect it to survive any sort of hard
intention. That's the surest way to destroy anything.

Silverblatt: The image that's coming to me through many of the things in
The Waterworks—also through *Lives of the Poets,* but throughout your
work—is the image of parents eating their young. Letting a younger generation go hungry, uneducated, untransformed by the knowledge of a previous
generation. Almost as if people will accept being orphaned and teach themselves, but if they turn to their own progenitors, they are not going to get
what they need. On the other hand, to write a book like *The Waterworks,* one

does turn to a previous generation of writers and teach oneself, I guess lonely, to write their sentences. So, I wondered about you and your forbearers.

Doctorow: It's true, I think, that every book is an answer to some other book, that every writer has the conversation or the communication not only with his readers, not only on a contemporary, lateral line, but with the past, always with the past, as if there were all these people sitting around in some wonderful, eventless heaven talking to each other. To the extent that you use a literary convention—whether you are aware of it or not, as I seem to have done in this book—I am responding as a hopeful child to Hawthorne, to Melville, to Poe, and maybe even to Edith Wharton. But, yes, there is no question about it. Whether this could be described as state of orphanage, I'm not sure. There seem to be a lot of children in the books, one way or another, and what McIlvaine accepts in *The Waterworks* is some sort of Darwinian principle that—although it's being argued in the church sermons and among the intellectuals—nevertheless governs, as new as it is, if it is new, the lives of the city, where everyone seems to be quite willing to sustain losses for the progress of the city. So, there are thirty or forty thousand vagrant children running around, most of whom will end up disastrously. Or there is no social policy that does anything about the veterans who have no arms or legs and that kind of thing. That we seem to be able to accept, even in our own day, enormous losses among our fellow citizens for our own comfort. And, there doesn't seem to be any way we can master, even in this post-coldwar enlightenment, the great domestic problems—if you want to use that terrible, political word—that afflict us. In that sense, the idea of orphanage, you see, becomes a very important, governing image of this book. For me, having these masters to rely on, whether consciously or not, is just the opposite of being an orphan: it's having a wonderful community of parents.

Silverblatt: Someone said to me recently there is no culture without altruism. I tend to think that the masters, whether it's Melville or Hawthorne—Melville, toward the end of his life impoverished and insane but still someone of whom his own little scrawled note remains true, "Stay true to the dreams of your youth"—that as opposed to these literary masters, the old men in *The Waterworks* are people who want to ensure their own lives in a permanent moment and care nothing for their own children or the children of strangers. Is there in selfishness a refusal to see to the children? Is there a sense that a generation of writers is abandoning children, that they are no longer being good masters? Is there the sense that the culture is not continuing itself or has stopped in some way? That the transmission has ended, and what there is instead is the transmission of selfishness from one generation to the next?

EL: Certainly there are political implications of that sort. The book does speak very clearly in terms of an attempt to invert the natural order of succession and primogeniture. One of the sons succeeding the fathers has very explicitly appeared during the past presidential election. This generation of Bill Clinton's that came up in the sixties was long ago thought to be totally unreliable and untrustworthy and not deserving of the mantle of power, and it was quite clear in the conflict in the debates between those two men [Clinton and Bush]. Every president since Eisenhower, I suppose, has been of that World War II generation and terribly shocked by the great anti-war uprising of their sons. So this does operate clearly. It may be, though, in general social terms, a loss of any kind of real serious, sincere communal ideal. Something has deteriorated from the way I think it used to be, although that itself might be an unwarranted sentimentality. But it just seems to me in the past, even when things were bad, there was always a sense that "something should be done about this," but I'm not sure that "something should be done about this" survives the political process today.

Silverblatt: Thank you. I've been speaking to E. L. Doctorow, thank you for being with us today.
Doctorow: Thank you.

An Interview with E. L. Doctorow

Michael Wutz / 1994

From *Weber Studies* 11 (Winter, 1994), 6–15. Used by permission.

Wutz: Looking back over your work, it seems to me that the years of the Cold War up through Vietnam are pretty much encapsulated in *The Book of Daniel*. Do the more recent political changes have any consequences for your fiction at all?

Doctorow: The Cold War went on for a long time—so long, that with the exception of the generation of writers now in or approaching their seventies, the working life of every one publishing today has been entirely circumscribed by it. So it's been a lifetime. The end of the Cold War didn't bring on any national sense of elation. Mentally we may still be in it, to a certain extent. And aren't those bombs still lying around? The population of the planet has doubled in the last fifty years or so, and in another thirty will double again., Some sort of post-humanistic fate is still a possibility. China is running out of potable water. Russia is close to anarchy. And a lot of raging fanatics are running around in Europe and the Mid-East. Not communist fanatics anymore but fanatics . . . who learned a lot about bellicosity from the super states. So the animus has been distributed. Perhaps the effect of all of this on anyone's fiction is the least of our problems.

Wutz: In 1988 Bill Moyers asked you why most prominent contemporary political fictions are written in Latin America and South Africa, but not in the United States. You responded to him by saying that "There's no critical fraternity today that has much regard for the political novel in America." I'm wondering whether this lack of critical response for political fiction that you see is, in any sense, related to the domineering presence of the New Criticism in the decades from, say, the 1940s to the mid, late 1970s? Put differently, is this political lethargy that you detect perhaps a kind of residue of an essentially ahistorical mode of critical-literary investigation?

Doctorow: I wouldn't pin it solely on the New Criticism. I grew up as a New Critic at Kenyon College. It was an historical response, you know, to a real lack of precision in critical thought. It was valuable in drawing attention to the text—in its presumption that the text itself could teach you everything

you needed to know about it. I think what you describe as lethargy has more
to do with the fact that with the Cold War the entire country, including a
large part of the intellectual community, turned right. Domestically, the Cold
War at its worst was a kind of civil religion with distinctly Puritan cruelties.
People were cowed. It's true that a generation rose up against the ideology in
the 1960s, but by the seventies they were pretty well mopped up. The ranks
of the public critics began to thin—the generations behind Edmund Wilson,
Irving Howe and Alfred Kazin disappeared into the academy. Fled, one might
say. There seemed to be a depoliticization of cultural life, generally. It was
clear the USSR was a terrible mistake. But the correlate to that was . . . that
anyone in America who wrote a political novel was writing a foolishly adversarial novel. It was possible according to Cold War orthodoxy to appreciate political novelists like Kundera from Czechoslovakia, or Coetzee or
Gordimer from South Africa, but the American political novel was an egre-
gious aesthetic error. A novel about an heroic CIA operative could be a good
story . . . but a novel about a conscientious objector was a political tract.

   Wutz: You've just lamented the demise of the critic who mediates between academia proper and the public at large. One influential critic, Fredric
Jameson, once observed (in an early draft of an essay which he later revised)
that what characterizes contemporary culture is "the gradual eclipse of histo-
ricity, the loss of any vital imaginative sense of the past, in all its radical
difference from us." And Jameson links this phenomenon with the products
of mass culture, such as nostalgia films, and also with your novel *Ragtime.*
He says that *Ragtime,* "better than any other recent novel strikingly drama-
tizes the transformation of the past, under postmodernism, into the sheer
images and stereotypes of that past, the displacement of the past as referent
with a new experience of the past as simulacrum and as pseudo-past." How
do you respond to a charge like that?

   Doctorow: Is it a charge? I haven't read the piece. I find it hard to believe
that a reasonably attentive reader, let alone a professional critic, would mis-
construe the irreverent spirit of that book. What makes it puzzling. . . . In *The
Book of Daniel,* written previous to *Ragtime,* I offered much the same critique
of nostalgia with Daniel's analysis of Disneyland—that is, the uses to which
history is put in terms of replacing the felt life with a few reductive images,
or lies of nostalgia, that rob the past of its true meanings. But I would have
to read the material you're citing to speak with certainty.

   Wutz: It seems to me that in the last hundred years, our literary landscape
has been dominated by this general bifurcation: there's modernism, which is

the period before the Second World War, and then there's postmodernism which, roughly speaking, is the period after. Are the terms modernism or postmodernism, in any sense, applicable to you or your work; where would you situate yourself within that spectrum?

Doctorow: I'm not sure I'm interested in situating myself in that way. I mean, certainly, I've used certain postmodernist techniques, but for what I think of as entirely traditional story telling purposes. What does that make me—a post-post-modernist?

Wutz: Notwithstanding your critique of American literary criticism, you're one of the few contemporary American novelists who is popular both with the critical establishment and with the general readership in this country. To what do you attribute this "double popularity," if that's the right term?

Doctorow: I don't know the answer to that. I honestly don't know. When one thinks of the size of the communities in the past that have produced periods of flourishing fiction, they were much smaller and more visible as class societies, so that, for example, Dickens writing about London could rely on certain things that everybody knew—certain types of people, the middle class, the merchant class, the class of tradesmen, the working class and the upper class, with self-portraying patterns of speech for each class. This is a large country and it claims to be classless, very volatile with periodic infusions of immigrant populations from various parts of the world. It is a pluralistic society; there's very little that we all have in common. But if you use a disreputable genre like the Western as I have, or play against the historical myths that everyone carries around in their mind, you may be making meaningful connections. I don't know if that's true. But I would offer that as an idea to consider.

Wutz: Keyword disreputable genre. *Welcome to Hard Times,* of course, is not the only novel that parodies such a genre. Your second (and least favorite) novel, *Big As Life,* is a sort of science fiction. And *Billy Bathgate,* your last published novel, plays off the crime novel, which could be seen as a disreputable genre as well. What is it that fascinates you about these "outlawed" forms of fiction, these subgenres that exist beyond the pale of the "literary"?

Doctorow: Well again, the use of the material of popular culture has always appealed to me because popular genres are meaningful and a source of analysis of who we are and what we're doing. The American affection for gangsters seems to me to be characteristically American. Those of us who pay our taxes and observe the speed limit have great admiration for lawless people; and the great operative myth of individualism in this country expresses itself to a degree beyond tolerance in the gangster. We like to watch our gangsters flaunt their brazen sociopathic ways and then we like to see them punished. The myth of the West of course is ours, and ours alone. So when you decide to use these materials, you rely on a certain kind of ground music that the reader has in his or her head, and you have the chance to write some counterpoint.

Wutz: Your first novel, *Welcome to Hard Times,* seems to address two issues that appear to be a constant of much of your work. For one, there is Blue who questions the myth of the American West; and two, he also meditates on the epistemological problem of containing experience in language. He realizes that the ledgers that he keeps do not allow him to "fix" truth— that's his own word—but that any verbalized experience is always already a construction. It seems to me that similar cases could be made for *The Book of Daniel,* for *Ragtime,* and also perhaps for *Loon Lake.* Would it be fair to say that this kind of, let me call it, double demystification—namely the unmasking of a received truth as myth and inquiring into the process of meaning making—is a fundamental continuity of your project as a novelist?

Doctorow: Well now that you've described that so well, I say—why not?

Wutz: What amazes me about your oeuvre is the uniqueness of each of your books. Each novel is radically different from the previous ones, each book has its own distinct voice; and you have, of course, always been resistant to the observation made by critics that you have a personal style, a signature of your own, if you will. Nevertheless, is there an essential Doctorow emerging from all of your writing, a kind of stylistic or thematic preoccupation that binds much, if not all, of your work?

Doctorow: I do feel that each book has its own identity and that I'm hidden in it. It's like those picture puzzles where you look at a tree and you're asked to find the wolves hiding in the leaves—that kind of thing. Nevertheless, by simply changing your focus, it seems to me you could bring into sharp relief certain preoccupations, thematic concerns, obsessions that are in every book. So, there again it has to be left to the critic. Different people see different things. There are always children in your books. Yes, you're right, a lot of children in my books. Or you play off myths, with popular culture and history. Yes, I do that. Your books all have different voices. Yes, that's true. So, you know, someone will have to take this further. I don't think it's my job to do that.

Wutz: Children, of course, do play a great role in American literature, not just in this generation of writers. It's almost a staple of much of American fiction. Could you please comment on the role of children in your fiction, and whether this centrality of children in recent American fiction is tied to a particular historical moment of this country.

Doctorow: Well, the first part is easy to answer. Children are the narrative sources of *Billy Bathgate* and *World's Fair.* The children's experience in *The Book of Daniel* frame, organize, and create the being of that book. The hidden narrator of *Ragtime* is probably the little boy in later times.

Wutz: Excuse me for interrupting here. Why do you say "probably"? Of late, that's a question that has received quite some attention within the critical community—whether or not the little boy is, indeed, the narrator.

Doctorow: Because he was hidden to me for so much of that book. At a certain point quite near the end he betrays a personal relationship to everything he has narrated and appears to be the son of Mother and Father, namely the little boy. I'm pretty sure that's who it is, but I'm not sure that that is essential for reading the book to know that. Now, to go back to the first part of the question, it seems to me writers have always used children, I'm not sure that's specific to our moment. Dickens, of course, Mark Twain, Robert Louis Stevenson, J. D. Salinger. There's a tremendous advantage writing from a child's point of view. You recover the capacity for wonder that you give up as an adult, that you've lost as an adult. You can rhapsodize the ordinary, which is empowering to a writer. Besides, you know, literature deals with hell and injustice and people going down under the weight of life, and the child is the symbol of the fully sensible mind and being who can't quite control experiences. Childhood is full sentient being and powerlessness combined, which most adults in this world can probably understand quite well.

Wutz: In your essay "False Documents" you suggest the fundamental permeability of our traditional concepts of fact and fiction. It's an essay about the breakdown or deconstruction of boundaries, about the ontological sameness of fact and fiction. As such, the essay also subverts what you have called *"the power of the regime"*—the Western world's belief in the hegemony of reason to construe reality. Your essay reminded me of the work of Gabriel García Márquez, because he also portrays a world in his narratives where fact and fiction interpenetrate in a peculiar way. Do you see any affinities between your own work and that of Márquez?

Doctorow: No, I don't. I see his work coming out of a wonderfully errant religious sensibility that simply overwhelms the physical world. I admire his work tremendously. He's a great prose poet, is what he is. But I don't feel a close connection with him.

Wutz: Repetition and reversal obviously play a great role *within* many of your individual novels. I'm wondering whether one could also speak of the repetition of certain scenes or characters *across* the boundaries of an individual text. I am thinking here of the black janitor Williams in *The Book of Daniel* who reappears as Smith in *World's Fair.* I'm thinking of Rochelle Isaacson's crazy mother, who is asthmatic, who speaks Yiddish, who is afraid of being poisoned, and who runs away frequently, and this woman reappears as a virtual double in the later novel, *World's Fair.* There's the fatal accident of the woman squashed against a schoolyard fence by a car that is witnessed by both Daniel and by Edgar; and both narrators, in fact, are as asthmatic as their grandmothers. Do you engage in some sort of intertextual recycling?

Doctorow: I suppose I do, but I wouldn't have called it that at the time I was doing it. One of the things I've found myself realizing is almost the sense that I have a repertory company of characters, and I keep changing their costumes and their looks, and maybe even altering their relationships. But they're my company of players and they play different roles, but they're beginning to appear to me as my loyal troop. There are certain things that you do, and then you still need to do, really. You know you see this most clearly in a writer like D. H. Lawrence. If you read any page of *The Rainbow,* just open the book at random, you will see the act of writing becoming very visible. He will describe a flood, for instance. There's this big flood in *The Rainbow,* and he'll do a paragraph on the flood, and he will not be satisfied, he will not have felt that he's sufficiently done the flood. So he gives you another paragraph where the same thing happens, but it's a little more, a few runs, a few changes on the original paragraph, and then a third paragraph. And so on, for pages. . . . And you see repetition, but it isn't repetition. It's just the writer having to do it until he's finished. Same thing in terms of recycling characters from book to book. All writers do this. Musicians do it, too. I mean Bach liked certain themes; you hear a theme in the violin concerto, you hear it again in double piano concerto, you hear it in the orchestral suite. Mozart, too. Artists like things, you know. An artist who uses paints likes certain colors, or he paints the same field, or the same set of still-life objects or the same nude, over and over. It's an admission by the artist not to have achieved perfection. If you achieve perfection, there's no reason to ever do anything again.

Wutz: The concluding segments of *The Book of Daniel* and *World's Fair* take place in a simulated and futuristic environment—the 1939 World's Fair and Disneyland—while the historical present of both novels is overshadowed by a war, in one instance the Second World War, in the other, Vietnam. Why this final juxtaposition between a technocratic vision of the future and a grim historical reality?

Doctorow: I'm not sure. Perhaps this is society's way of praying—constructing a future when the very possibility of a future is in doubt.

Wutz: In your essays and interviews, you have invoked the philosopher Walter Benjamin. How would you respond to the observation that Benjamin is present in much of your writing in the 70s, that he is almost a kind of kindred spirit. I'm thinking here in particular of Benjamin's wonderful reflections on the work of Nikolai Leskov, "The Storyteller," and his essay, "The Work of Art in the Age of Mechanical Reproduction." Both essays, it seems to me, raise a number of issues—such as the loss of an oral tradition and the consequences of technological replication—that are also present in . some of your work at the time.

Doctorow: Other people have talked about these issues, too. Albert Einstein, for instance. What did train travel do to our perception of the environment, when people could move faster than they could walk or ride a horse? What does it do to your understanding of music to be able to hear it over and over again by pushing a button, rather than waiting for the next time the orchestra or the pianist comes to town? These are significant questions. *Ragtime* is set in a period when motor cars were just beginning to make their way, and there are player pianos, and things were mass-produced resolutely. Benjamin is a philosopher of all of that. Novelists are not philosophers, they're rarely original thinkers, but somehow instinctively pick up on things that are articulated as ideas more articulately by other people.

Wutz: You have repeatedly said that your writing is largely the result of a process of trial and error, and that any rationale for the composition of a book is essentially a construct that is imposed in retrospect. Now, one reader of your work has suggested that *Ragtime* appears to have been produced by what he calls a "narratological assembly line," which refers of course to Henry Ford's invention in the text and to the novel's narrative speed (Harpham). I'm wondering whether such a sequential model suggests a degree of design and linearity that is at odds with your own process of composition.

Doctorow: I'm not crazy about the metaphor.

Wutz: Let me, for the moment, propose a different or perhaps a complementary model of composition. One of the most sustained image clusters in *Ragtime* is that of rags, which appears in numerous configurations, most prominently of course in the music from which the novel derives its title. How would you respond to the observation that *Ragtime* is both in terms of its thematic and its composition an assembly of narrative rags, "a crazy quilt of humanity"? Would such a patchwork approach to writing be closer to your experience as a novelist, and would such a model of composition accommodate the patterned randomness of the novel?

Doctorow: That's a little closer to the truth. With an assembly line, everything is pre-planned. A rag is both a tune and a rag. What is suggested is the impoverishment of the writer. The image of the writer as a ragpicker wandering through the streets, his disreputability and insecurity—I like that, in the sense that the materials of all novels are the lives the writer has lived or observed or heard about, these materials of rags, bits and pieces of thread, notions and stuff that he puts together somehow into something that didn't exist before. That can be worn, or used to keep warm.

Wutz: *Lives of the Poets* is not the first of your works to echo another work of literature in its title, in this case Samuel Johnson's book by the same title, of course. I'm thinking about the Dickensian overtones in *Welcome to Hard Times* and the biblical allusions in *The Book of Daniel*. What is your purpose in establishing these kinds of resonances?

Doctorow: Well, they may show I'm a different kind of novelist, from the writers I grew up on and took from. It's quite possible that you could not have a conversation like this with Dreiser. Hemingway would kick you out of the room. They wouldn't understand you, whereas I do. We may be in a period of literary ecology where writers are a little more educated, a little more self-conscious, and understand their books as answering other books. Every book inevitably is a response to some other book. Maybe our literature was better off when our writers were generally uneducated, coming up out of newspapers, rather than universities. I can imagine the fun Sam Clemens would have with a conversation like this.

Wutz: You have published individual pieces of short fiction in the past, but *Lives of the Poets* is your first published collection of short stories. Why the shift from a novel in the traditional sense to a series of shorter narrative forms?

Doctorow: Well I can't account for that. I started writing these pieces and I didn't know why, and because I'm not a short story writer but a novelist, I look for the connection among them. And the connection I found was the fictional writer who might have written them. And that led me to the novella that anchors the book. I think the case can be made that *Lives of the Poets* is a novel.

Wutz: *World's Fair* gives a vivid picture of the time when radio was the predominant means of entertainment, and we see how Edgar's imagination translates auditory signals into images. His was a culture of listening and imagining, not of televised seeing and passive absorbing. Your novel seems to celebrate this kind of imaginative engagement through radio broadcasts. Do you see in the radio a last technological stage of an oral culture that is based on the transmission of words? And as a follow-up to that, what affinities do you see between your own work as a novelist or storyteller and the radio?

Doctorow: I grew up listening to radio, and it left you room to participate. As I think I say in *World's Fair,* if you heard a car engine starting, you knew by the depth of the sound what kind of car it was. You always had to visualize the scene and the way the characters looked, even your favorite characters, The Lone Ranger, The Shadow—all these radio figures. And it is a form of oral storytelling. At some point when I was a boy, I thought nothing could be finer in life when I grew up than being a sound effects man for radio programs. The illusion of that was delightful to, thrilling to contemplate. Before I ever saw television, I'd heard about it and I thought this has to be great! You turn on a box and there's—a picture! And the very first reaction I had was one of extreme disappointment. The picture was flat, hermetic, oppressive. I was quite young at the time. I'd expected the same depth in the television picture as I had in my mind when I listened to radio shows. But it wasn't—it was this done deal. It was all there and it was one dimension and it was constrictive. And I'll never forget that impression I had—the flatness and the almost claustrophobic nature of the image pressed up against that screen. Yes, radio is oral culture and related to storytelling. I think that's unquestionable, because whether you hear it over the airwaves as it's dramatized with different voices or it's one person sitting and telling you this story and doing all the voices, you still have it in your mind, the depthless mind.

And you are your own director and costumer and hairdresser and lighting designer. The nature of visualization is profoundly different from mere vision. It's like a dream where things change radically from one thing to another and you don't mind—it seems logical and natural that they do.

Wutz: Billy Bathgate is the last in a series of your young male protagonists whose quest for selfhood and self-actualization is inextricably intertwined with the search for a father figure. Why do you come back to this linkage between paternity and identity?

Doctorow: Well, these are *Bildungsromane,* aren't they? And I think it's inevitable, this linkage. People say to me, why do you write books that take place in the past? Well, I say, we live in it. Any city you walk in is made of the decisions of the dead. And who can look in the mirror and not see his own father, his own mother? In Dickens, they don't know who their fathers are. Billy Bathgate doesn't know who his father is. It's maybe not knowing who your father is that requires this linkage. Knowing too well who your father is creates a different kind of problem entirely.

Wutz: Could you give us a sense of what you are working on at the moment? A preview of coming attractions?

Doctorow: A novel called *The Waterworks.* It takes place in New York City in the years after the Civil War. Its source is a little dream story I wrote some time ago with the same title. . . . "The Waterworks." I don't think I can sensibly say anything more about it.

Works Cited

Harpham, Geoffrey Galt. "E. L. Doctorow and the Technology of Narrative," *PMLA* 100 (1985): 81–95.
Jameson, Fredric, "Postmodernism and Consumer Society," *Amerikastudien/American Studies* 29 (1) 1984: 53–73.
Moyers, Bill. " 'World of Ideas' interview with E. L. Doctorow." (PBS Interview 1988).

The City, *The Waterworks,* and Writing

Michelle Tokarczyk / 1995

From *The Kenyon Review* 17 (Winter, 1995), 32–37. Used by permission.

The author of nine novels—*Welcome to Hard Times, Big as Life, The Book of Daniel, Ragtime, Loon Lake, Lives of the Poets, World's Fair, Billy Bathgate,* and *The Waterworks,* as well as a play, *Drinks Before Dinner,* and a collection of essays, *Hemingway, Poe and the Constitution*—E. L. Doctorow grew up in New York City and was educated at Kenyon College and Columbia University. A recipient of the PEN/Faulkner Award for fiction, the National Book Critics Circle Arts and Letters Award, and the National Book Award among others, Doctorow teaches creative writing at New York University.

MT: *I've been intrigued by your choices to set so many of your novels—* The Book of Daniel, Lives of the Poets, World's Fair, Billy Bathgate *and now* The Waterworks—*in New York City. How do you think being a New Yorker who has lived in the City for most of your life has affected your writing, your outlook in general?*

ELD: It was a very fortunate thing for someone who was going to be a writer to grow up at the cutting edge of American culture. In those days the country was more regionally directed than it is today. What went on in New York wasn't as well distributed, so there was a tremendous advantage to living here. New York was a very rich experience for a child. As a teenager, I used to go almost weekly to the Museum of Modern Art. I'd look at the permanent collection, look at the new work, go downstairs to the theater and see a foreign film. As a boy I went matter of factly to plays, to concerts. And as I grew up, I was a beneficiary of the incredible energies of European émigrés in every field—all those great minds hounded out of Europe by Hitler. They brought enormous sophistication to literary criticism, philosophy, science, music. . . . I was very lucky to be a New Yorker.

And, I was also in touch with, what turned out to be, although I couldn't realize it at the time, the last vestiges of Jewish immigrant culture. Those

vestiges were in my grandparents, and to a lesser extent in my parents, who
were born here. But it was enough for me to pick up on that wonderful sort
of beautiful trade-union spirit of the early twentieth century—the expectation
that this was a country where you could work out some justice for yourself
and everyone else in your situation if you worked at it. So I was lucky in that
sense. I was nourished by that Jewish humanist, not terribly religious, spiritu-
ality. I imagine that's another part of the New York mind-set.

– And then, of course, the place itself, the city as spectacular phenomenon.
All writers find a place for themselves, a home for their imaginations, and I
suppose the city is mine. It's the quintessential city—so much so that I've
felt at home in every city I've been anywhere in the world.

MT: *How did you come to* The Waterworks?

ELD: It began with the very short dream story in *Lives of the Poets,* "The
Waterworks." I never fully got that story out of my mind. I kept thinking
about it.

MT: *It is a puzzling and eerie story.*

ELD: I would think about it, and go on to a novel, and come back to it. I
understood eventually that image, the waterworks, meant I was in the industrial nineteenth century. Transporting water to the city, to any city, was a
great engineering feat of that time. Then, of course, the reservoir described
could have been the Croton holding reservoir at Forty-second Street and Fifth
Avenue.

MT: *Oh, I didn't know there had been one there.*

ELD: Where New York Public Library is now. The reservoir walls were
over forty feet high, twenty-five feet thick, and inward slanted. The style was
ancient Egyptian. You could walk from the street through these temple doors,
go up a flight of stairs, and come out on the embankment. People went up
there to take the air, to stroll about. That was the New York version of pastoral, Central Park not having been built yet. Once I was into the book I realized
how much of the nineteenth century city is still with us—not in just the
obvious architecture—Central Park, the Brooklyn Bridge, the Sixty-seventh
Street Armory, the row houses in the West Village, the Jefferson Market
Courthouse and so on—but even the shape of the streets, the widths, and the
names of them. My studio looks south over Soho to lower Manhattan. One
night a heavy fog came down and covered the World Trade center, covered
all the big glass, steel buildings of lower Manhattan, then the Woolworth

Building of the 1920s. The entire twentieth century was erased until all I could see was the ground-level city. It was the most uncanny experience: I was looking at the city that Melville walked in. I was looking at the nineteenth century. So in this way, step by step, the book proposed itself to me. In a sense the entire book is deduced from the story. For instance, the drowned boy who is carried off by the man in the black coat: I reflected on the uses of children in the nineteenth century. There were thirty to forty thousand vagrant children running around. Children who were unclaimed, who were totally on their own. People called them street rats. The city, my sense of the city of the time—New York in the post-Civil War—is what that story speaks to. And once I realized that, I was able to do the book.

MT: *Talking about the urchin children in nineteenth-century New York reminded me how much of your work is concerned with children. Particularly I thought about Billy Bathgate. I am very curious about him. He is, like Daniel Isaacson in* The Book of Daniel, *such a ruthless child. I wonder how you see his corruption.*

ELD: Billy Bathgate is everything that you would want a boy to be; he's bright, he's loyal, he's enterprising, he's observant, a quick learner. He has feelings, he is connected to his feelings, he works things out. But all these virtues are in service to the underworld, which fascinated him.

MT: *When I first read* Billy Bathgate *in the late 1980s I was reminded of crime's attraction—especially drug dealing—to many slum children. Criminal lives are incredibly dangerous but still alluring.*

ELD: Crime—along with sports and the arts—is the instant way up from the lower depths. They want the same things, those kids who sell drugs. They want what they see on television; they want the good life. They want a nice house, they want a car. A place in the world.

MT: *After* Billy Bathgate *came out, you published an essay "A Gangsterdom of the Spirit" in the* Nation. *I wondered if there was some connection between that gangsterdom you write about in the essay and the crime in* Billy Bathgate.

ELD: I suppose there may be some connection. It's not the kind of thing you can afford to think about in the writing. But it is a fact that this book about crime came to me in the 1980s. That's all I can say. It's a strange thing. I have never had the sense of enormous, indiscriminate power that would allow me at a given time to write any number of books. I have never had that feeling about myself. I find myself in a book and my understanding is: This is my book. There is nothing else I can do right now. At any given time you can do only the book that you are given to do.

MT: The Waterworks *is very interesting in the context of your other work. It seems that there are some recurring themes: Sartorius's quest for immortality reminds me of Ford and Morgan in* Ragtime. *McIlvaine's relentless search for the truth reminds me of Daniel's search for the truth about his parents' case.*

ELD: Comparisons to my other works don't occur to me because I don't think that way when I'm writing. If I did it'd probably worry me. The work has to dominate. That's where you live, in those specific sentences. But all writers have preoccupations, things they're attached to. So I suppose there must be recurring themes.

MT: *As I was thinking of the vagrant children Sartorius exploited, one of the things that came to mind was Stephen Dedalus's words in* A Portrait of the Artist as a Young Man, *"Ireland is a sow that eats its farrow." Are you perhaps suggesting something similar about American society during this period?*

ELD: I think what Joyce meant is something different. He's writing about Irish culture and a provincial repressive Catholicism that permeates every aspect of life and discourages vitality in the people. *The Waterworks* is a different sort of story. I think it's more a novel about all modern industrial culture, its presumption of continuous modernity, and the extent to which modernity is an illusion.

MT: *There seems to be a connection between the various kinds of evil depicted in the novel—Tweed's corruption, Sartorius's experiments, and slavery.*

ELD: Or among government, wealth, and science. But the discovery that came over me in writing the book was more the despair of being locked in history. I was very interested in the city's architecture, not only in the waterworks and the reservoir, but in the orphanage, and the grid layout of Manhattan. The narrator is quite sensitive to such things; in fact, at one point he talks of how architecture can inadvertently express the hideousness of a culture.

MT: *The main character, as a newspaper editor and reporter, reminds me of a writer as you've often depicted writers: that is, he searches out the truth. He's as relentless in his pursuit as Daniel in* The Book of Daniel.

ELD: I suppose *The Waterworks* is like *The Book of Daniel* in that each describes a process of discovery. Something is unfolded.

MT: *I was struck by the book's oral quality, by the sense that McIlvaine was indeed telling his story. I believe that when you wrote* World's Fair *you were striving for a sense of oral history. Were you doing so in* The Waterworks?

ELD: In *World's Fair* the oral history passages were set off from the main text. Here the narrator is meant to be talking all the way through. It's a spoken book. At one point I was thinking of indicating through another voice—in a monologue, afterword, or introduction—that McIlvaine in the last year of his life had dictated what he had to say to a stenographer. He says at one point, You have your motorcars and telephones and electric lights." He's looking back thirty years or so, you see, motorcars and electric lights and telephones being the glories of the period after the turn of the century. I always imagined he was dictating, that the unnamed stenographer—me possibly—became the captive audience. But I decided I didn't have to frame it all up, as Conrad does when an unnamed narrator gives us the scene—everyone sitting on the outerdeck smoking cigars, the sun going down over the Thames, as Marlowe begins one of his marathon monologues.

MT: *I had thought of Hawthorne and Poe as possible influences here, particularly because Hawthorne wrote sinister stories like "Rappaccini's Daughter" about scientific experiments.*

ELD: Undeniably. *The Waterworks* is a tale.

MT: *Aside from the narrative tale-telling voice, what other features of the book were particularly important for you?*

ELD: There are certain gifts that the book gave to me—for instance, the idea of the elusiveness of villainy. If you think about it, the old man Augustus Pemberton is never seen alive. His existence is reported secondhand from the newspapers or the fact that his son saw him. His factotum, Simmons, is found only after he's dead. As for Tweed, you never see more than a glimpse or two of him. He's a ruling ethos, a configuration of the clouds. As McIlvaine says, you can't really get your hands on these people. The only one who finally appears as a presence—in the end and after great delay—is Sartorius. His abusiveness, however, is not physical, it's intellectual. A man with his own standards, not society's.

MT: *In reflecting on* Lives of the Poets *especially, I've been thinking about something you said in an interview with Christopher Morris, "All writ-*

*ers have doubts about the value of their work as compared with, for example,
a well-made house."*

ELD: Words have no physical existence. Books are events in the mind.
You don't know as time passes if what was in your mind as you wrote is
really what's on the page. I find my view of my books shifts as I continue to
think about them, but certainly my relationship to the books that have been
done is distant. I think, "Well, all right, but with this new one I'm really
going to do it." You always have the "this one."

I meant . . . that you can look at a house and walk around it and live in it;
the windows are built so that the light comes in, the stairs are here, and you
know where the closets are. Space is measured and defined. The house is
solidly constructed, the floors are parqueted floors, and there's nice tile in the
bathroom.

MT: *Right, it's very solid.*

ELD: Several people can walk into the house and more or less agree that
it's a useful, livable house, but I'm not sure that the house of fiction is ever
something most people would agree on. I mean, there are obviously great
works that we admire. But I don't think self-satisfaction is very useful or
constructive for an author, even if I were capable of it to any great degree.
Maybe to people who write one book and stop. If you did something per-
fectly, what would be the need to go on? But it all operates in the mind.
Words are there . . . and not there. Books are, and are not. When you've
finished with a book, nothing will ever match the experience you've had
writing it.

Finding a Historical Line

Richard Marranca / 1996

From *The Literary Review* 39 (Spring, 1996), 407–14. Used by permission.

E. L. Doctorow does not feel that his novels are at all scholarly, despite the fact that most of them are somewhat historical. He does very little research, and does not write to convey any particular message. He feels that historical eras provide their own closure and a set of facts around which a fiction can be framed. Doctorow's feelings about New York City and his novel *The Waterworks* are discussed.

RM: *What's* The Waterworks *about?*

ELD: I just finished reading the page proofs, so it's a little hard for me to tell at this point. The book has to settle before you can provide a critical interpretation. It takes place in New York City in 1871, right after the Civil War, and the Tweed Ring is in power in the city government. The narrator is a newspaper editor of the *Telegram,* an evening newspaper. He has a free-lance writer, an interesting writer, who disappears. The book follows this editor's attempt to find out what happened to this writer. It's a far more complex story than that, a lot of characters and so on, but basically that's the central way the thing turns—someone disappears and someone else is trying to find him. The whole book is a process of discovery, and in the course of it more is discovered than could have been anticipated by the immediate situation.

Did you have to do a lot of historical research for writing it?

Well, I did a little reading in the period, but the images that move me do not deal with research. They were sort of phantom images of the time. As a matter of fact, the origins of the book are a story, a little three page dream story called "The Waterworks," published in a volume of stories called *Lives of the Poets.* And I never quite understood that story. It was a very evocative, and in attempting to understand why I wasn't through with it I began to project from it. The fact that it took place in the 19th century, which I didn't realize when I wrote it, and that it was in New York or near New York, also compelled me.

The Waterworks takes place in some unnamed locations at the reservoir and in the waterworks building next to it. A man sees a toy boat on the water that sinks; he goes into the waterworks and sees some men who have found an obstruction in the sluice gate and it's a child, the owner of the toy boat. That's basically what happens in the story.

The delivery of water was a very important technological advance in this country in the 19th century. New York didn't really have any water until the 1840s—until then they had bucket brigades when things caught fire. And of course there were all these terrible fires in New York.

For New York City, they brought water down from the Croton River upstate, and built a marvelous aqueduct all the way miles and miles down to the city. And they built a reservoir right in the middle of town, the Croton Holding Reservoir at 42nd and 5th Avenue, which is the sight of the New York Public Library now. It was a huge thing in the city, a broad expanse of water, practically like a lake. There were walls rising from the street, about 40 feet high and really thick—people used to stroll on the parapet. So I realized I could move my reservoir into town, which I did, and one thing led to another. And that's how the book began; that's not research. I start writing and get what I need when I go along. It's idiosyncratic, not methodical or exhaustive, certainly not scholarly.

Most of your novels have taken place in the past. Do you feel more comfortable writing about when you were a child? Or during the last century?

No, I never planned these things. A historical period gives you closure. In other words, you can write about a region, take an area to write about like Faulkner did, or Bill Kennedy, or you can take a period of time to write about, and it's the same nice kind of enframing of facts for you to build with. I don't have any particular affection for any period. Whatever images move me or evoke something within me are usually the reason for the books getting done.

Do you have an overall message in The Waterworks *that made you write it?*

There's an old-time movie producer named Sam Goldwyn and he used to say to critics of his movies that if you want a message go to Western Union. If I thought I had a message I'd deliver the message, I wouldn't write a book. A message is a message—another form entirely.

Is the novel connected to any concepts in your anthology, Jack London, Hemingway, and the Constitution?

I haven't thought about that. There's one piece in the book that might give you a sense of the period of the novel, "The Nineteenth New York." I wrote that for a magazine called *Architectural Digest,* which had been asking me for some years to write a piece for its New York issue. I finally did. I took some inspiration from the novel I was writing, and decided to write about New York in the 19th century. There are actually lines that overlap between the novel and the essay. I talk about that reservoir and about the architecture of the times and the fact that in so many of the neighborhoods today you see the 19th century still.

A surprising amount of the last century is still here, even though New York is supposed to be the town that tears itself down every fifteen or twenty years. In fact, there's Soho and the ironfront district, Cooper Union, Washington Square, Central Park, the row houses of Harlem and over on the West Side. That was one of the things that impelled me to write this book. I remember, as I more or less described it in the piece, looking south in my office window, which looks south over Manhattan, and it was a very foggy night and the fog came down and erased the World Trade Center, then it kept going down and erased the Woolworth Building; then the 1970s and 1960s glass and steel buildings, then it got down to the 1930s and 1920s and it was like some sort of archaeological inversion; and finally the fog got so low that all I could see were buildings five or six stories high and I realized that that was the 19th century. I was very moved by that. That's the way the mind operates. So you go around and try to get the feeling of things—the assertiveness of certain kinds of architecture and the world view behind it or the one coming, and it gives you a very good sense of what the culture must have been. I really responded to architecture. But that's the only piece in the anthology that connects to the novel.

The area you live in is very historical and lots of famous people lived there.
The West Village. Well, the Row House was an invention of the 19th Century.

Which are your favorite buildings in the city?
I like buildings that have grandeur without height. Like, for instance, the Metropolitan Museum of Art or the New York Public Library—these are, to me, very beautiful. The thing I like about other buildings also is the inadvertent way they express some outlandish cultural vision in the architect's belief that he was expressing taste. I don't really know that many buildings by name. I don't know if I have a favorite building.

In Ragtime *Stanford White is one of your main characters. Do you have any favorite characters from* Ragtime, *either real or fictional?*

No, I loved them all [with a smile].

Ragtime *was very innovative in style and substance. Everyone has talked about the blending of fact and fiction. You even bring this concept up in your anthology. Something about there being no fiction or nonfiction—just a text.*

That's the piece called "False Documents." I was sort of astonished with that one—people thought I was breaking the law somehow. It was an unforgivable transgression. Of course since then a lot of people have written freely on historical matters—probably in their own vision, filling in where the facts were not complete or where there's some mystery—going on about Lee Harvey Oswald or Ambrose Bierce. So, it seems to be accepted now, seems to be a permissible thing. At the time, there was some shock expressed by some critics, and I wrote the piece to deal with that, to deal with the naiveté. This was not on the part of the historians who are the first people who should know better. That there was indeed a phenomenology here and that reality is not a fixed star for everybody to observe; we're not in Newton's Universe anymore, we're somewhere else.

So that's how I came to that proposition. But if you think about the history of fiction, Defoe used an historical event, an outlandish case of a castaway named Selkirk, who came back to London. He was a bit crazy and dug a hole in his garden and lived there, rather than in his house. But Defoe knew that everyone in London knew that the idea of a castaway—a person who had been isolated on an island for years and years and had been rescued—was physically possible in those days. History invented the idea of the castaway but Defoe used that as a factual basis in his book in the presumption of its possibility and changed it into Robinson Crusoe who ended up expressing the values of the white European race.

And then Defoe claimed he was only an editor of the book, that he didn't make up a fiction. He said there really was a Robinson Crusoe who wrote these pages. And so, way back in the beginnings of the English novel authors have been meddling, going over the line between fiction and fact, claiming truth for themselves, even if they had to deny their own authorship as a device to persuade people that they are reading the truth. Besides that, a lot of public figures back in time discovered facts made fiction of themselves, so they're the ones who did that to their own lives. So we're not really crossing borders anymore. We're dealing with a fiction and doing a variant on it.

Has anybody called Ragtime *a postmodern novel? It's a very ambiguous term.*

Yeah, I've spoken to people who have asked me about postmodernism. I think I've used postmodern techniques in some of my work; I think in *Daniel,* perhaps *Ragtime, Loon Lake*—and always for traditional storytelling purposes. So is that postmodern? I don't think so. Maybe it's post-postmodern. That's what I am [laughing], a postpostmodernist.

Which do you think is your most political novel? Is it The Book of Daniel*?*

Well, on the face of it, on the surface, it seems to be the most concerned with political matters, being that it's about the 1950s and the political trial. In that sense the book is political. But I don't know if it's the most political thing I've written. Maybe this book, *The Waterworks,* is the most profoundly political thing I've written. *Billy Bathgate* was political. They're all political, and they're all nonpolitical.

I've noticed from your essays and from your novels that you are interested in mythology and how it is the matrix out of which so much originates. In The Book of Daniel, *for example, you mention the mythological and religious basis of law courts—how law courts look like altars. Are you interested in American mythology and the myths that underlie the culture?*

That's one of the things I said in the essay, "False Documents"—that people are making fictions of themselves. What I'm invading is the realm of myth: myth whose mask is history. And possibly one of the functions of reinvention, in this sense, is turning myth back into history. If myths aren't examined and questioned and dealt with constantly they harden and become dangerous. They become a structured belief and they make people insane. Society becomes monolithic and despotic, in one way or another.

That happened briefly in the 1950s, when the Cold War myths were quite calculatedly introduced into the population by politicians who needed the support for the policies of containment. And suddenly there was almost a civil religion and you could not blaspheme, could not dissent. There were loyalty oaths and trials and all sorts of hysteria, what we generally call Mc-Carthyism, but which was not confined to the McCarthy period. So, at that point the myths had taken over and become dangerous and inimical to a healthy free society.

But apart from that, in *Billy Bathgate* the myth has to do with the American love of transgression and sociopathic behavior. We're fascinated by gangsters. Most people are very law-abiding. But the basis of this free society, sort of the mythological underpinning, was supplied by revolutionists, over-throwers, men of violence. So while we like what we have and we're law abiding, anyone who comes along who's antisocial gets a little admiration. That's why we make so much of a fuss about gangsters. Of course we want to see them contradict the society, violate it, then we want to see then punished. *Billy Bathgate* dwells in that myth.

Well, in so many places you bring up the contradictions in America. We try to be a beacon to the world, while we let our cities turn to ruin . . . Arthur Salzman wrote an essay on our work, stating that you wish "to demythologize America." Is that an accurate statement?

I don't know that what I wish is a factor here, because what I write comes out of the book itself, and when I'm writing I'm in the book, thinking about it, rather than any intention I might have. I think of the books as having their own voices, kind of myself as realizing whatever the book has to be. In the course of it, if it turns out to be accessible or inaccessible, political or non-political, or demythologizing or remythologizing is not for me to say, not for me to delimit the experience of writing to anything as specific as that. It may be that the books do this, but that's for a critic to say. It's probably a mistake to look for authority for critical interpretation to the author of the book.

In the Massachusetts Review, *Peggy Knapp wrote an essay which compares* Daniel *to* Hamlet. *Did you read that or hear that comparison before?*

I think I met Peggy Knapp and I remember her mentioning she was going to do that piece. But there again I don't know if I was thinking of *Hamlet* at any time when writing the book or sought it as a model. I doubt, in any case, if it was conscious. If it were conscious it would have been inhibiting, wouldn't it? There are probably parallels that could be read into it that might be instructive. But I didn't go beyond hearing the thesis, and I also disclaim any intention to have used *Hamlet* as a model.

How much of the Rosenberg story is?

The law that was applied against them was in the novel; obviously the socio-political context in which that case was brought; certain things about the Isaacsons are shared with the Rosenbergs. They're a Jewish couple with two children, and they're radicals, leftists. That's about all. The Rosenbergs have two sons, the Isaacsons, a son and daughter. I never knew the members of that family or anybody connected with the case. When they were executed I was serving in the U.S. Army in Germany. It's all a little remote.

I started to write *The Book of Daniel* in the late 1960s, about '68. And this country was in great torment, with profound generational schisms. The country was just being torn apart by the war in Vietnam and that was probably the deepest division in our country since the Civil War. And the New Left, in all its manifestations, was going through its paces and confronting the larger society—everybody from the Yippies to the Black Panthers to the SDS, and many other varieties of counter-cultural dissent. The whole cultural scene was changing. This is when people started to wear jeans and men began to wear their hair long and to wear shirts without ties and dashikis.

That sounds like me.

So, cultural change was enormous. Rock music just swept everything away; there was no other music. There was enormous creativity with the popular music scene: Dylan and Baez and Paul Simon and all the great rock bands, some of which are still around. Grateful Dead, Stones, Beatles, and on and on and on. Things were never quite the same after the '60s. So I was thinking about all this and thinking about radicalism in general; this was the context for this kind of thinking. All of life was terribly politicized. There was also the whole civil rights thing going on at the same time—Martin Luther King and Freedom Summers, the troops surrounding Little Rock, and people trying to get a black student into the University of Mississippi, and there were riots and killings. You can't believe what was going on at this time.

So I began to think about the so-called moulet, people like Abbie Hoffman, spirited, totally anti-intellectual, self-inventing, spontaneous, satirical, using ridicule as a political act, staging public demonstrations, twitting the noses of the politicians. The point I'm trying to make is that I began to think about the New Left vis-a-vis the Old Left, which was very intellectual, very foreign, with nothing spontaneous about it; and certainly among the communists governed by a theory that had been developed in Europe.

So it was an attempt to find some sort of historical line between old and new and to write a big novel encompassing some sacrifice of radicals in this country, and I wrote *Daniel*. It is very hard for me now to compress it into, did you mean this or that? I meant the book.

You have an interesting essay on Hemingway in your anthology. Do you have any favorite American authors or people who influenced you such as Hemingway? You also wrote about Dreiser as well as Jack London, whom you said wrote the first "road novel."

Oddly enough, my affection for Dreiser was very late. Hemingway was an enormous influence on me when I was a young writer; Fitzgerald more so. I admired Faulkner very much, but I didn't feel any deep sympathetic response to him that I felt I could use, didn't feel a kindred spirit with Faulkner.

From the 19th century, Hawthorne and Melville meant a great deal to me, as well as Mark Twain. But those writers mean something to everybody. I particularly liked Hawthorne's definition of a romance: the idea of a sort of reality cured up into meaning, that you write a novel not from the accumulation of data the way the realists do but from structuring your story and using selective imagery. Well that's poeticism. One begins to turn out something that pushes in the direction of metaphor—or when you're not doing it absolutely correctly it falls into allegory, which Hawthorne lapsed into. But I was always moved by that, and by his setting books in the past. And Melville just blew me away, he was spectacular. And I loved Mark Twain. Those are some of them.

E. L. Doctorow

Michael Silverblatt / 1997

This interview originally aired on station KCRW, on the program "Bookworm," a project of Santa Monica college. Used by permission.

Silverblatt: Hello, and welcome to "Bookworm." My name is Michael Silverblatt. Today my guest is E. L. Doctorow. The occasion that brings him to my city, Los Angeles, is the soon-to-open musical adaptation of his novel *Ragtime*. And it is a pleasure to have had the opportunity to reread it, because twenty years ago when it was published in 1975—like many other people alerted to it by its publication in several chapters in the wonderful literary review, *The New American Review*—we had read two crucial chapters, and no one could wait, I mean so many people read that book the day it came out. I remember waiting at the bookstore for it the way one would wait for a Beatles album in those days. And so to read it now, the book thrusts forward very preciously details that I'd forgotten from my first reading, and I wondered: what is your relationship to your own prior work? Do you read it with surprise?

Doctorow: Well, eventually you stop reading it, shortly after it's published, at least I do, and then I find that as some time elapses, I will have some curiosity about the book, and I'll open it at any page and start to read it, but I'll seldom read more than three or four pages because I will find myself editing them, or if I'm quite caught up in them, I'll close the book because I don't want to reach a page that I'll start to edit. So either way, it's a short read I give it, but when I find lines that surprise me I'm very, very happy.

Silverblatt: I wanted to begin by quoting one that surprised me. I'm going to read it in its entirety because it seemed to me to be a passage that would be immediately identified as in *Ragtime* style but probably jostled aside in the memory for most readers. Father has gone on an expedition up north with Admiral Peary, and they catch and eat birds up there.

> The day before the expedition was to leave, Father went along with Matthew Henson and three of the Esquimos to the bird cliffs half a day's journey from the coast. They climbed the cliffs with sealskin bags hung over their shoulders

and collected dozens of eggs, a great delicacy in the Arctic. When the birds
flew up, chattering and circling, it was as if a portion of the rock cliff had come
away. Father had never seen so many birds. They were fulmar and auk. The
Esquimos held out nets between them and the birds flew into the nets and became entangled. The nets were taken up at the corners and became sacks of
immobile weighted feathers chirping piteously. When the men had caught all
they could carry, they made the descent and straightaway slaughtered the birds.
The fulmar, about the size of gulls, were wrung at the neck. But what amazed
Father was the means by which the small and inoffensive auk was done in. One
simply nudged the tiny heart in its breast. Father watched it done and then tried
it himself. He held an auk in one hand and with his thumb gently squeezed the
beating breast. Its head slumped and it was dead. The Esquimos loved the auklet
and customarily pickled it in sealskins.

First, what startles is the information itself. And then I guess what makes it
unforgettable on the second reading is that this book itself seems to be about
the extraordinary frailty and vulnerability of the heart and how easily it can
be broken.

   Doctorow: I like those lines. I'm trying to remember how they found
their way into the book. When I was a boy I read a lot of adventure, northern
adventure, you know, Jack London and things up in the Yukon and the Arctic,
and it was a territory that fascinated me. I also read some of the narratives,
the nonfiction narratives by the explorers Amundsen—it was wonderful—and
a writer named Peter . . . Seejal, I believe—maybe you could check that
out—who wrote about auks and the way they were killed. These things stay
in your mind. When you write a book, it's sort of a kitchen sink kind of form,
and when you are pressing on, you throw everything you can think of into it,
with of course the idea that somehow it will turn out to be relevant, even
though you may not know how when you use the material. Maybe a better
image for this way of working—appropriate for *Ragtime,* because of the private meaning of that title, *Ragtime* for me was always literally the use of
rags—is to take bits and scraps of discarded material and sew them together
to make something new, and so there is always a kind of rag bin up there in
the head that one can draw on.

   Silverblatt: The bit of the fragment, the bit of rag that I find happiest to
recount sewn into this tapestry quilt is the story "Michael Kohlhass" by
Heinrich von Kleist. That was a very funny time, because Kleist was an
author whom I did not know of, but there was a film by Eric Wilmer of "The

Marquise of O." There was a story by Donald Barthelme called "The Idiot" that parodied pieces of Kleist's text in which someone was applying to the famous writers school with pastiches based on Kleist. And there was Doctorow, whose character Coalhouse Walker and the incidents surrounding Coalhouse Walker are derived from the Kleist text. But the brilliance there is in seeing that what happens to a working class horse dealer in the halls of the emperors and his preceptors could happen to a black man wielding a Model T. Its incorporation or appropriation—the sense that the book doesn't want to invent very much, it wants to somehow inherit—this is a book that vends things second hand: Emma Goldman, Houdini, Kleist, a collection.

Doctorow: The source of what you use finally doesn't matter, because you're making a composition, whether you're using your own life (the inspirations you get from looking at pictures or from hearing something on the street or from something you know happens to someone else) or whether you are using historical materials. The sources don't matter as much as the act of composing. There are people who say to me about a book, "Is this autobiographical?" And I try to explain that the sources may be autobiographical, but a composition has been made, so it's fiction. We can no longer think of it as autobiographical. It doesn't matter where the material comes from.

Silverblatt: I'm speaking with E. L. Doctorow. We're talking about his twenty-two year old novel, *Ragtime,* and the new musical adaptation of it. One of the most arresting essays in Doctorow's book of essays, *Jack London, Hemingway, and the Constitution,* is an essay called "Standards" in which the form of the song is subjected to a rather severe examination or meditation. The folk song does fairly well, and certain songs from the past such as "A Bird in a Gilded Cage" are praised for their accuracy about the social condition of a young woman marrying an older man, but the songs that seem to get whapped around are those by the writers of Tin Pan Alley—old immigrants who've reduced knowledge into brief, cheerful songs. It is one of the most cynical and even condescending passages in all of Doctorow, so I wonder what brought you to your willingness to let Mr. Drabinsky et. al. adapt your novel?

Doctorow: I'm not sure that I entirely agree with your interpretation as to cynicism; there seems to be some irony in it. The songs that come in for some fun are not associated with show tunes. There is a separate category which I think are exempt from these standards . . .

Silverblatt: Standards?
ELD: The standards I'm talking about are the ballroom standards not

attached to any theater piece. In fact, the writers of theater music do stand outside this tradition of simplification and innocence. So many of the writers, like Cole Porter, Dorothy Fields and so on, were indeed university graduates, quite sophisticated. So, I don't see any conflict there, but if there is . . .

MS: (laughter) I like to make trouble . . .

ELD: No, it's not trouble . . . If there is, I resort to Scott Fitzgerald's famous line—the sign of intelligence is the ability to hold two contradictory ideas in one's mind at the same time and still function. The fact of the matter is that the people who have written the music and the lyrics, Stephen Flaherty and Lynn Ahrens, are extraordinarily bright and witty. It has a good deal of its own wit, which in proportion overall to the theater piece is not unlike the book. They have done some really remarkable things in knowing what moments in the story should be song and doing their version. I'll give you an example. I have a lot of fun in the book in the chapter when Father takes his little boy to the baseball game, and these are the days of John McGraw, the days when the immigrants played baseball. It was a very rude crowd, and they played a very rough game. The spiked each other—people like Ty Cobb, for instance—and spat. Spitting was a very big part of the game, and fighting and trying to murder one another on the base paths, and I tried to describe a game in which a fight erupts, throwing up big clouds of dust around second base, and so on. Well, they wanted to do something similar, but of course you can't stage a baseball game on stage that way, so what they did was to transform the moment into the stands—the father and the little boy sitting in the stands with all these fans who are as ugly in speech and vulgar and mean-spirited and angry, as the players are in the book. These people are shouting at the players during the course of the song called "What a Game!"

Silverblatt: Even on the CD, it's a very funny song.

Doctorow: So this is a kind of inversion of that moment, with all the feeling about the old time baseball players transformed or transferred to the people who watch them.

Silverblatt: When in fact I saw *Kiss of the Spiderwoman,* which was produced by Garth Drabinsky and adapted by Terrence McNally, what impressed me was that a very difficult book had been approached at the level of its difficulty. There had not been as in the movie an attempt to simplify either the sexuality or the difficulty or the ugliness of the material. I've read the script. McNally seems to have adapted the technique that he perfected in

Love, Valor and Compassion, of having the narrative hurtle forward by having the characters narrate acts that are not in fact occurring before you, and so the fast motion of the book *Ragtime* is accomplished on stage by this simple expedient.

Doctorow: It is a very astute way of dealing with a book that is of course heavily populated and highly eventful—to somehow make it work given the economies of the theater and the libretto and the immense amount of time taken up by an individual song. It's a great accomplishment of Terrence's. I think it's essentially Brechtian to have the characters speak of themselves in third person, before they step back into the scene and become what they just described. It is really a crucial invention for making the show work.

Silverblatt: It seems to me that one of the great virtues of the *Ragtime* of E. L. Doctorow, which I just reread with great pleasure, is that it is very *sec,* very dry: there is a passion there in the book, but you have to come to know the characters, their circumstances, the intricacies of plot to see how wet or moist it is underneath. There is very little of the kind of thing that is becoming the banner for this production of *Ragtime*—nostalgia about immigration, what my grandparents did, the travails of Ellis Island. It is not going on in this book, but it does on the CD of the musical, and I wondered how you feel about the earnestness of some the material.

Doctorow: It may be a little misleading if you are hearing the music out of context. My interpretation of the show is that it's hardly nostalgic, that it deals as you say with the level of difficulty, it engages the book's level of difficulty. The appearance of the immigrants on stage at Ellis Island—the fear they feel is given to the audience because of the way it is staged with these gates clanging down, stopping every few steps they take as they approach America. They finally get to the promised land and talk to the immigrant father who gets on his knees and kisses the ground, and they all sing about success. As they are singing about success, a transverse girder comes down because the basic set is the old Penn Station in New York City. As the girder comes down, someone else is singing about success over their heads. It's J. P. Morgan, an immensely fat man, and as he sings about success the girder begins to press the immigrants into the ground. It's only when Harry Houdini appears, another dead man, that there is the urge to sing about escape, and immigrants slowly and painfully push that girder up off their shoulders. Now this is hardly nostalgia for the days of the Lower East Side, and what follows afterwards shows misery and difficulty. He fails to earn a living.

He is badly shaken by a verbal assault on his little child and decides to leave New York.

Silverblatt: Now in the book the central realization about Henry Ford was that Ford discovered not only that cars are made of replaceable, exchangeable parts but that the men on the assembly lines making the cars are also exchangeable. This production of *Ragtime* is something that is happening in theaters internationally: a big production has been done in Toronto, one is being leveraged into place in Los Angeles, one is being planned in New York. As someone external to the process, how do you avoid the horrors that the book condemns that go into these makings and marketings of these juggernauts and several companies rivaling to replace each other? Do you have an ethic about that?

Doctorow: My ethical considerations have been concerned with the fidelity of the piece to the spirit and the overall attitude of the book. I think that they have honored that. There are inevitably things that I regret that are not on the stage that are in the book, people who didn't make the cut, as it were, characters like Sigmund Freud. I regret that there is not more of J. P. Morgan, who I thought made a wonderful, funny, brisk kind of character for the piece. I wanted a scene in the book which people have talked about over the years almost more than others that has to do with a meeting between Ford and Morgan in the Morgan library, in which Morgan suggests they are reincarnated men of wisdom who were meant to lead the world every time they come into it. Morgan is represented as planning to build his own pyramid, like a pharaoh of old. None of that is in the piece. But something else is there, given the constraints of the theater, which to me is remarkably close to the kind of feeling I've had writing a book about the things I'm writing: Emma Goldman has a very prominent part in the piece and talks about the struggles of working people and . . .

Silverblatt: . . . here in Los Angeles being played by the wonderful Judy Kay . . .

Doctorow: Yes, and it may be that by the time the show opens here or on Broadway I'll be less silent about it. I haven't seen the latest changes that have been made and won't for several weeks. But so far I think that the risk I've taken has panned out in that probably the show is likely to drive people to the book. All that marketing you see is something that no publishing house can ever dream of. But I'm not particularly concerned about about the size and the ambition of the producer and his organization for this show. It is an independent company; it isn't a great corporate conglomerate, and essentially the producing vision is one man's, Drabinsky's, who is very dynamic and passionate about what he is doing, very personally involved, so whatever the sense you may have from your vantage point of this kind of bulldozer approach to marketing is not the interior experience that I'm having. This is not to say that we haven't had our arguments. I've been giving them notes all the way through from the very beginning, responding to the workshop production, the meeting, the rehearsal periods, the Toronto production, both before and after it opened, and I'm continuing to do that. They have been quite responsive, and I don't get the feeling that anybody's trying to do something else than what I want done. So far it looks pretty good to me, but if it doesn't work out that way, I'll be glad to come back and discuss it with you.

Silverblatt: A final question to get back to (for me) the more important fact—the work of E. L. Doctorow and its own incarnations. When I was rereading the book *Ragtime* I was thrilled of course because I came to *Ragtime* having read subsequently *Loon Lake* and *World's Fair, The Book of Daniel* and *Lives of the Poets* and *Billy Bathgate.* And so of course the book contained seedlings of the future, and the themes of Doctorow are remarkably consistent. For instance, in *Ragtime* the billionaires dream of eternal life, of reincarnation, as they do in *The Waterworks.* It's a central concern of that book to live forever. The little boy, who seems at least in the final pages to have narrated *Ragtime,* is also one who is creative: he knows before the assignation of Ferdinand, that the archduke is in danger. That is very much the status of the boy in *World's Fair,* looking forward and looking back. The novelist seems to have this wonderful relationship—to look back on characters who are trying to guess what the future will be. The future is the novelist that is looking back on them, but I wondered about that consistency. It can't be defined, but are you aware of it as you work?

Doctorow: No, fortunately not. For many years people have been telling me that one book is so different from another, and I've always known that wasn't true. I think not only thematic preoccupations, over and over, but I sometimes think that basically I have a repertory of actors, and I give them different names in each book and put different costumes on them, but essentially they are the same spirits over and over who recur and return eternally in my working mind. But it is true that you don't want to know too well what you're doing; I think that is not a state of mind that is conducive to good work, and as soon as I learn something, possibly from an astute and decisive commentator such as yourself, I do my best to forget it. (Laughter)

Silverblatt: How do you do that?

Doctorow: Well it's very easy (laughter): I just take a diet soda or something that has a short term memory loss capacity in it. (Laughter)

Silverblatt: I've been speaking to E. L. Doctorow on the occasion of adaptation of *Ragtime* into a new musical opening in Los Angeles, playing now in Toronto, and opening eventually in New York City. Thank you for joining me.

Doctorow: My pleasure.

Index